Trading

for
dummies®
A Wiley Brand

Trading

4th Edition

Lita Epstein, MBA

Author of *Reading Financial Reports For Dummies*

Grayson D. Roze

Business Manager, StockCharts.com

for

dummies®

A Wiley Brand

Trading For Dummies®, 4th Edition

Published by: **John Wiley & Sons, Inc.,** 111 River Street, Hoboken, NJ 07030-5774, www.wiley.com

Copyright © 2017 by John Wiley & Sons, Inc., Hoboken, New Jersey

Published simultaneously in Canada

For general information on our other products and services, please contact our Customer Care Department within the U.S. at 877-762-2974, outside the U.S. at 317-572-3993, or fax 317-572-4002. For technical support, please visit https://hub.wiley.com/community/support/dummies.

Wiley publishes in a variety of print and electronic formats and by print-on-demand. Some material included with standard print versions of this book may not be included in e-books or in print-on-demand. If this book refers to media such as a CD or DVD that is not included in the version you purchased, you may download this material at http://booksupport.wiley.com. For more information about Wiley products, visit www.wiley.com.

Library of Congress Control Number: 2017941824

ISBN 978-1-119-37031-4 (pbk); ISBN 978-1-119-37033-8 (ebk); ISBN 978-1-119-37032-1 (ebk)

Manufactured in the United States of America

SKY10029830_091421

Contents at a Glance

Table of Contents

Introduction

T rading used to be the purview of institutional and corporate entities that had direct access to closed securities trading systems. Technical advances leveled the playing field, making securities trading much more accessible to individuals. After the stock market crash of 2000, when many people lost large sums of money because professional advisors or mutual fund managers didn't protect their portfolio principal, investors chose one of two options — getting out of the market altogether and seeking safety or finding out more about how to manage their own portfolios. Many who came back into the market ran from it again in late 2008, when the market saw its worst year since the Great Depression. In 2017, the stock market roared to a high of the Dow Jones Index topping 21,000, but will they be spooked again after the next correction?

The concept of buying and holding forever died after that 2000 stock crash; it saw some revival from 2004 to 2007 but then suffered another death in 2008. People today look for new ways to invest and trade. Although investors still practice careful portfolio balancing using a buy-and-hold strategy, they look much more critically at what they're holding and are more likely to change their holdings now than they were before the crash. Others have gotten out of the stock market completely.

Still others have moved on to the world of trading. Many kinds of traders ply their skills in the markets. The ones who like to take on the most risk and want to trade as a full-time business look to day trading. They never hold a position in a security overnight. Swing traders hold their positions a bit longer, sometimes for a few days or even a few weeks.

But we don't focus on the riskier types of trading in this book; instead, we focus on position trading, which involves executing trades in and out of positions and holding positions for a few weeks or months and maybe even a year or more, depending on trends that are evident in the economy, the marketplace, and ultimately individual stocks.

About This Book

Many people have misconceptions about trading and its risks. Most people think of the riskiest type of trading — day trading — whenever they hear the word *trader*. We're definitely not trying to show you how to day trade. Instead, we want to introduce you to the world of position trading, which is much safer, less risky, and yet a great way to build a significant portfolio.

Don't get the wrong idea; trading in securities always carries risks. You should never trade with money that you can't risk losing. That means trading with your children's education savings isn't a good idea. If you want to trade, set aside a portion of your savings that isn't earmarked for any specific use and that you believe you can put at risk without ruining your lifestyle.

Obviously, we plan to show you ways to minimize risk, but we can't promise that you won't take a loss. Even the most experienced traders, the ones who put together the best trading systems, don't have a crystal ball and periodically get hit by a market shock and accompanying loss. By using the basics of fundamental and technical analyses, we show you how to minimize your risk, how to recognize when the market is ripe for a trade, how to identify which specific sectors in the market are the right places to be, how to figure out which phases economic and market cycles are in, and how to make the best use of all that knowledge.

As you dip into and out of this book, feel free to skip the sidebars (shaded boxes). They contain interesting information but aren't essential to understanding important points of trading.

Within this book, some web addresses may break across two lines of text. If you're reading this book in print and want to visit one of these web pages, simply key in the web address exactly as it's noted in the text, pretending as though the line break doesn't exist. If you're reading this as an e-book, you've got it easy — just click the web address to be taken directly to the web page.

Foolish Assumptions

We've made a number of assumptions about your basic knowledge and stock-trading abilities. We assume that you're not completely new to the world of investing in stocks and that you're familiar with the stock market and its basic language. Although we review many key terms and phrases as we explore the basics of trading, if everything you read sounds totally new to you, you probably need to read a basic book on investing in stocks before trying to move on to the more technical world of trading.

We also assume that you know how to operate a computer and use the Internet. If you don't have high-speed access to the Internet now, be sure you have it before trying to trade. Many of the resources we recommend in this book are available online, but you need high-speed access to be able to work with many of these valuable tools.

Icons Used in This Book

For Dummies books use little pictures, called *icons*, to flag certain chunks of text. Here's what they actually mean:

TIP

Watch for these little flags to get ideas on how to improve your trading skills or where to find other useful resources.

REMEMBER

If there's something that's particularly important for you to remember, we mark it with this icon.

WARNING

The trading world is wrought with many dangers and perils. A minor mistake can cost you a bunch of money, so we use this icon to point out particularly perilous areas.

Beyond the Book

In addition to the material in the print book or e-book you're reading right now, this product also comes with some access-anywhere goodies on the web. When you just want a quick reminder of trading basics, check out the free Cheat Sheet at www.dummies.com; just search for "Trading For Dummies Cheat Sheet." There you'll find explanations on how to identify the beginning of bull and bear markets, how to trade in those types of markets, and how to develop your own trading system. We also recommend websites that offer trading information, analysis, and advice.

Before you can read charts, you need to create them. To help you get started creating and reading financial charts, we have partnered with StockCharts.com, one of the web's premier charting platforms. We've even arranged a 20 percent discount especially for *Trading For Dummies* readers toward a subscription on the website. Sign up today and get a free one-month trial of the site's advanced charting tools, resources, and more. The coupon code is SCC-DUMMIES-17. Access the trial as a *Trading For Dummies* reader at `http://stockcharts.com/sales/index.html`. If you're already a StockCharts member, use the discount code to renew your existing subscription.

Where to Go from Here

You're ready to enter the exciting world of trading. You can start anywhere in this book; each of the chapters is self-contained. But if you're totally new to trading, starting with Chapter 1 is the best way to understand the basics. If you already know the basics, understand everything about the various markets and exchanges that you care to know, have a broker picked out, and have all the tools you'll need, you may want to start with fundamental analysis in Part 2. Remember, though, to have fun and enjoy your trip!

1

Getting Started with Trading

IN THIS PART . . .

Know what you're getting into before you begin trading stocks by reviewing the ups and downs you'll encounter.

Get familiar with the various stock markets and the different types of market orders.

Pick an appropriate trading partner by finding a broker who's right for your trading style.

Figure out the minimum hardware and software requirements and check out recommended websites and programs.

Chapter **1**

The Ups and Downs of Trading Stocks

Making lots of money is the obvious goal of most people who decide to enter the world of trading. How successful you become as a trader depends on how well you use the tools, gather the needed information, and interpret the data you have. You need to develop the discipline to apply all that you know about trading toward developing a winning trading strategy.

Discovering how to avoid getting caught up in the emotional aspects of trading — the highs of a win and the lows of a loss — is key to developing a profitable trading style. Trading is a business and needs to be approached with the same logic you'd apply to any other business decision. Setting goals, researching your options, planning and implementing your strategies, and assessing your success are just as important for trading as they are for any other business venture.

In this book, we help you traverse these hurdles, and at the same time, we introduce you to the world of trading. In this chapter, we give you an overview of trading and an introduction to the tools you need, the research skills you must use, and the basics of developing all this information into a successful trading strategy.

Distinguishing Trading from Investing

Trading is not the same thing as investing. Investors buy stocks and hold them for a long time — often too long, riding a stock all the way down and possibly even buying more along the way. Traders, on the other hand, hold stocks for as little as a few minutes or as long as several months, and sometimes possibly even a year or more. The specific amount of time depends on the type of trader you want to become.

Investors want to carefully balance an investment portfolio among growth stocks, value stocks, domestic stocks, and foreign stocks, along with long-, short-, and intermediate-term bonds. A well-balanced portfolio generally offers the investor a steady return of between 5 percent and 12 percent, depending on the type of investments and amount of risk he or she is willing to take.

For investors, an aggressive portfolio with a mix of 80 percent invested in stocks and 20 percent in bonds, if well balanced, can average as high as a 12 percent annual return during a 20-year period; however, in some years, the portfolio will be down, and in others, it will go through periods of high growth. The opposite, a conservative portfolio with 20 percent invested in stocks and 80 percent in bonds, is likely to provide a yield on the lower end of the spectrum, closer to 4 percent. The volatility and risk associated with the latter portfolio, however, would be considerably less. Investors who have 10 or more years before they need to use their investment money tend to put together more-aggressive portfolios, but those who need to live off the money tend to put together less-aggressive portfolios that give them regular cash flows, which is what you get from a portfolio invested mostly in bonds.

REMEMBER

As a trader, you look for the best position for your money and then set a goal of exceeding what an investor can otherwise expect from an aggressive portfolio. During certain times within the market cycle, your best option may be to sit on the sidelines and not even be active in the market. In this book, we show you how to read the signals to decide when you need to be in the market, how to find the best sectors in which to play the market, and the best stocks within those sectors.

Seeing Why Traders Do What They Do

Improving your potential profit from stock transactions is obviously the key reason most people decide to trade. People who want to grow their portfolios rather than merely maintain them hope that the way they invest in them does better than the market averages. Regardless of whether traders invest through mutual funds or stocks, they hope the portfolio of securities they select gives them superior returns — and they're willing to work at it.

People who decide to trade make a conscious decision to take a more active role in increasing their profit potential. Rather than just riding the market up and down, they search for opportunities to find the best times and places to be in the market based on economic conditions and market cycles.

Traders who successfully watched the technical signals before the stock crash of 2008 either shorted stocks or moved into cash positions before stocks tumbled and then carefully jumped back in as they saw opportunities for profits. Some position traders simply stayed on the sidelines, waiting for the right time to jump back in. Even though they were waiting, they also carefully researched their opportunities, selected stocks for their watch lists, and then let technical signals from the charts they kept tell them when to get in or out of a position.

Successful Trading Characteristics

To succeed at trading, you have to be hard on yourself and, more than likely, work against your natural tendencies, fighting the urge to prove yourself right and accepting the fact that you're going to make mistakes. As a trader, you must develop separate strategies for when you want to make a trade to enter a position and for when you want to make a trade and exit that position, all the while not allowing emotional considerations to affect the decisions you make on the basis of the successful trading strategy you've designed.

TIP

You want to manage your money, but in doing so, you don't have to prove whether your particular buying or selling decision was right or wrong. Setting up stop-loss points for every position you establish and adhering to them is the right course of action, even though you may later have to admit that you were wrong. Your portfolio will survive, and you can always reenter a position whenever trends indicate the time is right again.

You need to make stock trends your master, ignoring any emotional ties that you have to any stocks. Although you may, indeed, miss the lowest entry price or the highest exit price, you nevertheless will be able to sleep at night, knowing that your money is safe and your trading business is alive and well.

Traders find out how to ride a trend and when to get off the train before it jumps the tracks and heads toward monetary disaster. Enjoy the ride, but know which stop you're getting off at so you don't turn profits into losses.

Tools of the Trade

The first step you need to take in becoming a trader is gathering all the right tools so you can open and operate your business successfully. Your computer needs to meet the hardware requirements and other computer specifics we describe in Chapter 4, including processor speed, memory storage, and screen size. You may even want more than one screen, depending on your trading style. High-speed Internet access is a must; otherwise, you may as well never open up shop.

We also introduce you to the various types of software in Chapter 4, showing you what can help your trading business ride the wave to success. Traders' charting favorites such as MetaStock and TradeStation are evaluated, along with Internet-based charting and data-feed services. We also talk about the various trading platforms that are available and how to work with brokers.

After you have all the hardware and software in place, you need to hone your analytical skills. Many traders advocate using only technical analysis, but we show you how using both technical and fundamental analyses can help you excel as a trader. (Part 2 covers fundamental analysis, and Part 3 discusses technical analysis.)

Taking Time to Trade More Than Just Stocks

The ways traders trade are varied. Some are day traders, while others are swing traders and position traders. Although many of the tools they use are the same or similar, each variety of trader works within differing time frames to reach goals that are specific to the type of trades they're making.

Position trading

Position traders use technical analysis to find the most promising stock trends and enter and exit positions in the market based on those trends. They can hold positions for just a few days, a few months, or possibly as long as a year or more. Position trading is the type of trading that we discuss the most in this book. After introducing you to the stock markets, the types of brokers and market makers with whom you'll be dealing, and the tools you need, we discuss the basics of fundamental analysis and technical analysis to help you become a better position trader.

Short-term swing trading

Swing traders work within much shorter time frames than position traders, rarely holding stocks for more than a few days and looking for sharp moves that technical analysis uncovers. Even though we don't show you the specifics of how to become a swing trader, we nevertheless discuss the basics of swing trading and its strategies in Chapter 17. You can also read about the basics of technical analysis and money-management strategies, both of which are useful topics to check out if you plan to become a swing trader. However, you definitely need to seek additional training before deciding to pursue this style of trading — reading *Swing Trading For Dummies* by Omar Bassal, CFA (Wiley), would be a good start.

WEATHERING A CHANGING MARKET

Housing stocks crumbled in the housing crunch. Financials were crushed in the credit crisis.

We can't claim any special foresight or knowledge to know when a stock is about to take a big plunge. We don't have a crystal ball. But we've been able to keep most of our money safe from the ravages of the down market since 2008. By using strategies that we discuss throughout this book, we can exit positions before giving back most of our accumulated profits — while many others unfortunately do just that.

An impending pullback is not illuminated with flashing beacons. There is no instant indicator telling us that it's time to sell everything. Instead, we close individual positions as each stock's technical conditions deteriorate. The tools we describe in this book enable us to recognize when risk levels have changed, when few stocks are attractive, and when simply leaving most of our trading capital in cash is the best course of action.

Getting credit in 2017 is much easier than it was 2009, but recovery from the housing crash in 2008–2009 is still weak. The stock market, on the other hand, has climbed. For example, the Dow Jones Index was at 8,000 in 2009 and topped 21,000 in 2017. Many traders and analysts expect another correction. We will weather this market with the majority of our trading capital intact as we take profits. Then we may make a little money by shorting a few stocks or buying some short or double-short exchange-traded funds. Thanks to the tools we show you in this book, we will be ready to trade aggressively when the technical condition of stocks begins improving again.

Day trading

Day traders never leave their money in stocks overnight. They always cash out. They can trade into and out of a stock position in a matter of hours, minutes, or even seconds. Many outsiders watch day traders in action and describe it as more like playing a video game than trading stocks. We discuss this high-risk type of trading in Chapter 18, but we don't show you the specifics of how to do it. If day trading is your goal, this book will only take you part of the way there. You discover the basics of technical analysis, but you need to seek out additional training before engaging in this risky trading style — check out *Day Trading For Dummies* by Ann C. Logue, MBA (Wiley).

Going Long or Short

Before you start trading, you absolutely have to know what stocks you want to buy and hold for a while, which is called *going long,* or holding a long stock position. You likewise have to know at what point holding that stock is no longer worthwhile. Similarly, you need to know at what price you want to *enter* or trade into a position and at what price you want to *exit* or trade out of a position. You may be surprised to find out that you can even profit by selling a stock without ever owning it, in a process called *shorting.* We discuss these vital trading strategies in Chapter 15.

You can even make money buying and selling options on stocks to simulate long or short stock positions. Buying an option known as a *call* enables you to simulate a long stock position, in much the same way that buying an option known as a *put* enables you to simulate a short stock position. You make money on calls when the option-related stock rises in price, and you make money on puts when the option-related stock falls in price.

When placing orders for puts and calls, you're never guaranteed to make money, even when you're right about the direction a stock will take. The values of options are affected by how volatile stock prices are in relationship to the overall direction (up or down) in which they're headed. We discuss options and how they work in greater detail in Chapter 19.

Managing Your Money

Managing your trades so you don't lose a bunch of money is critical. Although we can't guarantee that you'll never lose money, we can provide you with useful strategies for minimizing your losses and getting out before your stock portfolio takes a huge hit. The key is knowing when to hold 'em and when to fold 'em, and we cover that in great detail in Chapter 12.

WARNING

One thing that we can't emphasize enough is that you must think of your trading as a business and the stocks that you hold as its inventory. You can't allow yourself to fall in love with and thereby hang on to a stock out of loyalty. You'll find it especially hard to admit you've made a mistake; nevertheless, you have to bite the bullet and exit the position before you take a huge hit. You'll discover that housecleaning and developing successful strategies for keeping your inventory current are important parts of managing a trading portfolio.

Setting a target price for exiting a position before ever trading into it is the best way to protect your business from major losses. Stick with those predetermined exit prices and you'll avoid a major pitfall that many traders face — holding a position too long and losing everything. You obviously don't want to turn a profit into a loss, so as your position in a stock produces a profit, you can periodically raise your target exit price while continuing to hold the position to ensure that you keep most of that profit.

Understanding your risks — market risks, investment risks, and trading risks — helps you make better trading decisions. We review the different kinds of risks as they relate to specific situations at several points throughout the book.

Understanding Fundamental Analysis

You've probably heard the phrase "It's the economy, stupid." Well that's true, and we show you how understanding the basics of the business cycle can help you improve your trading successes. In Chapter 5, you find out how to identify periods of economic growth and recession and how these differing periods impact bull and bear stock markets. We also explore sector rotation and how to use it to pick the right sectors for your trading activities.

You can also discover plenty of information about how money supply, inflation rates, deflation, joblessness, and consumer confidence impact the mood of the market and stock prices and how the economy can be driven by how confidently (or not) political and monetary leaders speak out about it. We discuss the role of the Federal Reserve (Fed) and how when the Fed Chairman speaks, the markets listen.

Essentially fundamental analysis looks at company financial performance, as well as the performance of the economy, to analyze the future profit potential of a stock or other equity purchase. Understanding how the economy works isn't the only fundamental analysis tool that's important to you. You also need to read financial statements to understand the financial status of the companies you want to buy. We delve into financial statements in Chapter 6.

A company's income statements, on the other hand, give you a look at the results of the most recent period and provide a basis for comparison with prior years and periods. You can use these statements to look at whether revenues are growing, and if they are, by what percentage. You also can see how much profit the company is keeping from the revenue it generates. The cash-flow statement shows you how efficiently a company is using its cash and whether it's having problems meeting its current obligations. The balance sheet gives you a snapshot of a company's assets and liabilities and stockholder's equity.

You can use this information to develop your own estimate of a company's growth and profit potential. In Chapter 6, we show you how to do a few basic ratio calculations that you can use to compare similar stocks and then choose the one with the best potential.

TIP

Analysts use this information to project a company's financial growth and profits. You never should depend entirely on what analysts say, but you always should do your own research and collect the opinions of numerous analysts. One of the best ways to find out what analysts are saying and what aspects of the financial statements may raise a red flag is the analyst call. In Chapter 7, we explain how you can listen in on these calls and understand the unique language used in them to make better choices when selecting stocks. We also discuss the pros and cons of using analyst reports.

Getting a Grip on Technical Analysis

You use fundamental analysis to determine what part of the business cycle the economy is in and what industries offer the best growth potential. Then you use that information to select the best target companies and identify prices at which you'd want to buy their stocks.

After choosing your targets, you then use *technical analysis* to follow trends in the prices of the target stocks so you can find the right time to get in and ultimately to get out of a stock position. These targets become part of your stock-watch list. After you've established that list, you then use the tools of technical analysis to make your trades.

In Chapter 8, we introduce you to the basics of technical analysis, how it works, and how it needs to be used. Although some people think of technical analysis as no more than fortune-telling, others believe it yields significant information that can help you make successful trades. We believe that technical analysis provides you with extensive tools for your trading success, and we show you how to use those tools to be profitable.

Your first step in technical analysis is finding out how to create a chart. We focus on the most popular type — bar charting. In Chapter 9, you discover the art of deciphering simple visual stock patterns and how to distinguish between trends and trading ranges, all so you're able to spot when a stock moves from a trading range into either an upward or downward trend and know when you need to act.

In Chapter 10, we show you how to use your newfound skill of identifying trends to locate areas of support and resistance within a trend that ultimately help you find the right times to make your move. You find out how to read the patterns in the charts to identify trading signals and what to do whenever you've acted on a failed trading signal.

Chapter 11 fills you in on moving averages and how to use them to identify trends. You also find out about oscillators and other indicators that traders use for recognizing trading signals. As a newbie trader, you'll probably find that your greatest risk is *paralysis of analysis*. That's where you may find that you're having so much fun reading the charts or are just so confused about which chart has the right signal that you feel paralyzed by the variety of choices. We show you how to create and use a tiny subset of tools that is available in today's charting software packages to simplify your life and make your choices easier. You'll likewise discover how to use such odd-sounding but critical tools as an MACD indicator or a stochastic oscillator, and we help you take advantage of the powerful concept of relative strength.

Putting Trading Strategy into Practice

After you get used to using the tools, you're ready to put your new skills into practice making money. In Chapter 13, we show you how to put your newfound affinities for fundamental analysis and technical analysis together to develop and build your trading strategy. Using fundamental analysis, you can

» Determine which part of the economic cycle is driving the market.

» Determine which sector makes the most sense for stock trading.

» Figure out which sectors are in the best positions to go up.

» Find out which stocks are leading in the ascending sectors.

>> Evaluate where the Fed stands on the economy and which potential moves by the Fed can impact the strength of the market.

>> Evaluate and hopefully anticipate potential shocks to the market. Although doing so may seem like gazing into a crystal ball, you really can pick up some signs by checking out the key economic indicators. We show you what they are.

After you complete your fundamental analysis, we show you how to use your new technical analysis skills successfully. Using them, you find out how you can

>> Trade within the overall technical conditions.

>> Confirm which economic cycle a market is in by using index charts.

>> Determine whether an ascending sector is stuck in a range or ready to enter a new upward trend.

>> Determine whether leading stocks are stuck in ranges or ready to break out in upward trends.

Finally, we show you how to use your newfound skills to manage risk, set up a stop-loss position, and choose your time frame for trading.

In Chapter 14, we introduce you to techniques for using exchange-traded funds (ETFs) to ride the trends instead of taking the risk of finding just the right company in each sector. Sector ETFs have become a major trading tool for position traders who want to take advantage of sector rotation, which we talk about in Chapter 5.

After honing your skills, you're ready to start trading. So in Chapter 15, we focus on the actual mechanics of trading by

>> Discussing how to enter or trade into a position.

>> Explaining bid and ask prices.

>> Discussing the risks of market orders.

>> Explaining how to use limit and stop orders.

We also explore how to exit or trade out of a position and still stay unattached emotionally, when to take your profits, and how to minimize your losses, in addition to discussing potential tax hits and how to minimize them.

Now that you know how to research the fundamentals, effectively use the technical tools, and mechanically carry out a trade, the next step is developing and managing your own trading system, which we discuss in Chapter 16. We explore the basic steps to developing the system, which include

1. **Designing and keeping a trading log.**

2. **Identifying reliable trading patterns.**

3. **Developing an exit strategy.**

4. **Determining whether you'll use discretionary trading methods or mechanical trading. We explore the pros and cons of each.**

5. **Deciding whether to develop your own trading system or buy one off the shelf.**

6. **Testing your trading systems and understanding their limitations before making a major financial commitment to your new system.**

We also discuss assessing your results and fixing any problems.

REMEMBER

After you've designed, built, and tested your system, you're ready to jump in with both feet. The key to getting started: Make sure you begin with a small sum of money, examining your system and then increasing your trading activity as you gain experience and develop confidence with the system that you develop.

Trading at Higher Risk

Some traders decide they want to take on a greater level of risk by practicing methods of swing trading or day trading or by delving into the areas of trading derivatives or foreign currency. Although all these alternatives are valid trading options, we steer clear of explaining even the basics of how to use these high-risk trading alternatives. Instead, in Part 5 (Chapters 17 through 20) we provide you with a general understanding of the ways these trading alternatives work and the risks that are unique to each of them.

If you decide, however, that you want to take on these additional risks, don't depend on the information in this book to get started. Use the general information that we offer you here to determine what additional training you need to feel confident before moving into these trading arenas.

Remembering to Have Fun!

Although you are without question considering the work of a trader for the money you can make, you need to enjoy the game of trading. If you find that you're having trouble sleeping at night because of the risks you're taking, then trading may not be worth all the heartache. You may need to put off your decision to enter the world of trading until you're more comfortable with the risks or until you've designed a system that better accommodates your risk tolerance.

You may find that you need to take a slower approach by putting less money into your trades. You don't need to make huge profits with your early trades. Just trading into and out of a position without losing any money may be a good goal when you're just starting out. If you notice your position turning toward the losing side, knowing that you can trade your way out of it before you take a big loss may help you build greater confidence in your abilities.

REMEMBER

Making a losing trade doesn't mean that you're a loser. Even the most experienced traders must at times face losses. The key to successful trading is knowing when to get out before your portfolio takes a serious hit. On the other side of that coin, you also need to know how to get out when you're in a winning or profitable position. When you're trying to ride a trend all the way to the top, it sometimes starts bottoming out so fast that you lose some or possibly even all of your profits, causing you to end up in a losing position.

Trading is a skill that takes a long time to develop and is perfected only after you make mistakes and celebrate successes. Enjoy the roller coaster ride!

Chapter **2**

Exploring Markets and Stock Exchanges

B illions of shares of stock trade in the United States every day, and each trader is looking to get his or her small piece of that action. Before moving into the specifics of how to trade, we first want to introduce you not only to the world of stock trading but also to trading in other key markets — futures, options, and bonds. In this chapter, we also explain differences and similarities among key stock exchanges and how those factors impact your trading options. After providing you with a good overview of the key markets, we delve into the different types of orders you can place with each of the key exchanges.

Introducing the Broad Markets

You may think the foundation of the United States economy resides inside Fort Knox, where the country holds its billions of dollars in gold, or possibly that it resides in our political center, Washington, D.C. But nope. The country's true economic center is Wall Street, where billions of dollars change hands each and every day, thousands of companies are traded, and millions of people's lives are affected.

Stocks are not the only things sold in the broad financial markets. Every day, currencies, futures, options, and bonds also are traded. Although we focus on stock exchanges in this chapter, we first need to briefly explain each type of market.

Stock markets

The stocks of almost every major U.S. corporation and many major foreign corporations are traded on a stock exchange in the United States each day. Today, numerous domestic and international stock exchanges trade stocks in publicly held corporations; moreover, the only major corporations not traded are those held privately — usually by families or original founding partners that choose not to sell shares on the public market. *Forbes* magazine's top privately held corporations are Cargill, Koch Industries, Albertsons, Dell, and PricewaterhouseCoopers. Many of the large private corporations that are not traded publicly do have provisions for employee ownership of stock and must report earnings to the Securities and Exchange Commission (SEC), so they straddle the line between public and private corporations.

A *share of stock* is actually a portion of ownership in a given company. Few stockholders own large enough stakes in a company to play a major decision-making role. Instead, stockholders purchase stocks hoping that their investments rise in price so that those stocks can be sold at a profit to someone else interested in owning a share of the company sometime in the future. Investors may hold the stock to earn dividends, as well. Traders rarely hold the stock long enough for dividends to be a primary decision factor in whether to buy a stock. Therefore, after the company's initial sale of stock when it goes public, none of the money involved in stock trades goes directly into that company.

For the majority of this chapter, we focus on the two top stock exchanges in the United States: the New York Stock Exchange (NYSE) Euronext and NASDAQ (the National Association of Securities Dealers Automated Quotation system). We also introduce you to the world of electronic communication networks (ECNs), on which you can trade stocks directly, thus bypassing brokers.

Futures markets

Futures trading actually started in Japan in the 18th century to trade rice and silk. This trading instrument was first used in the United States in the 1850s for trading grains and other agricultural entities. Basically, *futures trading* means establishing a price for a commodity at the time of writing the financial contract. The commodity must be delivered at a specific time in the future. If you had a working crystal ball, it would be very useful here. This type of trading is done on a commodities exchange. The largest such exchange in the United States today is the

CME Group. *Commodities* include any product that can be bought and sold. Oil, cotton, and minerals are just a few of the products sold on a commodities exchange.

Futures contracts must have a seller (usually the person producing the commodity — a farmer or oil refinery, for example) and a buyer (usually a company that actually uses the commodity). You also can speculate on either side of the contract, basically meaning:

>> When you buy a futures contract, you're agreeing to buy a commodity that is not yet ready for sale or hasn't yet been produced at a set price at a specific time in the future.

>> When you sell a futures contact, you're agreeing to provide a commodity that is not yet ready for sale or hasn't yet been produced at a set price at a specific time in the future.

The futures contract states the price at which you agree to pay for or sell a certain amount of this future product when it's delivered at a specific future date. Although most futures contracts are based on a physical commodity, the highest-volume futures contracts are based on the future value of stock indexes and other financially related futures.

Unless you're a commercial consumer who plans to use the commodity, you won't actually take delivery of or provide the commodity for which you're trading a futures contract. You'll more than likely sell the futures contract you bought before you actually have to accept the commodity from a commercial customer. Futures contracts are used as financial instruments by producers, consumers, and speculators. We cover these players and futures contracts in much greater depth in Chapter 19.

Bond markets

Bonds are actually loan instruments. Companies and governments sell bonds to borrow cash. If you buy a bond, you're essentially holding a company's debt or the debt of a governmental entity. The company or government entity that sells the bond agrees to pay you a certain amount of interest for a specific period of time in exchange for the use of your money. The big difference between stocks and bonds is that bonds are *debt obligations* and stocks are *equity.* Stockholders actually own a share of the corporation. Bondholders lend money to the company with no right of ownership. Bonds, however, are considered safer because if a company files bankruptcy, bondholders are paid before stockholders. Bonds are a safety net and not actually a part of the trading world for individual position traders, day traders, and swing traders. Although a greater dollar volume of bonds is traded each day, the primary traders for this venue are large institutional traders. We don't discuss them any further in this book.

Options markets

An *option* is a contract that gives the buyer the right, but not the obligation, either to buy or to sell the underlying asset upon which the option is based at a specified price on or before a specified date. Sometime before the option period expires, a purchaser of an option must decide whether to exercise the option and buy (or sell) the asset (most commonly stocks) at the target price. Options also are a type of *derivative*. We talk more about this investment alternative in Chapter 19.

Reviewing Stock Exchanges

Most of this book covers stock trading, so we obviously concentrate on how the key exchanges — NYSE and NASDAQ — operate and how these operations impact your trading activity.

New York Stock Exchange (NYSE: ICE)

The U.S. stock market actually dates back to May 17, 1792, when 24 brokers signed an agreement under a buttonwood tree at what today is 58 Wall Street. The 24 brokers specifically agreed to sell shares of companies among themselves, charging a commission or fee to buy and sell shares for others who wanted to invest in a company. Yup, the first American stockbrokers were born that day.

A formalized exchange didn't come into existence until March 8, 1817, when the brokers adopted a formal constitution and named their new entity the New York Stock & Exchange Board. Brokers actually operated outdoors until 1860, when the operations finally were moved inside. The first stock ticker was introduced in 1867, but it wasn't until 1869 that the NYSE started requiring the registration of securities for companies that wanted to have their stock traded on the exchange. Registration began as a means of preventing the over-issuance (selling too many shares) of a company's stock.

From these meager beginnings, the NYSE built itself into the largest stock exchange in the world, with many of the largest companies listed on the exchange. Trading occurs on the floor of the exchange, with specialists and floor traders running the show. Today these specialists and floor traders work electronically, which first became possible when the exchange introduced electronic capabilities for trading in 2004. For traders, the new electronic-trading capabilities are a more popular tool than working with specialists and floor traders. Electronic-trading capabilities were enhanced when the NYSE merged with Archipelago Holdings in 2006. The exchange expanded its global trading capabilities after a merger with

Euronext in 2007, which made trading in European stocks much easier. NYSE Euronext was bought by Intercontinental Exchange (ICE) in 2013.

REMEMBER

You may not realize just how much the concept of supply and demand influences the trading price of a stock. Price swings of a stock are caused by shifts in the supply of shares available for sale and the demand created by the number of buyers wanting to purchase available shares.

The designated market makers

Designated market makers buffer dramatic swings by providing liquidity when needed, such as when news about a company breaks. If news that has a major impact on a stock's price breaks, designated market makers buy shares or sell the ones they hold in a company to make the trend toward a higher or lower stock price more orderly. For example, if good news breaks, creating more demand for the stock and overwhelming existing supply, the designated market maker becomes a seller of the stock to minimize the impact of a major price increase by increasing supply. The same is true when bad news strikes, creating a situation in which having more sellers than buyers drives the stock price down. In that situation, the designated market maker becomes a buyer of the stock, easing the impact of the drop in price. Designated market makers operate both manually and electronically to facilitate stock trading during market openings, closings, and periods of substantial trading imbalances or instability.

The floor brokers

The guys you see on the floor of the stock exchange, waving their hands wildly to make trades, are the *floor brokers*. They're actually members of the NYSE who trade exclusively for their own accounts. Floor brokers also can act as floor brokers for others and sell their services. But over 82 percent of trades take place electronically, so floor trading today is used primarily to trade a small group of extremely high-priced stocks not traded electronically.

Supplemental Liquidity Providers

In order to handle the volume of today's international marketplace, the NYSE established a new class of market participants called *Supplemental Liquidity Providers* (SLPs). These high-volume members of the exchange add liquidity to the marketplace. Each SLP is assigned securities for which he or she is obligated to maintain active trading of at least 10 percent in a trading day. SLPs must average 10 million shares exchanged in a day. They help generate more quoting activity to improve pricing and liquidity for stocks.

NASDAQ

NASDAQ, which stands for the National Association of Securities Dealers Auto-mated Quotations, was formed after an SEC study in the early 1960s concluded that the sale of *over-the-counter* (OTC) securities — in other words, securities that aren't traded on the existing stock exchanges — was fragmented and obscure. The report called for the automation of the OTC market and gave the responsibility for implementing that system to the National Association of Securities Dealers (NASD).

The NASD began construction of the NASDAQ system in 1968, and its first trades were made beginning February 8, 1971, when NASDAQ became the world's first electronic stock market. In 2007, NASDAQ combined forces with the Scandinavian exchange group OMX. Together, NASDAQ OMX operates 25 securities markets. It also provides trading technology to 70 exchanges in 50 countries.

Market makers

NASDAQ market makers compete with each other to buy and sell the stocks they choose to represent. Nearly 300 member firms act as market makers for NAS-DAQ. Each uses its own capital, research, and system resources to represent a stock and compete with other market makers.

Market makers compete for customers' orders by displaying buy and sell quota-tions on an electronic exchange for a guaranteed number of shares at a specific price. After market makers receive orders, they immediately purchase or sell stock from their own inventories or seek out the other side of the trades so they can be executed, usually in a matter of seconds. The four types of market makers are

>> **Retail market makers:** They serve institutional and individual investors through brokerage networks that provide a continuous flow of orders and sales opportunities.

>> **Wholesale market makers:** They serve primarily institutional clients and other brokers or dealers who aren't registered market makers in a particular company's stock but who need to execute orders for their customers.

>> **Institutional market makers:** They execute large block orders for institu-tional investors, such as pension funds, mutual funds, insurance companies, and asset-management companies.

>> **Regional market makers:** They serve companies and individuals of a particular region. By focusing regionally, these market makers offer their customers more extensive coverage of the stocks and investors in a particular area of the country.

NASDAQ continues to be the leader in electronic trading. Its system, called the NASDAQ Crossing Network, enables fully anonymous trade execution to minimize the market impact of trading.

Over-the-counter and bulletin-board stocks

Stocks that do not meet the minimum requirements to be listed on NASDAQ are traded as *over-the-counter* or *bulletin-board* stocks (OTCBB). The OTCBB is a regulated quotation service that displays real-time quotes, last-sale prices, and volume information for the stocks traded OTCBB. These stocks generally don't meet the listing qualifications for NASDAQ or other national securities exchanges, and fewer than two (and sometimes zero) market makers trade in these stocks, making buying and selling them more difficult.

Amex (now NYSE MKT LLC)

When the NYSE moved indoors, some stocks still weren't good enough to be sold on the exchange. Those stocks were called *curb traders* and ultimately made up what became known as the American Stock Exchange (Amex), which moved indoors in 1921. Amex lists stocks that are smaller in size than those on the NYSE yet still have a national following. Many firms that first list on Amex work to meet the listing requirements of the NYSE and then switch over.

The Amex trading system was integrated into the NYSE trading system after the merger with the NYSE was completed in 2008, and its named changed to the NYSE Alternext. Then in 2009, the name was changed to NYSE Amex Equities. In May 2012, the name changed again to NYSE MKT LLC.

LISTING REQUIREMENTS

NASDAQ has the easiest minimum listing requirements of all the broad-market exchanges. The New York Stock Exchange (NYSE) has the toughest requirements to meet for companies to be listed. In addition to listing requirements, companies on the exchanges must conform to certain rules, including publishing quarterly reports, soliciting proxies, and publicly announcing developments that may affect the value of the securities.

Electronic communications networks (ECNs)

Many traders look for ways to get around dealing with a traditional broker. Instead they access trades using a *direct-access broker*. We talk more about the differences in Chapter 3. A new system of electronic trading that is developing is called the *electronic communications network* (ECN).

ECNs enable buyers and sellers to meet electronically to execute trades. The trades are entered into the ECN systems by market makers at one of the exchanges or by an OTC market maker. Transactions are completed without a broker-dealer, saving users the cost of commissions normally charged for more traditional forms of trading.

Subscribers to ECNs include retail investors, institutional investors, market makers, and broker-dealers. ECNs are accessed through a custom terminal or by direct Internet connection. Orders are posted by the ECN for subscribers to view. The ECN then matches orders for execution. In most cases, buyers and sellers maintain their anonymity and do not list identifiable information in their buy or sell orders.

In the last few years, ECNs have gone through consolidation. Inet was acquired by NASDAQ. Archipelago now operates under the NYSE umbrella as NYSE Arca Options. Instinet, which serves primarily institutional traders, has an agreement for after-hours trading with E*Trade.

Understanding Order Types

Buying a share of stock can be as easy as calling a broker and saying that you want to buy such and such a stock — but you can place an order in a number of other ways that give you better protections. Most orders are placed as day orders, but you can choose to place them as good-'til-canceled orders. The four basic types of orders you can place are market orders, limit orders, stop orders, and stop-limit orders.

REMEMBER

Understanding the language and using it to protect your assets and the way you trade are critical to your success as a trader. The next few sections explain the nuances of placing orders so you don't make a potentially costly mistake by placing a market order when you intended to place a limit order. Putting a stop-limit order in place may sound like the safest way to go; however, doing so may not help you in a rapidly changing market.

Market order

When you place a *market order,* you're essentially telling a broker to buy or sell a stock at the current market price. A market order is the way your broker normally places an order unless you give him or her different instructions. The advantage of a market order is that you're almost always guaranteed that your order is executed as long as willing buyers and sellers are in the marketplace. Generally speaking, buy orders are filled at the *ask price* (the price at which the holder of the stock is willing to sell), and sell orders are filled at the *bid price* (the price at which a buyer is willing to buy). If, however, you're working with a broker who has a smart-order routing system, which looks for the best bid/ask prices, you sometimes can get a better price on the NASDAQ.

WARNING

The disadvantage of a market order is that you're stuck paying the price when the order is executed — possibly not at the price you expected when you placed the order. Brokers and real-time quote services quote you prices, but because the markets move fast, with deals taking place in seconds, you'll probably find that the price you're quoted rarely is the same as the execution price. Whenever you place a market order, especially if you're seeking a large number of shares, the probability is even greater that you'll receive different prices for parts of the order — 100 shares at $25 and 100 shares at $25.05, for example.

Limit order

If you want to avoid buying or selling stock at a price higher or lower than you intend, you must place a *limit order* instead of a market order. When placing a limit order, you specify the price at which you'll buy or sell. You can place either a buy limit order or a sell limit order. Buy limit orders can be executed only when a seller is willing to sell the stock you're buying at the limit price or lower. A sell limit order can be executed only when a buyer is willing to pay your limit price or higher. In other words, you set the parameters for the price that you'll accept. You can't do that with a market order.

The risk that you take when placing a limit order is that the order may never be filled. For example, a hot stock piques your interest when it's selling for $10, so you decide to place a limit order to buy the stock at $10.50. By the time you call your broker or input the order into your trading system, the price already has moved above $10.50 and never drops back to that level — thus, your order won't be filled. On the good side, if the stock is so hot that its price skyrockets to $75, you also won't be stuck as the owner of the stock after purchasing near the $75 high. That high will likely be a temporary top that quickly drops back to reality, which would force you to sell the stock at a significant loss at some point in the future.

Some firms charge more for executing a limit order than they do for a market order. Be sure that you understand the fee and commission structures if you intend to use limit orders. If your broker charges for limit orders, you may want to change brokers.

Stop order

You may also consider placing your order as a *stop order*, which means that whenever the stock reaches a price that you specify, it automatically becomes a market order. Investors who buy using a stop order usually do so to limit potential losses or protect a profit. Buy stop orders are always entered at a stop price that is above the current market price.

When placing a sell stop order, you do so to avoid further losses or to protect a profit that exists in case the stock continues on a downward trend. The sell stop price is always placed below the current market price. For example, if a stock you bought for $10 is now selling for $25, you can decide to protect most of that profit by placing a sell stop order that specifies that stock be sold when the market price falls to $20, thus guaranteeing a $10 gain.

You don't have to watch the stock market every second; instead, when the market price drops to $20, your stop order automatically switches to a market order and is executed.

The big disadvantage of a stop order is that if for some reason the stock market gets a shock during the news day that affects all stocks, it can temporarily send prices lower, activating your stop price. If it turns out that the downturn is merely a short-term fluctuation and not an indication that the stock you hold is a bad choice or that you risk losing your profit, your stock may sell before you ever have time to react.

The bottom can fall out of your stock's pricing. After your stop price is reached, a stop order automatically becomes a market order, and the price that you actually receive can differ greatly from your stop price, especially in a rapidly fluctuating market. You can avoid this problem by placing a stop-limit order, which we discuss in the next section.

Stop orders are not officially supported on the NASDAQ. However, most brokers offer a service to simulate a stop order. If you want to enter a stop order for a NASDAQ stock, your broker must watch the market and enter the market or limit order you designate as a stop when the stock reaches your specified sale price. Some broker-dealers won't accept a stop order on some securities and almost never accept a stop order for OTC stocks. If you intend to use stop orders, make sure that you

>> Check with the brokers you're planning to use to ensure that they accept stop orders.

>> Find out what your brokers charge for stop orders.

>> Review how your broker's stop orders work, so you don't run into surprises.

After all, you don't want to execute a stop order and end up selling a stock that you didn't intend to sell or at a price you find unacceptable.

Stop-limit order

You can protect yourself from any buying or selling surprises by placing a *stop-limit order*. This type of order combines the features of both a stop order and a limit order. When your stop price is reached, the stop order becomes a limit order rather than a market order.

A stop-limit order gives you the most control over the price at which you will trade your stock. You can avoid a purchase or sale of your stock at a price that differs significantly from what you intend. But you do risk the possibility that the stop-limit order may never be executed, which can happen in fast-moving markets where prices fluctuate wildly.

For example, you may find that deploying stop-limit orders is particularly dangerous to your portfolio, especially when bad news breaks about a stock you're holding and its price drops rapidly. Although you have a stop-limit order in place, and the stop price is met, the movement in the market may happen so rapidly that the price limit you set is missed. In this case, the limit side of the order actually prevents the sale of the stock, and you risk riding it all the way down until you change your order. For example, say you purchased a stock at $8 near its peak. On the day the company's CEO and CFO were fired, the stock dropped to $4.05. You may have had a stop-limit order in place to sell at $5, but on the day of the firing, the price dropped so rapidly after the company announced the firing that your stop-limit order could not be filled at your limit price.

TIP

Stop-limit orders, like stop orders, are more commonly used when trading on an exchange than in an OTC market. Broker-dealers likewise can limit the securities on which stop-limit orders can be placed. If you want to use stop-limit orders, be sure to review the rules with your broker before trying to execute them.

Good-'til-canceled order

You can avoid having to replace an order time and again by using a *good-'til-canceled* (GTC) order. GTC orders are placed at a limit or stop price and last until the order actually is executed or you decide to cancel it. A GTC order won't be executed until the limit price is reached, regardless of how many days or weeks it takes.

You can choose to use this type of order whenever you want to set a limit price that differs significantly from the current market price. Many brokerage firms limit how much time a GTC order can remain in place, and most of them charge more for executing this type of order.

Other order types

Less commonly used order methods include contingent, all-or-none, and fill-or-kill orders. *Contingent orders* are placed on the contingency that another one of your stock holdings is sold before the order is placed. An *all-or-none order* specifies that all the shares of a stock be bought according to the terms indicated or that none of the stock should be purchased. A *fill-or-kill order* must be filled immediately upon placement or be killed.

Chapter **3**

Going for Broke(r): Discovering Brokerage Options

As an individual, you can't trade stocks — or bonds, or options, or futures — unless you have a broker or are a broker yourself. That doesn't mean, however, that you have to work with a human being to trade stocks. Online brokers and direct-access brokers enable you to make trades electronically, so you never need to speak with a human being for these processes unless you're having a technical problem.

The differences among brokers are based on prices, services, and special capabilities. High-volume swing traders and day traders typically require the services of a direct-access broker, while position traders can and do trade successfully with more traditional discount, online, and full-service brokers. In this chapter, we help you understand the brokerage options that are available, the types of accounts you can establish, and the basic trading rules you must follow.

Why You Need a Broker

Unless you plan to get your brokerage license from the National Association of Securities Dealers (NASD) and set up shop yourself (which is hard — and expensive — to do), you need to work with a broker to be able to buy and sell stocks. How you choose a broker is based on the level of individual services you want. The more services you want, the more you pay for your ability to trade.

As an individual, you can open your account with a brokerage house, but if you work with a human being, that person is considered a broker. Brokerage houses or brokerage services are also usually referred to as brokers for short.

REMEMBER

For now, just be aware that on one side of the spectrum is the full-service broker who does a lot of hand-holding and offers stock research and advice and other human-based services. When using a full-service broker, you pay a significant commission for each stock trade. In the middle are discount brokers that offer fewer services but charge less per trade. On the opposite side of the spectrum are direct-access brokers, who offer few human-based services and instead provide extensive trading platforms so you can trade electronically and access the stock-exchange systems directly on a real-time basis.

Exploring Types of Brokers and Brokerage Services

Before you can pick the type of broker that best fulfills your needs, you need to understand the kinds of services that each kind of broker provides. After you gain an understanding of your options and select the types of services you want, you then need to carefully research each of the brokers that match your needs. Within each classification are good and bad brokers. We give you the tools for researching brokerage firms in the sections that follow.

Full-service brokers

If you want someone to assist you with buying decisions and implementing those decisions, you need to check out full-service brokers. They offer extensive research and other services. Usually, they call you with trading ideas. All you need to do is say yes or no. You pay a transaction fee for trades plus a commission percentage based on the dollar volume. You can invest in stocks, futures, options, bonds, mutual funds, money-market funds, and variable annuities. You can work with a full-service broker by telephone, mail, fax, or Internet. Most have websites you can access for information, and many allow you to enter your own trades.

Here is an example transaction fee schedule for one of the better-known full-service brokers (others can be as much as twice as high):

Transaction Size	Commission Rate
$0–$6,000	2% of principal
$6,001–$10,000	$30 plus 1.5% of principal
$10,001–$25,000	$80 plus 1% of principal
$25,001–$100,000	$205 plus 1% of principal

Alternatively, some full-service brokers do permit you to make all the trades you want per year for a fee of 0.30 percent to 2.5 percent of the total assets in your brokerage account. Using language common to traders, that's 30 to 250 basis points. You have to have more than $10 million in an account to get the lowest fee. Traders with less than $100,000 pay closer to the 2.5 percent of assets to access the unlimited trading features.

WARNING

Just because you choose to use a full-service broker doesn't mean you can just sit back and let your money grow after placing it into an account. Brokers make money on commissions for the exchange of stocks. If they have no transactions during a given month, they don't get paid. Unscrupulous brokers recommend trades to their customers to generate new commissions even when those decisions are not necessarily the best investment advice for their clients. This practice is often referred to as *churning*.

Even the research arms of many full-service brokerage houses are scrutinized by the Securities and Exchange Commission (SEC) primarily because their analyses didn't accurately reflect the values of stocks in companies that used the firms' investment-banking capabilities in the past. Analysts tend to see their firms' clients through rose-colored glasses when providing research reports, especially when their firms make a lot of money by providing investment-banking services to those companies. We talk about changes that have been implemented to improve analyst services in Chapter 7.

REMEMBER

Just because you choose to work through a full-service broker doesn't mean you can sidestep doing your own research. You always need to perform due diligence, independently researching your stock purchases. Although you certainly can use the research arm of your brokerage firm, it shouldn't be your sole source of research on any stock you're thinking about buying or that you already hold.

TIP

If you're planning to be a trader, then do your own research and implement your own trading strategies. Why pay for the services of a full-service broker? We really don't recommend that you waste your money on the additional costs of maintaining a full-service brokerage account or paying the high transaction fees and commissions.

Discount brokers

Many discount brokers offer the same services as full-service brokers, including research. The big exception is that you don't get individual attention or unsolicited advice on what to buy or sell. Some discount brokers send out monthly newsletters with stock recommendations; most don't trade futures or sell variable annuities. You can access a discount broker by telephone, mail, fax, or Internet. To get the lowest fees on trades, you need to do your own trades by accessing the broker's website.

The big difference to you, as an individual trader, is that you can save a lot of money on trading costs, provided you know what you're doing and you understand the language of stock trading. Transaction fees for online trades can range from as low as $5 up to about $30 with a discount broker. If you want special services requiring a broker's assistance, you can work with a human being. Depending on the discount brokerage firm and the level of service required, fees can range from $25 to $50 per trade. Some discount brokers provide broker-assisted trades using a commission rate schedule similar to the ones offered by full-service brokers, but it has lower fees per trade. If you get involved in more-complicated trading transactions that require human assistance, costs can rise significantly. Anytime you're planning to use a broker's assistance, be sure you understand any additional costs that may be charged to your account for that assistance.

Direct-access brokers

If you want to bypass the traditional brokers and trade directly through an exchange or market maker, you need to open your account with a direct-access broker so you can use one or more of the electronic communications networks (ECNs) to make your trades. Traders usually download software onto their PCs so they can access the ECN directly using their Internet connections.

Traders using direct-access brokers typically get real-time NASDAQ Level I quotes, which show the latest bid and ask prices, quote size, last trade, and volume.

Direct-access brokers also offer NASDAQ Level II access. NASDAQ fees are higher for Level II, and the brokerage may also charge an additional fee for this type of access. In addition to what you see in a Level I quote, you also find the number of market makers participating in the market for any one stock.

A NASDAQ Level II quote screen shows the best bid price and the best ask price for specific stocks from participating market makers. All the bid and ask prices are ranked from best to worst. Some direct-access brokers combine NASDAQ Level II information and ECN book data to show the complete market depth for a specific stock. The ECN book isn't a printed book like you would expect to find on a bookstore shelf. It's a compilation of all the trades and the bid and ask quotes available on all the electronic networks.

Traders can review the quotes and select which market maker or ECN to use for each transaction. Most full-service and discount brokers make that choice for you when you're working with them. A few discount brokers are providing access to ECNs.

TIP

When working with direct-access brokers, one key difference is that the software you use may reside on your own computer and not on your broker's server, which greatly accelerates the speed at which you can trade. Again, some discount brokers provide software to enable you to receive direct raw data on your home computer, but their software isn't as sophisticated as what direct-access brokers have to offer. We cover software issues in detail in Chapter 4.

REMEMBER

We often talk about how you can miss trading at the prices you want, especially in fast-moving markets. Well, having direct access doesn't guarantee that you won't miss a price, but your chances of catching those prices are better because you don't have to wait for pages to download from your broker's server. Of course, for this advantage to work for you, you must have high-speed Internet access, which can include DSL, cable, or satellite access.

Working with a direct-access broker gives you a steady stream of raw financial data — the actual trades, current bid and ask prices, trading volume, and market statistics. The trading software that you load onto your computer determines how this data is organized and presented on your computer monitor. Providing better access is how direct-access brokers distinguish their services from other brokers.

Software prices and access fees vary greatly and can cost you as much as $300 per month. The fees sometimes can be waived, especially if your trading volume is high enough — typically about 50 or more trades per month. As you can see, you have to make regular trades for a direct-access broker to be more cost-effective than a discount broker. That said, even some discount brokers offer limited direct access using less-sophisticated software.

Proprietary trading firms

Proprietary (or *prop*) trading firms enable traders to use at least some of the firm's capital in addition to or instead of their own. Depending on the firm, traders share the gains and may (or may not) share the losses. You can't just walk in and expect to trade with one of these firms. You must have an NASD Series 7 license combined with a proven history of trading in the equity markets. Some proprietary trading firms may also require that you have a Series 55 and Series 63 license. The firm you work with trains you in its trading style, but proprietary trading is not usually an option for beginners. Some proprietary trading firms do offer to bring in beginners or relatively inexperienced traders to train who don't meet licensing requirements upfront, but the fees for this training can be steep.

Futures brokers

Unless you're working with a full-service brokerage firm, you may have to open a separate account with a futures broker if you want to trade commodities or other types of futures. Futures brokers must be licensed by the NASD in a way that differs from stockbrokers. Many direct-access brokers provide futures brokerage services, but you can't always find them at a discount broker. We talk more about trading futures in Chapter 19.

Services to Consider When Choosing a Broker

You can't choose your broker purely on the basis of price. You need to know what types of services are offered to enable you to make the types of trades you want to make. When researching brokers, check out the types of orders supported, whether they can offer you data tools, what types of charts they provide, and whether they can give you ECN access if you want to make your own trades electronically.

Types of orders supported

As we mention in Chapter 2, not all brokers provide stop orders for OTC and NAS-DAQ trades. The NASDAQ has no facility for handling stop orders, so the broker must monitor your stop prices and enter either market or limit orders if your price is triggered. Although monitoring stop prices usually is done automatically, not all brokers offer the service. If you know you'll be using stops with many of your trades, you need to find a broker who provides those services. Some discount brokers provide those services if you're willing to pay for them.

As such, you also need to compare not only prices for those services but also the respective brokers' reputations for effectively and efficiently providing those services. If you want to place contingent orders (see Chapter 2), you may discover that few discount brokers offer that service, even for a price.

WARNING

As you trade, you definitely need to steer clear of brokers who accept *payment for order flow,* a practice in which some exchanges or market makers pay brokerage firms for routing orders to them. Firms can make a penny or more per share, but the SEC requires the firm to inform you whether it receives payment for order flow when you first open an account and thereafter on an annual basis. Each time a firm receives a payment for order flow, it must disclose that information on the trade confirmation. If you see an indication on one of your trades that your broker received this type of payment, you have the right to request notification in writing about the source and type of payment related to that transaction. These payments may encourage unethical brokers to steer orders away from the best prices and toward the market maker offering such payments.

Data tools

The type of data to which you want to have access is crucial. Most brokers provide basic stock quotes, usually in real time, and some may even offer market data providing a much deeper look at the market that includes not only current sales information but also previous sales information. If you want access to a higher level of data, you need to open your brokerage account with a firm that provides the level of data that you need, or you may buy it from a third party. Again, pricing for differing data tools can vary among brokerage firms. Firms that offer you ways of getting this data through your home computer (as opposed to accessing it from their servers) charge more, but you'll receive the information quicker. The faster your Internet connection, the more quickly and reliably you receive this information. Data feeds may also include critical tools such as stock screeners, option analytics, rating service information, and news feeds. We cover data tools in greater detail in Chapter 4.

Charts

Data fed into your home computer is raw stock-market data. How this information is formatted on your computer and which charts you're able to build from it depend on the software that your broker provides. Charting software can be critical to your ability to make trading decisions. Your broker may charge you to use the software but usually discounts or waives the fee based on the size of your portfolio or your volume of trading activity.

TIP

Many free charting alternatives are available online, including StockCharts.com, which we used to produce the charts for this book. We talk about charting capabilities in Chapter 4.

ECN access

If direct access to stock exchanges and market makers is important to you, then you need to find a broker that provides ECN access. You don't have to open an account through a direct-access broker; some discount brokers do provide ECN access. Be sure to check out the section "Choosing the Right Broker for You," later in this chapter.

Knowing the Types of Brokerage Accounts

You can open your brokerage accounts in a couple of different ways: as a cash account or a margin account. However, if you open a margin account, you also must open a cash account. You also may open separate accounts for retirement savings. Because retirement accounts have more restrictions, your trading alternatives are more limited in those accounts, but that isn't necessarily a bad thing. You shouldn't be risking your retirement funds on speculative trading anyway.

Cash accounts

The traditional brokerage account is a *cash account,* which also is known as a *Type 1 account.* With a cash account, you must deposit the full cost of any purchases by the settlement date of the transaction. At many brokerage houses prior to 2002, you were permitted to place an order to buy stock even if the cash was not yet in your account. As long as the money was deposited within three days of the completion of the transaction, you could make the purchase. Today, however, few brokers give you that kind of flexibility. Most brokers require funds to buy stocks to be in your cash account before you can place an order. The amount of cash you need to have on deposit varies by broker; some let you open an account for as little as $100 or $1,000, but others require as much as $10,000 or more to open a new cash account.

Margin accounts

You don't have to have as much cash on hand to buy stock when you open a *margin account,* which also is known as a *Type 2 account.* This type of account enables you to borrow certain amounts of money using cash or securities already in the account as collateral. Because using a margin account essentially is buying stocks or bonds on credit, each respective brokerage firm has its own screening procedure to determine whether you qualify for the loan and can buy on margin.

The Federal Reserve requires a $2,000 minimum deposit to open a margin account, and it currently limits the amount you can borrow on margin to 50 percent of the initial purchase price. Not all stocks can be bought on margin. Some brokerage firms enforce even stricter margin rules, especially if you choose to invest in volatile stocks. When buying stocks on margin, you pay an interest rate on the margin loans, but most brokerage firms charge relatively low rates to encourage the transaction business. Be sure to check out the "Margin requirements" section later in this chapter.

When opening a margin account, the firm also requires you to sign what's called a *hypothecation agreement,* which stipulates regulations for the account and permits the broker to have a lien on your account whenever the balance in your account falls below the minimum maintenance margin (more about that in a moment). The agreement also enables your broker to loan your shares to short sellers. That's where shorted stock comes from. We talk more about short selling and the mechanics of margin trading in Chapter 15.

WARNING

You're taking a risk by purchasing shares of stock with borrowed money and using shares you own as collateral. If your stock holdings fall in value below the minimum maintenance margin requirement, your broker can force you to sell stock you don't want to sell and use other assets you may not want to use to cover the outstanding loan. The risks and regulations for using a margin account are described more fully in the section on margin requirements, later in this chapter.

Options

If you want to trade options, your broker will require you to sign a special options agreement acknowledging that you understand the risks associated with trading options or derivative instruments. This practice became common after brokers were sued by some clients because they suffered huge losses when trading options and claimed they were unaware of the risks. The agreement protects the broker from being sued if you lose a lot of money, so you need to know what you're doing when dealing with derivatives (see Chapter 19).

IRAs and other retirement accounts

IRAs and other accounts in which you're saving for retirement — such as 401(k)s or 403(b)s — sometimes allow you to trade options, but margin trading is not allowed at all. These limitations are for your protection to avoid risking major losses in your long-term investments that never should be put at such high levels of risk. The Internal Revenue Code limits the amount you can contribute each year to all retirement accounts.

Although you may be able to find a brokerage firm that allows you to trade using options — puts and calls, which are a type of option (see Chapter 19) — you nevertheless risk penalties for certain trading activities that occur in your retirement account whenever the IRS determines the account is being used for trading purposes rather than long-term investing. Officially, the Internal Revenue Code prohibits the "IRA or Keogh Plan account holder from loaning money to the account. Likewise, the holder cannot guarantee borrowing by the account or cover its losses." That's why margin accounts, which entail a type of borrowing, aren't allowed.

REMEMBER

Because these accounts are either tax-free or tax-deferred, you can't write off any losses in them against any gains from investments held outside of them in other taxable accounts. In other words, you don't have the same tax-planning choices with IRAs or retirement accounts to offset gains and losses. All money taken out of an IRA at retirement is taxed at your current income tax rate. This differs from stocks held outside an IRA. For these stocks, you can use stock losses to minimize the tax you may have to pay on stock gains. If you hold the stock for longer than a year, you're taxed based on the lower capital gains rate of 15 percent for most taxpayers (some low-income taxpayers qualify for a rate as low as 0 percent) rather than your higher current income tax rate, which can be as high as 35 percent for some taxpayers.

Here are some additional trading limitations of retirement accounts:

>> **Margin is not allowed.** Using funds within a retirement account as collateral for trading on margin isn't permitted. It's against the law. You won't find a broker that will permit you to place retirement funds in margin accounts.

>> **Short positions are prohibited.** Speculative trading using short positions, which is a common trading strategy for futures contracts and widely used by experienced stock and bond traders, requires a margin account. When someone shorts a stock, he or she borrows the stock and sells it in the hope of buying it back later for less. Selling short requires the use of margin and is therefore not permitted in a retirement account. We talk more about short selling in Chapter 15.

>> **Trading policies are more stringent.** All brokers have more stringent trading policies for retirement accounts. Before you open a retirement account, check with your broker about its trading limitations to be sure they match your intentions for the account.

>> **Options trading may not be permitted.** If you're an experienced trader, you can find some brokerage firms that allow options trading in your retirement account. Not all types of options, however, can be traded in a retirement account. The ones that you most likely can trade are covered calls, long call and put positions, or cash-secured puts. We talk more about puts and calls in Chapter 19.

Choosing the Right Broker for You

Before beginning a search for the right broker, you must first decide what type of trader you want to be and what services you need. If you want to be a position trader, or one who trades infrequently, your best bet is either a full-service or a discount broker. Making the choice between full-service and discount brokers depends on how independently you want to operate as a trader. If you want advice on your stock-investing plans, you need to seek out a full-service broker, but we certainly don't recommend this expensive option. Before risking your money on trading, however, you need to be comfortable enough with the language and mechanics of trading and how to conduct your own research. If you don't need the services of a direct-access broker, your best bet is to select a discount broker.

Considering more than price

Your choice of brokers should be based on much more than who can offer you the cheapest price. Although price definitely is a factor in your selection of broker, it's one of many factors you need to consider. The most important factors are the services that your broker offers and how effective and efficient the broker is in carrying out those promised services. Look for brokers that offer smart order-routing capabilities, but steer clear of the ones that accept payment for order flow (see the earlier section "Types of orders supported").

REMEMBER

You may find a brokerage firm that provides all the bells and whistles at the cheapest price, but if its systems break down at a critical trading moment and you're not able to implement your trades when you want to, those bells and whistles mean nothing, and not being able to rely on them can result in huge losses. Look for brokers that allow you to test-drive a demo version of order-entry systems. Also, if you want to trade using a mobile device, be sure your broker offers one that is dependable.

Doing a little research

If you expect to become an active and successful trader and want full access so you can trade electronically through the exchanges, you more than likely need to research direct-access brokers. If, however, you believe that your volume of trades per month will be lower than 50, you may want to consider a discount broker that offers access to ECNs. Basically, your choice of brokers comes down to the types of services and accounts you need and which broker offers the best mix for what you want to do and pay.

Your first step is to make lists of your financial objectives, the types of trading you want to do, and the services you know you're going to need. After committing those factors to memory, talk with other traders you know and be sure to find out what their experiences have been with various brokers.

TIP

You can also research and compare ratings of brokers on the Internet. Try these websites:

>> **Kiplinger:** Kiplinger picks the seven best online brokers for investors and explains why at http://www.kiplinger.com/slideshow/investing/T023-S003-best-online-brokers/index.html.

>> **Barron's:** Barron's publishes an annual survey of the best online brokers every March. Here is the one from 2016: http://www.barrons.com/articles/best-online-brokers-fidelity-wins-in-barrons-2016-survey-1458363203.

>> **Stocks and Commodities:** This magazine (www.traders.com) also periodically reviews brokers and trading platforms. Subscription is required.

TIP

After narrowing down your choices, check out the disciplinary histories of the brokerage firms you're considering. You can easily do that by calling a toll-free hotline operated by the Financial Industry Regulatory Authority (FINRA) at 800-289-9999, or checking its website at www.finra.org to find out what disciplinary actions (if any) have been taken by securities regulators or criminal authorities. On the front page of the FINRA website, you'll see "Broker Check" at the top right of the page. You can use this to check the background of brokers. FINRA also has a Securities Helpline for Seniors you can call: 844-574-3577. You also need to call your state regulator to be sure the specific broker you're thinking about working with is licensed to do business in your state. This information can be crucial. If you work with an unlicensed broker who goes out of business, you may not have any way of recovering any lost funds, even if an arbitrator or court rules in your favor.

Understanding how you'll be paying

After conducting your initial research into brokerage firms and narrowing down your choices, be sure you understand how the brokerage firms are paid by

>> Reviewing each firm's fee and commission schedule. The schedules should include the fees or charges you're required to pay when opening the account and what you pay to maintain and close the account.

>> Finding out how your broker is compensated if you're planning to work with a human being rather than trade online. Many brokers receive higher compensation when they sell their firm's own products, so they may try to steer you toward them rather than another product that may be a better match for your trading objectives. Rarely are brokerage products good trading vehicles.

TIP

One other level of protection that you need to check on is the broker's membership in the Securities Investor Protection Corporation (SIPC). Although SIPC membership won't insure you against losses caused by market declines, the SIPC does give you some protection if your brokerage firm faces insolvency. You can find out more about the SIPC at www.sipc.org.

Getting to Know the Rules

After you pick your broker, you must be sure you know the trading rules. Although federal law mandates margin requirements, sets trade settlement rules, and bans free riding (nope, we're not talking about horseback riding here), brokerage firms sometimes have even more stringent rules for their clients. We review the federal requirements here, but you need to check with your broker to find out any additional rules it imposes.

Rules for stock trading fall under the jurisdiction of the Federal Reserve, which specifies its stock trading regulations in *Regulation T*. Rules spelled out under Regulation T encompass margin accounts, broker–dealer accounts, securities transactions, credit extended based on securities, and other factors related to securities markets. We don't review all the specifics here, but instead we home in on three key areas that impact your trading choices — margin requirements, trade settlement, and free riding.

Margin requirements

The Federal Reserve's Regulation T specifies how much you can borrow when you use a margin account to purchase new shares of stocks on margin. This *initial margin requirement* permits you to borrow up to 50 percent of the cost of the new shares. For example, if you open a new margin account with a $10,000 cash deposit, you buy up to $20,000 worth of stock. After your $20,000 purchase, your account will have a cash balance of $0, an equity balance of $10,000, and a margin balance of $10,000. At this time, all your equity is committed to this trade, so you can't enter any new positions unless you deposit additional funds.

If the stock price increases, your equity balance increases. If the stock price decreases, your equity balance decreases. In either case, your margin balance remains the same, $10,000. The only way to reduce the outstanding margin balance is to deposit extra cash into your account or sell the shares of stock.

When your stock price increases, your equity balance increases and you may use the increased equity as collateral to borrow additional money to buy additional shares of stocks. You may borrow up to the value of the increased equity balance, which increases your margin balance.

However, if your equity balance decreases, NASD rules (Rule 431 and Rule 2520, respectively) regulate the minimum equity position permitted in your account. Currently, the minimum is 25 percent of the total value of all margined securities if one is a pattern day trader (more about day trading in Chapter 18). Some brokers may require more.

For a pattern day trader, if the total value of the stock falls below $13,332, then the equity balance in your initial $10,000 portfolio will be less than 25 percent of the total remaining value. The math is simple: 25 percent of $13,332 is $3,333. Your cash balance is still $0, and your margin balance is still $10,000. Subtract $10,000 from $13,332 to determine your equity balance, which is $3,332. Your equity balance is less than 25 percent of your total account balance.

When this occurs, your broker will call and demand additional collateral to support the outstanding margin loan. This is a *margin call.* You may meet your margin-call requirements by depositing more cash, or you may deposit fully paid, unmargined securities from another account. If you don't deposit additional collateral, your broker is permitted to sell up to four times the amount of stock required to meet your margin call and may sell any of the stocks in your portfolio.

If you have more than a few positions, margin calculations become complex. It helps to think about it like this: When initiating a new position, you can never borrow more than half of the position's value. To maintain sufficient collateral, your broker will insist that the value of your stocks be more than enough to cover the loan. Therefore, if your equity balance falls below 25 percent of the total portfolio value, your broker will ask for additional collateral in the form of a margin call.

As a trader, you should never satisfy a margin call. Instead, you should close the offending position(s). It's possible that an extraordinary event may cause the value of your stocks to fall below the amount owed on your outstanding margin loan. If this happens, your broker will close your positions, but you must still repay the debt. Unlike a cash account, you can lose more than 100 percent of the money you deposit into a margin account.

Not all stocks can be bought on margin and neither can all stocks be used as collateral. If you want to trade on margin, be sure you understand the margin requirements imposed by your broker. Some brokerage firms require even stiffer requirements to maintain a margin account, especially if you trade volatile or lightly traded stocks.

If you trade any security in the same day in a margin account, be sure you understand the FINRA rules for day-trading activity. Your broker or the FINRA will consider you a *pattern day trader* after you buy or sell any security on the same day in a margin account and execute four or more such trades during a five-day business period (excluding Saturdays, Sundays, and holidays). If you're pegged as a pattern day trader, you're required to maintain $25,000 in your margin account, which can seriously impact your day trading and other trading activities.

Settling trades

When you place an order to buy a stock, you must settle that transaction in three business days. This *settlement cycle* is known as *T + 3*. The brokerage firm must receive your payment for any securities you buy no later than three days after the trade is executed. Today, many brokers require that the cash be in your account before placing the trade unless you have a margin account set up. If you're selling a stock, it's probably being held in your brokerage account and will be taken out of that account on the day of settlement. Options and government securities trade on a *T + 1* settlement cycle, which means these transactions settle the next trading day.

Free riding

No, we're not talking about hopping a train on the sly. *Free riding* in the stock-trading world can get you in a bunch of trouble, so keep reading. Basically it means that you must pay for a stock before you can sell it, and because settling a stock transaction takes three days, that means, in theory, you can actually buy a stock and then place an order to sell it before the stock purchase actually settles. You can actually buy and sell a stock without any cash because of the lag time in settling the account.

This is a cash account problem. Although many swing and day traders actually turn around stock purchases and sales that quickly, they typically trade in a margin account and are able to sidestep the problem. Margin traders use the unsettled proceeds of a trade as collateral to borrow money until the trade is settled. Still, day traders and swing traders must have enough cash or buying power in their accounts to cover all purchases of stock.

Formally, this rule is found in Section 220 of Regulation T, which states that in a cash account a brokerage firm may buy a security on your behalf — or sell a security — if either of the following applies:

>> You have sufficient funds in the account.

>> The firm accepts in good faith your agreement to make a full-cash payment for the security before you sell it.

If you do ever buy and sell a security before the settlement cycle (T + 3) is complete — or even on the same day — and without sufficient cash in your account, a brokerage firm can make what is called an *intraday extension of credit* (a loan), but it exposes the firm to increased risks — especially the risk that you may overextend your financial resources and may not be able to settle your trades. Most brokerage firms require active traders who buy and then sell securities within the settlement cycle to conduct those activities within a margin account.

WARNING

If you take a free ride and haven't made some type of credit arrangement with your broker, your broker is likely to freeze your account for 90 days. During that 90-day period, the broker requires you to pay for any purchase on the date that you make the trade. In other words, you lose the option of settling your trades within three days. Some brokerage firms require you to have enough cash in your account to complete the transaction before you make the trade so you thus avoid even the risk of free riding.

We talk more about these rapid forms of trading (swing trading and day trading) in Chapters 17 and 18.

Chapter **4**

Putting Your Key Business Tool to Work: The Computer

B ack in the old days, you'd call your broker to enter an order and then wait for your broker to phone back and report the fill price. Active traders? They'd hang out in the broker's lobby, watching the ticker, boasting over winning trades, commiserating over losing trades, and shooting the breeze.

If you kept charts, you either made them yourself or had them delivered by postal carrier in book form. They arrived at the end of each week. If you couldn't afford that extravagance, you'd buy monthly summaries and update them yourself.

Every retail investor bought and sold stocks the same way. The pros had the advantage, but it was more or less a level playing field for the rest of us.

Today, you'd be hard-pressed to find a ticker-tape machine in any brokerage office. The Internet has changed everything. You can still buy chart books, but now they're delivered via the Internet, and so are stock prices, real-time intraday charts, and research reports. You can enter orders online, have your orders filled within seconds, and receive notification showing the order's price almost as quickly.

Online brokers provide a vast array of research and trading tools for their clients. Real-time streaming quotes, proprietary and third-party research, sophisticated charts, and extensive order-entry capabilities make today's traders better informed and better equipped than ever before.

If you're anything like us, you're going to spend plenty of time with your trading platform. It pays to spend a little time thinking about what information you need now, how you'll use it, and what you may need in the future. With just a little foresight, you can set up your trading platform so it's effective today and yet still be able to be upgraded without completely disrupting your day-to-day activities.

In this chapter, we review the basic computer hardware you need to access all there is to offer for traders, explore the software options you want to consider for managing your trading activities, and discuss various trading platforms and data-feed alternatives. Finally, we give you a road map to the options available on the Internet.

Making Use of Your Computer

Although tracking the market and charting stock prices by hand is an excellent learning exercise — it gives you a feel for the market that you can't get by reviewing computer-generated charts — we doubt that you'd want to travel to the local library or your broker's office to research the stocks that interest you. The wealth of online information that can help you improve your trading results is simply remarkable. This section lists some of the things you can do with your computer.

Identifying trading candidates

With your computer, you can do all of the following:

>> Display and interpret price charts

>> Research stocks, bonds, IPOs, options, and futures

>> Read analyst reports and company reports to the SEC

>> Screen stocks for technical or fundamental constraints

>> Monitor economic reports, earnings reports, and business news

>> Monitor market indexes, sectors, and trading statistics

Managing your account

With a computer and an Internet connection, you can manage your account, which involves some or all of the following:

>> Entering and executing trades and monitoring open orders

>> Controlling and tracking order routing

>> Receiving almost instantaneous fill reports

>> Monitoring and analyzing your portfolio and all open positions

>> Tracking profits and losses

>> Analyzing your trading history

Improving your trades

You can become a better trader by doing the following:

>> Evaluating trading systems and testing trading ideas

>> Keeping trading logs to audit your trading performance

>> Monitoring the tax consequences of your trades

>> Staying in touch with other traders

Finding Price Charts

Price charts show the history of a stock's price over time. These charts contain useful trading information that is revealed with careful analysis. Reading, interpreting, and understanding what you see in a price chart are described in Chapters 8 through 11 (Part 3).

There are two kinds of online charts: real-time charts and delayed-price charts. Although the charts may be identical, the prices shown in the charts are not. Real-time charts display current price data updated within a few seconds of the trade. Delayed-price charts don't show the most current trades. Instead, the prices shown on the chart are at least 15 to 20 minutes old.

Although real-time charts are desirable, they're a necessity only for extremely active short-term traders. Analyzing the market and developing your trading plan are best done before the market in which you plan to make your trades opens, or after it closes. Delayed-price charts are more than adequate for these planning and analysis activities.

Fortunately, price charts are easy to find. If your broker doesn't provide an adequate charting package, you can find excellent charting tools on dozens of online sites. Most of the charts on free websites display 20-minute delayed prices. You may have to pay $9.95 to $39 a month for Internet charts that update in real time (and put up with Internet banner ads if you have to go outside your broker's environment).

At a minimum, you need control over the time frame and the types of charts displayed. For example, you probably want 1-minute, 5-minute, 15-minute, and 60-minute charts to go with daily, weekly, and monthly charts. Other features to look for include these:

>> Trading volume. (It's critical.)

>> Moving averages to show average prices over time. You want at least two types, simple moving averages and exponential moving averages, and you want control over the period being averaged. Moving averages are discussed in Chapter 11.

>> Indicators and oscillators to help evaluate a stock's direction and momentum. We use the MACD (moving average convergence divergence) indicator and the stochastic oscillator. Indicators and oscillators are discussed in Chapter 11.

>> A variety of chart styles, including bar charts and candlestick charts. Bar charts are the most popular stock charts, and they're the ones we use throughout this book. We describe how to read and interpret them in Chapter 9. Candlestick charts display the price data using a slightly different format that some traders prefer. The analysis techniques in this book work for both styles.

>> Ability to display data in a log or semi-log format. This allows equal percentage price changes to appear the same on the price chart, which is helpful for comparing the price movements of two differently priced stocks. For example, if a $10 stock rises to $20, that's a 100 percent price change. If a $50 stock rises to $100, that's also a 100 percent price increase, but it will look like a much larger price increase on a standard price chart. Use a log or semi-log format to show similar percentage changes so they look the same on the chart.

>> Ability to group charts together so you can quickly scan open positions or trade candidates.

>> Ability to show support and resistance levels, draw trend lines, and make annotations.

Although many excellent online charting alternatives are out there, they typically aren't as flexible or configurable as the ones offered in stand-alone charting packages or integrated trading platforms. And you probably won't have access to trading-system development and testing software that's required to create and test your own trading system. The advantages and disadvantages of online charts, stand-alone charting packages, and integrated trading platforms are discussed in the following sections. We discuss methods for developing and testing personalized trading systems in Chapter 16.

Checking out Internet charts with delayed prices

You can use delayed-price charts to identify support and resistance levels, display moving averages, find emerging trends, and select possible entry and exit points for tomorrow's trading day.

TIP

Here are a couple of sources for online charts:

>> **BigCharts (`www.bigcharts.com`):** BigCharts is part of the CBS MarketWatch family. The site is free and offers an excellent charting package with plenty of options, including interactive charts, industry analysis, and stock screeners. You can define a list of favorite charts for quick review. News and market commentary are also provided.

>> **Investor's Business Daily (`www.investors.com`):** Investor's Business Daily (IBD) publishes its proprietary ranking system online and in its daily paper. Using the stock-picking methodology developed by publisher William O'Neil, the site provides charts and rankings by relative strength and earnings growth. They're available by subscription.

Considering Internet charts with real-time prices

Although most online brokers provide support for real-time prices, not all provide real-time charting capabilities. If your broker doesn't offer what you need and you find that delayed prices are just too frustrating, you can find a number of sites that offer real-time price charts. Real-time, browser-based Internet charts usually aren't free. They're generally priced between $9.95 and $39 per month.

Sites offering real-time charts include the following:

>> **StockCharts (www.stockcharts.com):** Chip Anderson started StockCharts early in Internet history. He's one of the few independents still around, and for good reason — the site is excellent. We use charts from this website throughout this book and have partnered with StockCharts for this book. StockCharts offers many excellent free charting tools, but the best parts are available by subscription. Advanced features include real-time intraday pricing, the ability to create and store chart annotations, the ability to create large lists of your favorite charts, the ability to define custom chart settings, and the capability of creating custom scans based on technical indicators.

>> **FreeRealTime.com (www.freerealtime.com):** The free capabilities of this site are fairly limited, and you'll have to put up with banner ads and the occasional full-page ad that display before the page you want appears. The free portion of this site uses data from electronic communications networks (ECNs), not data from the major stock exchanges. Unfortunately, ECNs don't trade all stocks, so real-time charts and quotes may not always be available. And ECN prices may not always match prices on the major exchanges, but they'll be very close. If you can put up with these limitations, the charts and price quotes are in real time. And they're free.

Looking into charting software

Before taking a step up toward a stand-alone charting application, make sure you explore the tools provided by your broker and other brokers and by websites offering Internet charts. Some of these online tools are powerful and may be more cost-effective than a stand-alone package.

Stand-alone charting software, however, often provides capabilities beyond what you can find online. For example, charting software packages offer system testing but rarely are part of a website's tool set.

Several packages are available; two examples include

>> **MetaStock (www.metastock.com):** MetaStock comes in two flavors, a standard end-of-day trading package and a professional version for real-time traders. Each offers a variety of analysis tools, technical indicators, system development and testing capabilities, and access to fundamental stock data.

>> **TradeStation (www.tradestation.com):** TradeStation is the gold standard of charting software. It is powerful, flexible, and configurable, and it's designed to work the same way institutional trading platforms do. You can fully automate your trading system by programming your strategies into the system and then

having TradeStation execute them in real time. (Whether you should do so, however, is open for discussion.) It also supports direct access to all ECNs and stock exchanges.

Many other charting packages are available, but these two packages are widely used and give you a good basis for comparing all the other available products.

REMEMBER

The drawback to stand-alone charting software is the expense. In addition to the price of the software, you need a data provider to deliver end-of-day or intraday market prices. When selecting a charting software package, make sure it supports the data service you plan to use. They must work together.

Data service vendors include

>> MetaStock (www.metastock.com)

>> eSignal (www.esignal.com)

Digging Up Fundamental Data

Fundamental data — corporate information such as revenue, earnings, and cash flow — isn't as perishable as price data or trading statistics, but accessing these numbers directly from your trading platform as they're updated is a nice feature. Some platforms also include other key fundamental information such as GDP growth, inflation indicators, and jobs reports. We discuss analysis of fundamental data in Chapters 5, 6, and 7 (Part 2).

TIP

Many brokers provide access to at least some fundamental data, but if you'd like to run the numbers yourself, these online sources can review the raw financial data:

>> *The Wall Street Journal* (www.wsj.com): *The Wall Street Journal* is available online by subscription. It provides access to a wide variety of information including stock quotes, stock valuation indexes, fundamental ratios, industry comparisons, insider transactions, earnings estimates, and stock analysis reports. Delayed-price charts also are available. A digital-only subscription is $99 for six months. You can get digital access plus a paper version delivered to your home at the price of $111 for six months.

>> **Edgar** (www.sec.gov/edgar.shtml): All publicly traded companies are required to file 10-Q and 10-K quarterly and annual reports electronically with

the Securities and Exchange Commission (SEC) through its Electronic Data Gathering Analysis and Retrieval system (EDGAR). These reports are available to everyone online at no charge.

Accessing Analyst Reports

Sometimes you can find these research reports at your local library, especially for big outfits like Standard & Poor's and Value Line. Many analysts sell research in the form of investment newsletter subscriptions.

TIP

We've used several of the following subscription services through the years, with varying degrees of success:

>> **Standard & Poor's (`www.standardandpoors.com`):** Registration is required, but access is free.

>> **Value Line (`www.valueline.com`):** The Value Line Investment Survey has been around for a long time. It profiles many of the major corporations and provides a variety of stock screens based on proprietary models. It also offers opinions on current economic and market climates. Some reports and updates are available on the site at no charge, but a subscription is required to access the complete site.

>> **Briefing.com (`www.briefing.com`):** This site has free and subscription components. Advanced features include access to analysts' upgrades and downgrades as they're released, access to updated earnings guidance, an IPO calendar, notification of changes in stock indexes, and quite a bit more.

>> **Morningstar (`www.morningstar.com`):** Morningstar probably is best known for its analysis of mutual funds, but it also provides extensive stock analysis, editorial commentary, a stock-screening tool, and a thorough snapshot tool that shows financial performance, fund ownership, and recent fund transactions. A subscription is required to access premium content.

Selecting a Trading Platform

You'll find as many different approaches to trading as you'll find traders. Fortunately, almost as many alternatives for setting up your trading environment also exist.

As technology develops and expands, online brokers are providing increasingly powerful trading tools for their clients. These tools include market research, charting capabilities, streaming prices, and news services. If your broker doesn't offer a specific service, you probably can find it offered on the Internet.

Before putting your computer to work as a trading platform, you need to understand the two primary techniques for delivering trading tools and services. The first uses your Internet browser to enter orders and deliver all information. The other approach uses a stand-alone software program, an *integrated trading platform*, to interact with your broker and your brokerage account.

For the most part, integrated trading platforms are married to specific brokerage firms. Some brokers provide you with a choice. For example, Charles Schwab's CyberTrader offers the integrated software-based system StreetSmart Edge or the use of web-based and mobile app trading tools. TD Ameritrade offers Trade Architect or thinkorswim. E*Trade offers E*Trade Pro and E*Trade Mobile. You may want to try out all three and see which one best fits the way you want to trade.

REMEMBER

The approach that suits you best depends somewhat on your trading style, cost considerations, and your computer's configuration. You may find that the level of service your broker offers depends on the size of your account or your trading volume. You have to balance your cost with your actual information needs.

Integrated trading platforms typically are direct-access systems. We discuss both direct-access brokers and traditional online brokers in Chapter 3. Although direct-access systems are offered in browser-based configurations, active day traders and swing traders may require a completely integrated, direct-access trading platform.

Browser-based trading environments

For most new traders, trading volume starts out relatively small, with perhaps five or fewer trades each month. Your time frame for holding a position probably is measured in days to weeks or weeks to months. You probably won't be making many intraday trades, except to automatically exit a position after a stop price is hit. In that case, a browser-based trading environment certainly is good enough to get you started and may be all you ever need.

These systems may be tightly integrated or somewhat disjointed, depending on the way the broker implements them. Some brokers, for example, automatically fill in order-entry screens with as much data as can be gleaned from your account. Others make you type all the data into the order screen by hand, which can be cumbersome and time-consuming. Some brokers provide pop-up order confirmation and fill reports, and others make you continuously press the Enter key while waiting for a trade execution to show in your account.

Pros

For the most part, almost any Internet-ready computer can support a browser-based trading platform. Although trading platforms use Windows most often, even Mac or Linux systems can be used for most browser-based applications.

Much of the browser-based information your broker offers is available to all clients, regardless of account size or trading volume. If your broker doesn't offer something you want, you usually can find it elsewhere on the Internet, either for free or for a modest fee.

Cons

When compared to an integrated software solution, browser-based trading is relatively slow, requiring you to open many browser windows and manually update account information. Depending on how well your broker implements these systems, a bit more typing may be necessary to enter and execute your orders.

WARNING

On some browser-based trading platforms, your Internet session may be disconnected whenever your screen is inactive for an extended period of time. At best, this kind of interruption can be frustrating. Similarly, some configurations depend on your using a specific browser or may require that you download and install a special browser plug-in to operate correctly.

Integrated trading platforms

For very active traders, especially day traders and swing traders, and for traders looking to develop personalized trading systems, an integrated trading platform that doesn't rely on your Internet browser can be a better solution. You typically download these software programs, install them on your computer, and then use them to access your brokerage account and trading tools. They range from rudimentary text-based applications with modest graphing capabilities to sophisticated technical-analysis programs that enable you to design and implement custom trading systems.

The most sophisticated of these platforms provides an institutional-level trading experience. Some, for example, permit trading baskets that enable you to simultaneously enter orders for a number of different stocks. Others help you to define hot keys for fast order entry.

You'll also find that integrated trading platforms provide support for sophisticated strategies. The most flexible among them give you the ability to enter contingent orders, where, for example, a stock's price may trigger an option order, or the execution of one order automatically cancels another. Several brokers offer the service of email or text message alerts when a stock hits a price you've specified or an indicator reaches a preset level. One broker even gives you the ability to automatically execute trades based on recommendations from well-known and reputable advisory services.

Pros

These trading platforms typically are faster and easier to use and customize than browser-based applications. The best among them have system-testing tools that help you fine-tune your personal trading strategies.

Cons

Integrated trading platforms can be expensive. Unless you have a large account balance, your broker may charge you either a monthly fee or base the access on your making a minimum number of monthly trades.

Furthermore, these platforms often require up-to-date computer equipment with a fast processor and plenty of storage to run well. Older equipment doesn't run this software satisfactorily. And it's likely you'll need to use the Windows operating system.

Features to consider

When selecting a trading platform, look for the capabilities you need today with an eye toward future expandability. You may want to consider the features in the three lists that follow.

Trading tools to look for include the following:

>> Stock trading

>> Support of sophisticated option-trading strategies

>> Futures trading, especially single-stock and index futures

>> NASDAQ Level II access

>> Direct-access trading and ECN book data

>> Watch lists

>> Automatic email or text message notification when a stock hits your price point

Analysis tools to shop for include these:

>> Sector analysis

>> Proprietary and third-party analysts' reports

>> News feeds (Dow Jones, Reuters, and so on)

>> Real-time charting capabilities

>> Time and volume sales reports

Account-management tools that you may need include the following:

>> Real-time account balances

>> Real-time updates of buying power and margin exposure

>> Portfolio-management tools

>> Open-order status

TIP

If you intend to manage your trading throughout the day using a mobile application, be certain that whatever trading platform you choose provides a mobile app that can be used on the mobile devices you own. Some platforms only offer mobile apps for specific devices, such as Apple or Android. You want to be able to integrate your activities across your mobile, desktop, and laptop devices.

Determining Computer Requirements

Few new traders actually need a fully integrated direct-access trading platform to begin trading or to trade profitably. But if you're considering a new computer system, the hardware and software requirements for these high-powered platforms may be of benefit. Otherwise, you may be unable to upgrade your new computer to run these applications.

Weighing Windows versus Mac versus Linux

Most trading platforms are designed for Windows, but die-hard Mac and Linux fans aren't completely locked out. If you're starting with a browser-based approach, almost any modern, Internet-ready computer can handle the task. Browser-based Internet tools usually work equally well on any hardware or operating system. Sadly, some sites require functions provided by a specific browser, but that is becoming increasingly rare.

If you're planning to buy new computer hardware for trading, we recommend that you avoid Mac hardware or Unix/Linux operating systems. Although Mac and Linux support browser-based applications at least as well as Windows, you may be unable to upgrade if ever you want a more integrated trading platform. We don't know of any commercially available trading platforms for independent traders (as opposed to institutional traders) that run on Linux or Mac OS X.

Configuring your computer system

Regardless of whether you decide to employ a browser-based approach or an integrated trading platform, you need a reliable computer with sufficient horsepower, memory, and storage space.

Some of today's high-powered, integrated trading software requires equally high-powered computer systems. We give you general hardware guidelines in this section, but if you decide you want a computer that can be upgraded to handle a high-performance integrated trading platform, you also need to check with specific software vendors to identify any special hardware requirements. You also need to be certain that your hardware supports your software.

Software vendors often claim that their products can run on relatively modest hardware configurations; however, you'll probably be disappointed and frustrated with system performance under such conditions. These software packages run much better on a computer that surpasses the system requirements. Trading platforms — especially testing applications and multichart, multiwindow, multimonitor displays — consume considerable amounts of system resources and can make many computers run unbearably slow.

The following minimum configurations easily support browser-based solutions. Upgraded configurations, however, may be required to adequately support fully integrated trading environments.

>> **Central processing unit (CPU):** At a minimum, you need a 1.6 GHz processor, but something much faster works better. Trading applications tend to rely on making many mathematical calculations, so you want to avoid the value-priced CPU chip sets. Look instead for systems that are primarily designed for graphics applications. Ideally, you should select a dual-core processor.

The slowest machines being sold today are rated in gigahertz multiples, and most modern machines have enough CPU horsepower to run charting application programs. However, high-end programs like TradeStation take advantage of specialty hardware such as multi-CPU and hyperthreading configurations. Check with software manufacturers for specific details.

>> **RAM:** 1GB of RAM is the absolute minimum, but you probably want more. Memory is inexpensive compared with other hardware upgrades, and having too much of it is next to impossible. Error-correcting memory may buy only extra peace of mind, but it doesn't cost much more than standard memory.

>> **Available disk space:** 1GB of free disk space should be enough when starting out, but you need much more for long-term storage of real-time price data, which is useful for developing and testing your own trading system. Chapter 16 discusses methods to personalize a trading system.

>> **Operating system:** If you're running a Windows environment, you need to be running at least Windows XP. Although browsers and software applications will run on older versions of Windows, XP gives you more stability and reliability than earlier versions of Windows. For trading applications, you want the most reliable system you can find and afford. Windows XP may not be bulletproof, but it's so much better than its predecessors that you definitely want to upgrade to that version or a newer one if you haven't already.

>> **Video card:** Although you may be able to squeak by using a shared-memory video system (it shares some of your RAM), you're better off with a stand-alone video card that relies on its own video memory. A minimum configuration for a single monitor requires at least 128MB of video memory, but 256MB of video RAM is better. You may even want 1GB whenever you opt for a single video card that supports dual monitors.

>> **Monitor size:** Modern, high-resolution LCD monitors are excellent and inexpensive. A 17-inch monitor probably is the smallest you should consider. Bigger is better. Even more important than size is the monitor's resolution. Anything less than 1024 x 768 resolution is useless for reading chart detail, but you'll want more. If you're going with a single monitor setup, you should consider a 20- or 22-inch monitor with resolution up to 1920 x 1200.

>> **Dual monitor configurations:** Some traders swear by the dual monitor configuration. The idea is to pull up your charts on one monitor and everything else on the other. Many video cards support dual monitors.

>> **Network interface:** You need some way of accessing a high-speed Internet connection (see the next section). Most computers now come with either a built-in Ethernet port or an extra Ethernet Interface Card. Either works fine.

>> **Power supply:** We recommend that you use an uninterruptible power supply (UPS). A UPS is relatively inexpensive and provides an extra measure of security. Some protect against lightning strikes. If you live in an area where power fluctuations are common, a UPS is a must.

Accessing the Internet

You must have reliable Internet access, and that means a high-speed connection — either DSL or cable Internet will work fine. Some very active day traders spring for a fractional T1 or dedicated T1 line for an additional measure of reliability, but either approach is expensive. A backup connection is a good idea. Consider a wireless laptop card or even a second high-speed Internet connection.

A dial-up connection is not fast enough or reliable enough for trading. Only about 3 percent of the population uses dial-up, but if you're one of those few, look for an alternative as soon as possible.

WARNING

Because of security concerns, avoid wireless networks unless you're absolutely certain that you know how to configure the network to keep prying eyes from seeing your private trading and account information. This is true for your mobile apps as well.

Picking a browser

Any modern browser probably will do. Although stumbling across a site that uses some browser-specific functions is a possibility, that scenario is becoming increasingly rare. Microsoft Edge is bundled with the Windows operating system at no additional charge. It will serve your needs well enough. Mozilla Firefox (www.mozilla.org) and Google Chrome (www.google.com/chrome/) are other excellent — and free — choices. The key is to choose a browser that will give you the best results with your charting system and broker.

Securing your computer

WARNING

The Internet is a dangerous place. You must protect your computer system and its data against attacks by vandals, hackers, and thieves. Make sure you have modern virus-scanning software, and keep your virus definitions up to date.

Norton's AntiVirus program gets good reviews and seems to do the job just fine. It can automatically update its virus definitions. You can get more information about Norton's program at www.symantec.com. McAfee Security's VirusScan also gets high marks from those in the know. Additional information is available on the web at www.mcafee.com.

We also recommend that you use a firewall. The Windows firewall is sufficient. Third-party firewalls like the free ZoneAlarm firewall from Check Point Software Technologies (www.zonealarm.com) also work well. ZoneAlarm monitors your connection to the Internet and is able to detect trojans and worms that are trying to call home. This ability is increasingly critical. In addition, you should consider installing a hardware firewall to provide an additional layer of security. Most routers include a hardware firewall and allow you to share your Internet connection with multiple computers.

Finally, keeping up to date with your operating system's security patches, especially when you're running Windows, is important. More viruses are written for Windows than for any other operating system.

You can configure Windows to automatically check for system updates. You can find instructions for how to set up automatic updates on a Windows computer and make sure all your system patches have been applied at the Windows Update site (http://windowsupdate.microsoft.com).

2

Reading the Fundamentals: Fundamental Analysis

Chapter **5**

Fundamentals 101: Observing Market Behavior

You hear plenty about recession and inflation. You know both can mean bad economic news, but do you really understand what they mean and why they happen? Regardless of what the economic gurus do, the economy cycles between periods of economic growth and recession. If growth becomes overheated, periods of inflation are likely. Inflation can also be caused when the value of the currency falls. For example, when the value of the U.S. dollar falls, it causes an increase in the price of imports and commodities like oil for U.S. residents. That, in turn, impacts the price of just about every other good sold in the United States.

The Board of Governors of the Federal Reserve (Fed) oversees moves that are made in monetary policy in the United States, and the legislative and executive branches of government are responsible for tax changes and other fiscal policy moves. The actions of the Fed and the government can minimize the impact of inflation or recession and spur economic growth, but nothing can be done to erase economic cycles. Markets and traders try to anticipate these cyclical moves with an eye toward recording gains. This chapter helps you understand which economic indicators tend to lead these cycles and how you can use them to understand the current state of the markets and the economy.

The Basics of the Business Cycle

The old adage "What goes up must come down" is as true for the economy as it is for any physical object. When a business cycle reaches its peak, nothing is wrong in the economic world; businesses and investors are making plenty of money and everyone is happy. Unfortunately, the economy can't exist at its peak forever. In the same way that gravity eventually makes a rising object fall, a revved up economy eventually reaches its high and begins to tumble.

The peak is only one of the four distinct parts of every business cycle — peak, recession, trough, and expansion/recovery (see Figure 5-1). Although none of these parts is designated as the beginning of a business cycle, here are the portions of the business cycle that each represents:

>> **Peak:** During a *peak,* the economy is humming along at full speed, with the gross domestic product (GDP — more about that later in this chapter) near its maximum output and employment levels near their all-time highs. Income and prices are increasing, and the risk of inflation is great, if it hasn't already set in. Businesses and investors are prospering and very happy.

>> **Recession/contraction:** As the saying goes, all good things must come to an end. As the economy falls from its peak, employment levels begin to decline, production and output eventually decline, and wages and prices level off but more than likely won't actually fall unless the recession is a long one.

>> **Trough:** When a recession bottoms out, the economy levels out into a period called the *trough.* If this period is a prolonged one, it can become a depression, which is a severe and prolonged recession. The most recent depression in the United States was in the late 1920s and 1930s. Output and employment stagnate, waiting for the next expansion.

>> **Expansion/recovery:** After the economy starts growing again, employment and output pick up. This period of expansion and recovery pulls the economy off the floor of the trough and points it back toward its next peak. During this period, employment, production, and output all see increases, and the economic situation again looks promising.

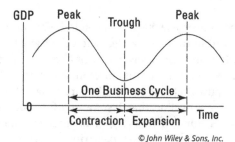

© John Wiley & Sons, Inc.

FIGURE 5-1:
The basic
business cycle.

Understanding how periods of economic growth and recession are determined

How do you know which part of the business cycle the economy is in? Officially, you don't usually find out until months after that part of the cycle has either started or ended. The National Bureau of Economic Research (NBER) officially declares the peaks and troughs. The NBER is responsible for formally announcing the ends of peaks and troughs and signaling when a recession (end of a peak) or expansion (end of a trough) starts. You can see a table explaining the peaks and troughs since 1857 at www.nber.org/cycles/cyclesmain.html.

The NBER identified December 2007 as the peak of the most recent economic expansion, but it didn't make that pronouncement until December 2008. By the time the peak was declared, the market had been in a downtrend for 15 months, including the sharp selloff in September 2008. The trough of June 2009 was not pronounced until September 2010, and as of this writing, we're still waiting for the next peak as the United States climbs out of its worst recession since World War II. The NBER determined that the recession lasted 18 months. Previously, the longest postwar recessions were those of 1973 to 1975 and 1981 to 1982, both of which were 16 months long.

As you can see, the time lag between events and when the NBER makes its announcements can be lengthy. But it can get worse. For example, the NBER declared on November 26, 2001, that the peak of the last business cycle was reached March 21, 2001. That was eight months later. The end of the trough for this cycle, November 2001, wasn't announced until July 17, 2003. In other words, the economy was in a period of expansion/recovery for 20 months before the NBER made it official.

WARNING

Unfortunately for all concerned, information that the NBER needs to make its official announcements isn't always immediately available. The process of collecting economic data and revised preliminary estimates of economic activity takes time. Estimates and data don't become available immediately after a particular part of any business cycle ends. As a result, before drawing any conclusions, the NBER must wait until it sees a clear picture of what's happening with the economy. Although many economists identify recessions and expansions based on at least two quarters (six months) of economic data, NBER uses its own models. Still, a growth spurt that lasts one full quarter doesn't indicate the start of an expansion, nor does a decline that lasts a quarter indicate the start of a recession. Bearing that in mind, a time lag of at least six months is typically required before the NBER even considers declaring a recession or a recovery, which effectively renders the official announcement useless for traders.

The peak of a business cycle occurs during the last month before some key economic indicators begin to fall. These indicators include employment, output, and new housing starts. We talk more about economic indicators and which of them are critical for traders to watch in the section "Understanding Economic Indicators," later in this chapter. However, because neither a recession nor a recovery can be declared until enough data is accumulated, finding a way around the time lag of official information is impossible.

Signals that the economy was weakening became clear to the markets as early as summer 2007, when the major indexes hit their peaks. Looking at an earlier business cycle, you can see the whole process. Just as in 2007, clear signs that the economy was headed toward a recession were seen as early as the spring of 2000, which is when the NASDAQ index hit its peak and began its downward spiral. The effects of the recession took a bit longer to hit the other major exchanges, but they started a downward trend by the summer of 2000. Just like in 2008, job losses had started mounting by mid-2000, and many economists were already sending alarms that the economy was headed into a recession.

Even though the NBER announced the official beginning of that recession as March 21, 2001, and the official end of the trough and beginning of the recovery as November 2001, no significant recovery was seen in the markets until October 2002. Job growth remained anemic as of early 2004. The first sign of job growth was seen during the fourth quarter of 2003, after nearly three years of job losses. That economic expansion finally picked up steam and ultimately lasted through 2007.

Using economic indicators to determine the strength of the economy

Considering the amount of lag time between events and official pronouncements, we're sure you're wondering how you can determine which part of the cycle the economy is in and how you, as a trader, can use this information. Most economists attribute changing business cycles to disturbances in the economy. Growth spurts, for example, result from surges in private or public spending. One way public spending can surge is during a war, when government spending increases and companies in industries related to the war effort prosper. They often need to increase hiring to fulfill government orders. Employees at these companies usually receive increases in their take-home pay and start spending that extra money. As consumer optimism increases, other companies must fulfill consumers' wants and needs, so production and output also increase in companies that are unrelated to national defense.

When these same factors work in reverse, the start of a recession is sure to follow. For example, a cut in government spending will likely result in layoffs at related industrial plants, reduced take-home pay, and finally declines in output and production in order to cope with reduced spending.

In addition to government spending, a decision by the Fed to either raise or lower interest rates causes another major disturbance in the economy. When interest rates rise, spending slows, and that can lead to a recession. When interest rates are cut, spending usually goes up, and that can aid in spurring an economic recovery.

Even though the Federal Reserve has kept interest rates at near zero since the financial crisis began in 2007, recovery has been very slow. The Federal Reserve raised the target rate to 0.75 percent in late 2016 for the first time since the financial crises of 2007 began, and it is expected to raise rates several times in 2017.

Another school of economic thought disagrees with the notion that government policy or spending is responsible for changes in the business cycle. This second group of theorists believes that differences in productivity levels and consumer tastes are the primary forces driving the business cycle. From this point of view, only businesses and consumers can drive changes in the economic cycle. These economists don't believe that governmentally driven monetary or policy changes impact the cycle.

REMEMBER

Which camp you believe is not critical; the key is picking up the signs of when the economy is in a recession and when it's in an expansion. Peaks and troughs are flat periods (periods where the high or low stays primarily even before moving in the opposite direction) and are impossible to identify until months after they end. As a trader, you can identify shifts in buying and spending behavior by watching various economic indicators. By doing so, you can discover when the economy is in the early stages of a recovery or recession or if it's fully into a recession or recovery.

Relating bull markets and bear markets to the economy

You've probably heard the terms *bull market* and *bear market*. To find out what they mean, you first need to understand how economic cycles affect the stock market. *Bulls* are people who believe that all is right with the world and the stock market is heading for an increase. They definitely think the economy is expanding. *Bears* are people who believe the economy is heading for a downturn and stocks will either stagnate or go down. A *bull market* is a market in which a majority of stocks are increasing in value, and a *bear market* is a market in which a majority of stocks are decreasing. Bears definitely believe the economy is either in a recession or headed that way.

Regardless of whether the bulls or the bears are right, you can make money as a trader. The key: Identify the way the market is headed and then buy or sell into that trend. During a bear market, traders make their money by selling short, or taking advantage of falling prices (find out more about that in Chapter 15). Traders sell short by borrowing stock from their broker and then selling it with the hope of making a profit when the price falls.

Even during a bear market, some stocks offer opportunities for traders to make money, including oil and gas stocks and real-estate investment trusts (REITs). Petroleum stocks and REITs pay higher dividends and, therefore, are most attractive when the rest of the market is falling or showing no growth potential. During a bull market, riding a stock through recovery but getting out before a fall is key. We talk more about trends and what they mean in Chapter 10.

Employing a Sector Rotation Strategy

In general, the markets are divided into *sectors,* and at any given time some of those sectors are expanding, even during a bear market. Some traders are adept at rotating their investments from one sector to another that is more likely to benefit from the part of the business cycle that's driving the economy. This basic trading strategy is called *sector rotation.*

The guru of traders who want to take advantage of sector rotation is Sam Stovall, chief investment strategist for Standard & Poor's, who wrote the classic on sector rotation, *Sector Investing,* in 1996. Stovall developed the sector rotation model shown in Figure 5-2. As you can see, he found that market cycles tend to lead business cycles. Markets tend to bottom out just before the rest of the economy is in a full recession. The start of a bull market, on the other hand, can be seen just before the rest of the economy starts its climb toward recovery. Markets reach their tops first and enter a bear market before the general economic indicators show a peak.

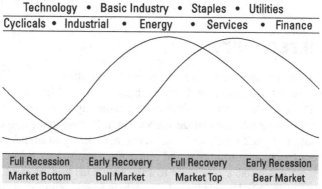

FIGURE 5-2:
The sector rotation model.

© John Wiley & Sons, Inc.

As a trader, you can take advantage of this knowledge by knowing which sectors are more likely to rise during the various parts of a market cycle. You need to buy into the sectors with stock prices that are likely to rise, or you can sell short the sectors in which prices are expected to fall. We discuss short selling in Chapter 15.

The following sections explain how to identify the different phases of recovery and recession and which sectors are most affected during those periods. Then we give you an overview of what to be on the lookout for if you want to use a sector rotation strategy.

Early recovery

You can spot an early recovery when consumer expectations and industrial production are beginning to rise while interest rates are bottoming out. That scenario was evident during the economic cycle discovered during the fall and early winter months of 2003. During the early stages of recovery, Stovall found that industrial, basic industry, and energy sectors tend to take the lead.

We started seeing the early signs of recovery in late 2011 and 2012, as unemployment began to fall, but full recovery was not seen until 2016. The market's rise to an historic high over 18,000 of the Dow Jones Industrial Index (DJII) didn't happen until April 2016, so investors finally believe we are on the road to recovery since the market collapse in 2007–2008. That's considerably more than double the low the Dow hit in March 2009 — 7,056.48. In November 2016, the market was still seeking top, and the Dow topped 21,000 in March 2017.

Full recovery

When the economy has fully recovered, you start seeing signs that consumer expectations are falling and productivity levels and interest rates are flattening out. These factors were seen during the economy's period of full recovery leading up to the economic peak in December 2007. During that period, companies in the consumer staples (such as food, beverages, and household items) and services sectors (such as automotive and electronic repair, hair salons, and dry cleaning services) exhibited a tendency to take the lead, and interest rates had actually started to fall. As knowledgeable investors know, when that happens, it's only a matter of time before a recession follows. Investors know that the staples of life are needed even in times of recession, so the stocks of those companies tend to benefit.

Early recession

When the economy reaches the earliest part of a recession, consumer expectations fall more sharply and productivity levels start to drop. Interest rates also begin to drop. Most of the 2.5 million job losses during the 2001 economic downturn occurred during late 2001 and early 2002. During 2001, the Federal Reserve cut interest rates 11 times to try to ease the concerns about the upcoming recession. The Fed started to raise rates in 2004 but then lowered them again in 2007 during the mortgage crisis. At the time of this writing, the Fed's funds rate (the interest rate the Fed charges to member banks) was 0 percent, and by 2016 the target rate was just 0.25–0.50. In total, from December 2007 to early 2010, 8.7 million jobs were lost. In February 2013, nonfarm payroll employment was still 3 million jobs lower than at the start of the recession in December 2007. While employment has improved since 2013, the recovery in 2016 was still seen as weak, and the number of unemployed totaled 7.6 million in February 2017.

Utilities and finance sector stocks are the most likely to see rising prices during the first part of a recession, because under those circumstances investors seek stocks that provide some safety (because owning them involves less risk) and pay higher dividends. Gold and other valuable mineral stocks also look good to investors seeking safety. Though the financial sector did not follow this pattern in the 2008 recession, it is still typical to see banks, insurance companies, and investment firms perform well during the early parts of a recession.

Full recession

Although it may not make much sense intuitively, a full recession is when you first start seeing indications that consumer expectations are improving, which is shown by increased spending. However, industrial productivity remains flat, and businesses won't increase their production levels until they believe consumers are actually ready to spend again. Additionally, interest rates continue to drop because both business and consumer spending are slow, so demand for the money weakens while competition for new credit customers grows between banks and other financial institutions. During a full recession, cyclical (such as car manufacturers or construction-related industries) and technology stocks tend to lead the way. They will likely be the companies most beaten down in a full recession, so they will be good candidates to lead in the next recovery. Investors look to safety during a recession, so companies that satisfy that need tend to do best.

Sector rotation

Someone once said that the stock market predicted 15 of the last 8 recessions. And although it's true that the market isn't a terribly precise economic prognosticator, that's sort of beside the point. Economic indicators can help you understand the big picture, which, in turn, can help you make better trading decisions.

REMEMBER

Of all the economic tools available, sector rotation analysis is probably the most valuable. Even if the sector rotation model can't help you identify an economic cycle, it can identify sectors and stocks that are ripe for further study.

When you trade, you want the strongest stocks in the strongest sectors, which is why you should monitor sector performance carefully. Knowing the sectors that are performing best enables you to anticipate which sectors are likely to begin outperforming and which are likely to fade. Using those projections, you can start monitoring stocks in those up-and-coming sectors. For a sector to outperform, the stocks within it must also outperform. You need to be monitoring those stocks before they begin their runs.

TIP

Plenty of data is available to help you separate the strongest sectors from the ones that are underperforming. *Investor's Business Daily*, for example, ranks nearly 200 industry groups by price performance. You can also monitor sectors by following exchange-traded funds (ETFs), such as the Select Sector SPDRs (Standard and Poor's Depository Receipts), at http://www.sectorspdr.com/sectorspdr/.

TIP

You can easily see what's happening in various sectors using StockCharts Performance Charts at http://stockcharts.com/freecharts/perf.php?. At the bottom of the chart, you see a series of predefined performance charts from which to choose. Select S&P sector ETFs to quickly get a visual overview of which sectors are performing well and which sectors are not. Figure 5-3 gives an example.

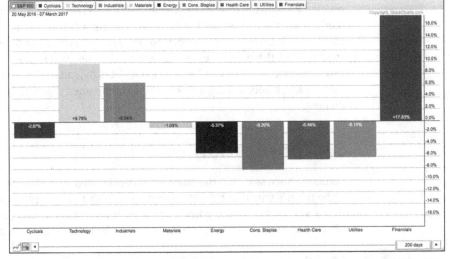

FIGURE 5-3:
S&P sector ETFs (exchange-traded funds).

Chart courtesy of StockCharts.com

Understanding Economic Indicators

The key to knowing where, as a trader, you are during the business cycle is watching the economic indicators. Every day that you open your newspaper, you see at least one story about how the economy is doing based on various economic indicators. Popular indicators track employment, money supply, interest rates, housing starts, housing sales, production levels, purchasing statistics, consumer confidence, and many other factors that indicate the state of the economy.

Economic indicators are useful to your trading. Some are definitely more useful than others. We don't have the space here to describe each of the indicators, so instead, we focus on the ones that can provide you with the most help in making your trading decisions.

Interest rates

Watching the Federal Open Market Committee (FOMC) of the Federal Reserve (which includes the seven members of the Board of Governors, the president of the New York Federal Reserve Bank, and presidents of 4 of the other 11 Federal Reserve Banks) and tracking what it may or may not do to interest rates is almost a daily spectator sport in the business press. Although members of the FOMC meet only eight times per year, discussions about whether the Federal Reserve will raise or lower interest rates serve as fodder for stories published on at least a weekly, if not daily, basis. Every time the Fed chairperson speaks, people look for indications of what the Fed may be thinking. Speeches by other members of the Fed likewise are carefully dissected between FOMC meetings. Most press coverage shortcuts all this by saying the Fed may raise or lower interest rates.

REMEMBER

The key reason for you to be concerned: A change in interest rates can have a major impact on the economy and thus on how you make trades. An increase in rates is likely to slow down spending, which can lead to an overall economic slowdown. For the most part, when the Fed raises interest rates, it's because the board believes the economy is overheated, which can fuel the risk of inflation. An increase in interest rates can reduce spending and thus ease overheating. If, on the other hand, the Fed fears an economic downturn or is trying to fuel growth during a recession, the board frequently decides to cut interest rates to spur spending and growth.

TIP

In addition to following press reports covering speeches and congressional testimony by members of the Fed, you can also get a good hint about what the Fed is thinking by reading the Beige Book, which is a report compiled by the 12 Federal Reserve Banks. Summaries about current economic conditions in each of the 12 districts are circulated to Federal Reserve Board members two weeks prior to the FOMC meeting, at which monetary policy, including interest rates, is set. The summaries are developed through interviews with key business leaders, economists, market experts, and others familiar with each individual district. You can read the Beige Book online at www.federalreserve.gov/monetarypolicy/beigebook/default.htm. You can find out about past FOMC statements at www.federalreserve.gov/newsevents/press/monetary/2016monetary.htm. These links give you access not only to current issues of the Beige Book and FOMC statements but also to information from those two sources dating back as far as 1996. They can provide an excellent overview of economic trends and possible shifts in Federal Reserve monetary policy.

Money supply

The money supply is a key number to watch because growth in money supply can be a leading indicator of inflation in situations when the money supply is greater than the supply of goods. When more money than goods is around, prices are likely to rise. Commodities and money traders should keep close watch over these three aggregates — money supply, inflation, and goods and services.

The Fed tracks two monetary aggregates: M1 and M2. *M1* includes money used for payments, such as currency in circulation plus checking accounts in banks and thrifts. Currency sitting in bank vaults and bank deposits at the Fed is not part of M1, but instead is part of the monetary base. *M2* includes M1 money plus retail nontransaction deposits, which is money sitting in retail savings accounts and money market accounts. You can follow the money stock measures for M1 and M2 at `www.federalreserve.gov/releases/h6/`. When you track the money base using M2, you can track the total amount of money sitting in someone's account or circulating in the economy.

The Fed decided in July 2000 that it would no longer set target ranges for growth rates of the monetary aggregates. In the late 1970s, money supply drove the Fed's decision-making process. As money supply grew to what was considered out of hand, the Fed kept raising interest rates until they were so high that many believe the Fed moves actually caused the recession in the early 1980s. After that time, managing interest rates became a higher priority than managing money aggregates. The Fed didn't kill the idea of target ranges for the money supply until it was certain that managing interest rates alone would help stem inflation. Now that the Fed has proved interest-rate management works, it no longer sets a target for monetary aggregates.

Inflation rate

Several key economic indicators point you toward ways of identifying the risk of inflation. The primary overall indicator is gross domestic product; it's released quarterly by the U.S. Department of Commerce's Bureau of Economic Analysis (BEA). You can also follow monthly trends by keeping your eye out for the consumer price index, the producer price index, and retail sales data, as described in the list that follows:

>> **Gross domestic product (GDP)** represents the monetary value of goods produced during a specific period in the economy. In the United States, GDP is released quarterly in three different versions. The first version, which includes advance data for the previous quarter, is released at 8:30 a.m. on the last business day of the months of January, April, July, and October. Preliminary data is released a month later, and the final numbers are released a month

after that. GDP is important to traders because it indicates the pace at which the economy is growing. In the GDP, you'll find numbers for consumer spending, private domestic investment, government or public spending, and net exports. Essentially, it includes all information about labor and property involving business activities inside the confines of the United States. If GDP fails to meet expectations set by the analysts or exceeds market expectations, stock prices will be affected, at least temporarily.

TIP

For a glimpse of what may be in store for the future, pay attention to the rate that inventories are increasing. It can be a leading indicator that growth is slowing or consumer demand is changing.

Even though the final official numbers are released quarterly, the advance reports and preliminary reports give you a good indication of what to expect in the final numbers. You can get full details about the GDP reports at www. bea.gov/national/index.htm#gdp. You can track the release schedule for the GDP reports and other government statistical reports at this location as well. Often the report is posted at the Bureau of Economic Analysis early in the morning before the actual release and embargoed until the official release time, so as a trader you may be able to get a heads up before the news is actually reported by the press.

>> **The Consumer Price Index (CPI)** measures the cost of a representative basket of goods and services, including food, energy, housing, clothing, transportation, medical care, entertainment, and education. Each type of cost is weighted. For example, medical costs are weighted more highly in recent years because they're rising at a faster pace, especially as the current population ages. In addition to the broad CPI, a core rate is issued that excludes food and energy, which are considered more volatile.

TIP

The core rate is an indicator you can watch for general price shifts. The financial markets, in general, look for a rate of increase in the range of 1 percent to 2 percent; anything higher may be a sign of inflation and can cause at least a temporary shock to stock prices. Any shock to stock prices obviously can be an opportunity for traders.

The CPI is released by the U.S. Department of Labor about 8:30 a.m. around the 15th of each month and reflects data from the previous month. You can track the CPI at the website of the Department of Labor's Bureau of Labor Statistics at www.bls.gov/cpi.

>> **The Producer Price Index (PPI)** is thought of more as a basket full of other indexes that affect domestic producers, including goods manufacturing, finishing, and agricultural and other commodities. The Department of Labor collects more than 100,000 prices each month from 30,000 production and manufacturing firms to calculate this basket. The markets pay close attention to this index, because even though it isn't as powerful an inflation index as the

CPI, it gives traders clues about what to expect in the next CPI release. The PPI is released a couple of days before the CPI, at 8:30 a.m. usually around the 13th of each month, and it reflects data from the previous month. You can track PPI data at www.bls.gov/ppi.

>> **Retail sales data** tracks information about (you guessed it) retail sales by large corporations and by small mom-and-pop retail outlets. The U.S. Census Bureau, which is a part of the Department of Commerce, surveys hundreds of firms each month using a random sampling of retail outlets that make federal insurance contributions to collect this data, which is particularly important whenever you're trading stocks in the retail sector. The survey looks at changes in retail numbers from month to month. When the number is a negative number, it means sales levels decreased from the previous month. This type of negative news can be a shock to stock prices, especially for companies in the retail sector. The data is released about two weeks after it's collected, or at 8:30 a.m. about the 12th of each month. You can track it online at www.census.gov/retail.

Deflation

In addition to watching the economic indicators discussed in the previous section for inflation, traders also need to watch the numbers for signs of deflation. Serious concern about the possibility of deflation takes center stage when prices start falling. *Deflation* occurs when a sustained period of falling prices takes place. The Great Depression of the 1930s was a classic period of deflation. Many economists believe that printing more money cures deflation because (as mentioned earlier in the "Money supply" section) increases in the money supply normally lead to increases in prices when more money is around than goods to be purchased.

During periods of deflation, increasing the money supply isn't necessarily the answer. Some economists believe injecting more money into the economy is risky, especially when production capacity is in excess and producers continue to produce goods even though prices are falling. Whereas, in other economic situations, producers commonly stop producing when prices fall.

In early 2004, Japan faced a continuing period of deflation even though its central bank had lowered rates to an effective negative interest rate and continued printing money in attempts to prop up its sagging pricing structure, and yet prices were continuing to drop. Some economists believe the Japanese experienced a liquidity trap. No matter how much money Japan printed, prices continued downward in a deflationary spiral.

Jobless claims

The Employment Situation Summary, another report from the Bureau of Labor Statistics (BLS), is one of the most important leading indicators to watch. This report is the first critical economic indicator released every month and frequently sets the expectations for the rest of the reports that month. For example, signs of a weak labor market reported in the Employment Situation Summary usually are a strong indication of poor retail sales and other possible negative reports later in the month. The summary also breaks down data by industry, such as construction and manufacturing. For example, a significant drop in employment numbers for the construction sector is a strong sign that the housing starts report will also be negative.

This report can send shock waves through the financial markets, especially if the numbers that are released vary greatly from expectations. Stock prices definitely fall whenever the report doesn't meet expectations or employment statistics show signs of weakness. On the other hand, stock prices can rise dramatically whenever the report indicates better-than-expected numbers. As is true with any shock to the market, changes in prices are temporary unless other indicators also exhibit the same trend or tendency.

REMEMBER

The reason why the employment report can drive markets so strongly is that the information it contains is a timely assessment of the overall market because it includes data that is only a few days old. This report is widely recognized as the best indicator of unemployment and wage pressure. Rising unemployment can be an early sign of recession, while increased pressure on wages can be an early sign of inflation. The report also is a broad-based snapshot of the entire labor market, covering 250 regions of the United States and every major industry.

The BLS (www.bls.gov) releases the report at 8:30 a.m. on the first Friday of each month with data for the previous month. The two key parts of the report that traders need to watch are

>> Unemployment and new jobs created

>> Average weekly hours worked and average earnings

Another employment indicator traders like to watch is the employment cost index (ECI). It's especially relevant during actual times of inflation or when fear exists that an inflationary period may be imminent. The ECI is a quarterly survey of employer payrolls that tracks movement in the cost of labor, including wages, benefits, and bonuses. Wages and benefits make up 75 percent of the index.

The BLS surveys more than 3,000 private-sector firms and 500 local governments to develop the index. The ECI, which reports data from the previous quarter, is released on the last business day in January, April, July, and October.

Consumer confidence

Keeping an eye on consumer confidence is another way of casting a glance into the future of the market. When confidence is high, consumers are more likely to spend. The best overall index for monitoring consumer confidence is the Consumer Confidence Index (CCI), which is put out by The Conference Board. This index is compiled through a sampling of 5,000 households and is widely respected as the most accurate indicator of consumer confidence.

Although minor changes in the CCI are not strongly indicative of a problem, major shifts can be a sign of rocky waters ahead. Most people who watch the CCI look for three- to six-month trends. The Fed, as an example, looks closely at consumer confidence when determining interest rate policy, which as you know can greatly affect stock prices. When confidence is trending lower, the Fed is more likely to lower interest rates. Stock markets love to hear about the Fed lowering interest rates. Confidence levels that are trending higher can be a warning of a pending inflationary period. A rapidly rising trend in consumer confidence can lead the Fed to raise interest rates to cut off inflation; moreover, a rise in interest rates can send stock prices lower.

The Conference Board releases the CCI at 10 a.m. the last Tuesday of each month. The biggest weakness of this index is that it isn't based on actual spending data. Instead, it's a survey of planned spending. You can track the CCI online at www. conference-board.org/data/consumerconfidence.cfm.

Business activity

A number of key economic indicators can give you a good idea of what business is doing and how that information may impact the stock markets. Key business indicators to watch include

>> **The National Association of Purchasing Managers report (NAPM):** One of the first economic indicators released each month is the NAPM report, which surveys purchasing managers and provides reviews of new orders, production, deliveries, and inventories. This report is released at 10 a.m. the first business day of each month and reflects data compiled from the previous

month. You can track this report online at www.ism.ws/ismreport/index.cfm.

>> **Durable goods orders:** The Department of Commerce releases another critical economic indicator of business activity in the area of durable goods orders. This indicator measures the dollar volume of orders, shipments, and unfilled orders of durable goods, or types of merchandise that have a life span of three years or more. This report serves as a leading indicator of manufacturing activity and can move the stock market, especially when its numbers vary from expectations. You can track the durable goods orders online at www.census.gov/indicator/www/m3/index.html.

>> **Housing starts and building permits:** This report is also released by the Department of Commerce. It can be a leading indicator of the direction the economy will take. When the number of permits rises, a positive economic indicator results. About 25 percent of investment dollars are plowed into housing starts, and that makes up about 5 percent of the overall economy. The report is broken down by regions — Northeast, Midwest, South, and West — so you can also get a strong indication of the strength of the economy on a regional basis. You can track this indicator online at www.census.gov/construction/bps/.

You can also track other reports on myriad industries at www.census.gov/manufacturing/cir/index.html.

>> **Regional manufacturing surveys:** Each Federal Reserve Bank district compiles data from regional manufacturing surveys that can help you find a score of indicators including new orders, production, employment, inventories, delivery times, prices, and export and import orders. Positive reports indicate an expanding economy. Negative reports indicate a contracting economy. The most closely watched is the Philadelphia regional surveys at www.philadelphiafed.org/research-and-data/regional-economy/. If you're trading in regional stocks, following the manufacturing surveys from the Federal Reserve Banks in key regions that you follow can help you determine the direction of the economy for the areas most relevant to the stocks you're trading.

TIP

You can get a lot of this information and more about the U.S. economy on the mobile app developed by the U.S. Census Bureau, Bureau of Labor Statistics, and Bureau of Economic Analysis. It's called America's Economy, and it's available for Apple and Android at www.census.gov/mobile/?intcmp=sldr1. This app provides real-time updates for 16 key economic indicators.

Using Data from Economic Indicators

You can see that plenty of data is available, but not all of it is relevant to the types of stocks you want to trade. Organizing your data collection and tracking the trends can make choosing economic signs and analyzing which part of the business cycle is driving the markets easier for you. Here are a few steps that can make this task much easier:

1. **Maintain a calendar of the release dates for the key economic indicators you decide to follow.**

   REMEMBER

   The markets may move in anticipation of this data, so if you know that a key economic indicator is about to be released, be sure to watch stock price trends for the possible impact the anticipated release may be having on the market.

2. **Know the parts of the economy that are most impacted by the economic indicators you're following.**

   For example, the GDP strongly suggests the path of economic growth, but the PPI and CPI are strong measures of inflation.

3. **Know which economic indicators are most important to the market.**

   For example, in times of inflation, economic indicators that reveal key data regarding inflation are the biggest market movers. If the markets are worried about growth, the growth components of GDP and other indicators will have the greatest potential for moving the markets.

4. **Know what the market is expecting to see in the numbers.**

   The actual number is not as critical as whether that number was expected by the markets. Surprises are what move the markets.

   REMEMBER

5. **Know what parts of the economic indicator are important.**

   Newspapers may write headlines for shock value, but the parts of the index they cover may not be critical to your decision making. For example, traders know that food and energy components of the CPI are volatile, so the more important number to watch is the core CPI, which doesn't include food and energy. The news media may focus only on the more volatile number.

6. **Don't overreact to a newly announced economic indicator that didn't meet market expectations.**

   Indicators frequently are revised after they're initially issued. The difference may merely be related to a revision and not an indication of a shift in the business cycle. However, be sure to check information about revisions to the previous month and how those revisions have impacted the current month's trend.

7. **Monitor the trends.**

On your calendar, keep track of key components of each economic indicator that you watch. Follow the trends of the most important data components to get a good idea of where the business cycle is headed.

REMEMBER

Keeping a tight watch on economic indicators is the best way for you to determine at what point the economy is in a new business cycle. Waiting for official pronouncements is much too late. By the time they're released, that phase of the cycle may be over and a new cycle may be driving the markets.

Chapter **6**

Digging Into Fundamental Analysis

Most traders don't worry about the fundamentals. These numbers include the general economic and market conditions that impact a stock (see Chapter 5 for an overview of these), as well as the financial information known about a company's activities and its financial successes and failures. Instead, traders tend to focus entirely on technical analysis and trends that can be seen using that type of analysis.

Taking the time to analyze the fundamentals of a stock puts you one step ahead of the trading crowd. Using fundamental analysis, you can determine how a stock's price compares with those of similar companies based on earnings growth and other key factors, including business conditions. This chapter helps you understand critical parts of fundamental analysis and how you can use the information gathered from it to make better trading decisions.

When starting a fundamental analysis, select an industry or business sector that interests you for possible stock purchases. Sometimes a particular company piques your interest, and you start your research by looking at the major players in that company's sector or by turning to the sector's fundamentals. Regardless of how you start, you need to narrow down your list of the companies you want to compare to the ones that are in similar businesses within the sector so you can find the best opportunity. You also want to be sure the stock trades well by looking at its daily volume of trades. Stocks with low trading volume can be hard to get into and out of, making them riskier stocks.

Most of the tools used in fundamental analysis require you to compare at least two companies operating in similar business environments to understand the meaning of the information. For the purposes of discussion in this chapter, we look at two big players in the home-improvement retail sector: Home Depot and Lowe's. If you've followed the business conditions in this sector, you know that both faced a severe downturn after the housing bubble burst in 2007. Housing still hasn't fully recovered, and Home Depot didn't build any new stores in 2016. The expansion of Lowe's has primarily been in Canada with the purchase of Canada's RONA.

Before discovering the tools of fundamental analysis, you first must understand how to read key financial statements, including the critical parts of the income statement, cash-flow statements, and the balance sheet.

Checking Out the Income Statement

The *income statement* is where a company periodically reports its revenues, costs, and net earnings. It's basically a snapshot of how much a company is earning from its operations and any extraordinary earnings that may have impacted its bottom line during a specific period of time. From the income statement, you can determine the impact of taxes, interest, and depreciation on a company's earnings and forecast earnings potential.

Every income statement has three key sections: revenue, expenses, and income. The revenue section includes all money taken into the company by selling its products or services minus any costs directly related to the sale of those products or services (called *cost of goods sold*). The expenses section includes all operating expenses for the company not directly related to sales, as well as expenses for *depreciation* (writing off the use of equipment and buildings — tangible assets), *amortization* (writing off the use of patents, copyrights, and other intellectual property or intangible assets), taxes, and interest.

The income section includes various calculations of income. Usually you find one calculation that shows earnings after operating expenses and before interest, taxes, depreciation, and amortization called *EBITDA*. This is followed by net income, which is the bottom line showing how much a company earned after all its costs and expenses have been deducted. Public companies must file financial reports with the Securities and Exchange Commission (SEC) on a quarterly and annual basis.

TIP

You can read any public company's financial reports at the Edgar website (www. sec.gov/edgar.shtml).

A year's worth of figures doesn't show you much, so you need to look at the trends throughout a number of years to be able to forecast growth potential or assess how well a company is doing compared with its competitors. We discuss a number of good sources for finding fundamental information in Chapter 4.

Both quarterly and annual reports are important. Comparing a company's results on a quarter-to-quarter basis gives you an idea of how well the company is meeting analysts' expectations and its own projections. For example, looking at results for the first quarter of 2017 versus the first quarter of 2016, you can see whether a company's earnings are increasing or decreasing in a similar market environment. While for some types of companies the first quarter is generally productive, other types of companies, such as retail stores, depend mostly on fourth-quarter holiday results, so you need to know what's expected in earnings for the various quarters.

While quarterly results allow you to monitor results from similar time periods, annual statements give you a summary for the year. You can also compare current-year results to the results over a number of years to see at what rate the company is growing.

Revenues

The first line of any income statement includes the company's sales *revenues*. This number reflects all the sales that the company generated before any costs are subtracted. Rather than go to all the trouble of showing their math (net sales = gross sales − any sales discounts, adjustments for returns, or other allowances), most companies show only net sales on their income statements. From these figures, you want to see obvious signs of steady growth in revenues. A decrease in revenues from year to year is a red flag that indicates problems and that it's probably not a good potential trading choice.

Cost of goods sold

The *cost of goods sold* (also known as *cost of merchandise sold* or *cost of services sold*, depending on the type of business) is an amount that shows the total costs directly related to selling a company's products or services. The costs included in this part of the revenue section include purchases, purchase discounts, and freight charges or other costs directly related to selling a product or service.

Gross margins

The *gross margin* or *gross profit* is the net result of subtracting the cost of goods sold from net sales. This figure shows you how much money a company is making directly from sales before considering other operating costs. You calculate the gross profit by subtracting costs of goods sold from net revenue. The gross margin is a ratio calculated by dividing gross profit by net revenue. Watching year-to-year trends in gross margins gives you a good idea of a company's profit growth potential from its key revenue sources.

You can calculate a gross margin ratio by dividing a company's gross profit by its net revenue:

$$\text{Gross margin ratio} = \text{Gross profit} \div \text{Net revenue}$$

The gross margin ratio, expressed as a percentage, considers revenue from sales minus the costs directly involved in making those sales and is a good indicator of how well a company uses its production, purchasing, and distribution resources to earn a profit. The higher the percentage, the more efficient a company is at making its profit.

TIP

By comparing gross margin ratios among various companies within the same industry or business sector, you can get an idea of how efficient each company is at generating profits. Investors favor companies that are more efficient.

To give you an idea of how to use this ratio and others in this chapter, we compare figures from two of the leaders in the home-improvement retail sector: Home Depot and Lowe's. Tables 6-1 and 6-2 present the gross profits section from the past three annual income statements (information taken from Yahoo! Finance) for each company. Table 6-3 compares the gross margin ratios for the two companies.

TABLE 6-1   Home Depot Gross Profits*

Fiscal Year Ending	1/31/2016	2/1/2015	2/2/2014
Total Revenue	88,519,000	83,176,000	78,812,000
Cost of Revenue	58,254,000	54,787,000	51,897,000
Gross Profit	30,265,000	28,389,000	26,915,000

*All numbers are in thousands.

TABLE 6-2

Lowe's Gross Profits*

Fiscal Year Ending	1/29/2016	1/30/2015	1/31/2014
Total Revenue	59,074,000	56,223,000	53,417,000
Cost of Revenue	38,504,000	36,665,000	34,941,000
Gross Profit	20,570,000	19,558,000	18,476,000

All numbers are in thousands.

TABLE 6-3

Comparing Gross Margin Ratios by Year

Fiscal Year Ending	2016	2015	2014
Home Depot	34.2%	34.1%	34.2%
Lowe's	34.8%	34.8%	34.6%

You can see that Lowe's is slightly more efficient at using its production, purchasing, and distribution resources than Home Depot, because Lowe's has consistently higher gross margin ratios. Both companies maintain their gross margin year to year with minimal change. The advantage of using this ratio, rather than the actual revenue and profit numbers for comparison, is that it makes comparing large companies with small companies within the same business or industry sector much easier. Even though Home Depot's sale volume is considerably higher, the ratio enables you to compare how efficiently each company uses its resources.

Expenses

WARNING

The next section of the income statement shows the expenses of operating the business, including the sales costs and administrative costs of business operations. When comparing a company's year-to-year results, you need to watch for signs of whether expenses are increasing faster than a company's gross profits, which can be an indication that a company is having a problem controlling its costs and doesn't bode well for future profit growth potential.

When you see expenses drop from one year to the next while gross margins increase, that's usually a good sign and means a company likely has a good cost-control program in place. The potential for growth in future profit margins is good.

Gross profits and expenses that rise at about the same rate is neither a significant positive nor negative sign. When that happens, the best way to get a reading on how a company is controlling its expenses is to compare its expenses with the expenses of other companies in similar businesses.

Interest payments

The interest payments portion of the expense section of an income statement gives you a view of a company's short-term financial health. Payments shown here include interest paid during the year on short- and long-term liabilities (more about those in the "Looking at debt" section, later in this chapter). These payments are tax-deductible expenses, which help reduce a company's tax burden.

To determine a company's fiscal health, use the *interest expense number* and the *earnings before interest and taxes* (EBIT) number, which is usually shown on the income statement. If not, you can calculate it by subtracting interest and tax expenses from operating income (which is gross profit minus expenses, also usually shown on the income statement). You can use this figure to determine whether the company is generating sufficient income to cover its interest payments using the interest coverage ratio. You can calculate the company's *interest coverage ratio* (expressed as a percentage, this ratio provides a clear-cut indicator of a company's solvency) using this formula:

$$\text{Interest coverage ratio} = \text{EBIT} \div \text{Interest expenses}$$

REMEMBER

Companies with high interest coverage ratios won't have any problems meeting their interest obligations, and their risk of *insolvency* (going belly up) is low. On the other hand, a low interest coverage ratio is a clear sign that a company has a problem and may face bankruptcy. Whether an interest coverage ratio tends to run high or low depends a great deal on the type of industry or business a company is in. Comparing the interest coverage ratios of several companies in the same industry or business is the best way to gauge, or judge, the value of the ratios.

Table 6-4 shows annual EBITs and interest expenses from three successive annual income statements for Home Depot, and Table 6-5 shows the corresponding numbers for Lowe's.

TABLE 6-4   **Home Depot Interest Payments***

Fiscal Year Ending	1/31/2016	2/1/2015	2/2/2014
EBIT	11,940,000	10,806,000	9,178,000
Interest	919,000	830,000	711,000

All numbers are in thousands.

TABLE 6-5　　　**Lowe's Interest Payments***

Fiscal Year Ending	1/29/2016	1/30/2015	1/31/2014
EBIT	4,419,000	4,276,000	3,673,000
Interest	0	0	0

All numbers are in thousands.

Table 6-6 shows the respective interest coverage ratios for Home Depot and Lowe's.

TABLE 6-6　　　**Comparing Interest Coverage Ratios**

Fiscal Year Ending	2016	2015	2014
Home Depot	7.7	7.7	7.7
Lowe's	-	-	-

Both companies are in a good position to make their interest payments. Lowe's currently shows no interest payments, so there is plenty of room to take on debt if needed. Home Depot has 7.7 times more income than it needs. Analysts generally consider a company in trouble whenever its interest coverage ratio falls below 3.

Tax payments

Corporations are always looking to avoid taxes, just like you. The *income tax expense* figure on the income statement shows the total amount that a company paid in taxes. A corporation pays between 15 percent and 38 percent of its income in taxes, depending on its respective size; however, corporations have many more write-offs they can use to reduce their tax burdens than you have as an individual tax-payer. Most large corporations have teams of tax specialists who spend their days looking for ways to minimize taxes. When looking at tax payments, reviewing how well the company you're interested in manages its tax burden compared with other similar companies is important.

Dividend payments

Companies sometimes pay a *dividend*, or part of the company profits, for each share of common stock that an investor holds. This dividend is distributed to shareholders usually once every quarter after the company's board of directors reviews company profits and determines whether to pay and how much the dividend will be. Paying dividends is not a tax-deductible expense for companies that pay them.

In the past, traders have preferred growth stocks that don't pay dividends. However, recent changes in the way dividends are taxed may have altered the way traders view dividend-paying stocks. Dividends are taxed at the same rate as ordinary income. Qualified dividends, dividends of a U.S. stock or foreign stock that qualifies, are taxed at a 0 to 15 percent tax rate. To collect a *qualified dividend*, you must hold the stock for at least 60 days prior to the ex-dividend date, which is the date of record on which the shareholder will be paid. For example, if the ex-dividend date is January 15 and you buy the stock on January 16, you're not entitled to the dividends. The dividends go to the person who owns the stock on the ex-dividend date.

Profitability

You now can use the income statement to quickly check your company's profitability by using one or both of two ratios — the operating margin and net profit margin. The *operating margin* looks at profits from operations before interest and tax expenses, and the *net profit margin* considers earnings after the payment of those expenses.

You calculate operating margin using this formula:

Operating margin = Operating income ÷ Gross profit or net sales

You calculate net profit margin using this formula:

Net profit margin = Earnings after taxes ÷ Gross profit or net sales

Table 6-7 shows the gross profits, operating incomes, and earnings after taxes from three successive annual income statements for Home Depot, and Table 6-8 shows the corresponding numbers for Lowe's.

TABLE 6-7   Home Depot Profitability*

Fiscal Year Ending	1/31/2016	2/1/2015	2/2/2014
Gross Profit	30,265,000	28,389,000	26,915,000
Operating Income	11,774,000	10,489,000	9,166,000
Earnings After Taxes	7,009,000	6,345,000	5,385,000

*All numbers are in thousands.

TABLE 6-8 Lowe's Profitability*

Fiscal Year Ending	1/29/2016	1/30/2015	1/31/2014
Gross Profit	20,570,000	19,558,000	18,476,000
Operating Income	4,971,000	4,792,000	4,149,000
Earnings After Taxes	2,546,000	2,698,000	2,286,000

*All numbers are in thousands.

Table 6-9 compares the respective profitability margins for Home Depot and Lowe's.

TABLE 6-9 Comparing Profitability Margins

Fiscal Year Ending	2016	2015	2014
Operating Margin			
Home Depot	38.9%	36.9%	34.1%
Lowe's	24.2%	24.5%	22.5%
Net Profit Margin			
Home Depot	23.2%	22.4%	20.0%
Lowe's	12.4%	13.8%	12.4%

You can see from the numbers in Table 6-9 that Home Depot did considerably better than Lowe's in 2016. Both stores continued their recovery since the housing downturn of 2007, but Home Depot's recovery is much stronger. In the previous edition of *Trading For Dummies,* we reported that Home Depot's operating margin was 27.5 percent in 2012 and Lowe's was 18.9 percent.

Looking at Cash Flow

When you review income statements, you're looking at information based on accrual accounting. In *accrual accounting,* sales can be included when they're first contracted, even before revenue from them is collected. Sales made on credit are shown even if the company still needs to collect from the customer. Expenses are recorded as they're incurred and not necessarily as they're paid. However, the income statement definitely does not show a company's cash position. A company that's booking a high level of sales can have a stellar income statement but nevertheless be having trouble collecting from its customers, which may put that company in a cash-poor situation. That's why cash-flow statements are so important.

You can get an idea of your favorite company's actual cash flows from the adjustments shown on its *cash-flow statement*. The three sections to this statement are operating activities, financial activities, and investment activities. Cash-flow statements are filed with the SEC along with income statements on a quarterly and annual basis.

Operating activities

Looking at cash flow from *operating activities* gives you a good picture of the cash that's available from a company's core business operations, including net income, depreciation and amortization, changes in accounts receivable, changes in inventory, and changes in other current liabilities and current assets. We talk more about these accounts in the later section "Scouring the Balance Sheet."

Calculating cash flow from operating activities includes adjustments to net income made by adding back items that were not actually cash expenditures but rather were required for reporting purposes. Depreciation is one such item. Similarly, expenses or income items that were reported for accrual purposes are subtracted out. For example, changes in accounts receivable are subtracted out because they represent cash that hasn't been received. Conversely, changes in accounts payable represent payments that haven't yet been made, so the cash still is on hand.

The bottom line: This section of a company's cash-flow statement shows actual *net cash from operations*. Table 6-10 compares three successive years of cash flow from operating activities at Home Depot and Lowe's.

Looking at the numbers in Table 6-10, you can see that Home Depot's cash position is on an upward trend, while Lowe's cash position went down from 2015 to 2016. Both Lowe's and Home Depot's cash positions have topped their cash flow from operating activities prior to the housing crash. In 2007, Home Depot's cash flow from operating activities was $7,661,000, and Lowe's was $4,502,000.

TABLE 6-10   **Total Cash Flow from Operating Activities***

Fiscal Year Ending	2016	2015	2014
Home Depot	9,373,000	8,242,000	7,628,000
Lowe's	4,784,000	4,929,000	4,111,000

All numbers are in thousands.

For all companies, one of the largest adjustments to cash flow is depreciation. *Depreciation* reflects the dollar value placed on the annual use of an asset. For example, if a company's truck will be a usable asset for five years, then the cost of that truck is depreciated over that five-year period. For accounting purposes on its income statement, a company must use *straight-line depreciation,* a method of calculating depreciation in which the company determines the actual useful life span of an asset and then divides the purchase price of that asset by that life span. Each year, depreciation expenses are recorded for each asset using this straight-line method. Although no cash is actually paid out, the total amount of depreciation is added back to the cash-flow statement.

For tax purposes, companies can be more creative by writing off assets much more quickly and thus reducing their tax burdens at the same pace. One type of write-off — dealing with Section 179 of the Internal Revenue Code — enables a company to deduct the full cost of an asset during its first year of use. Other methods enable a company to depreciate assets sooner than the straight-line method, but not as soon as the 100 percent permitted by Section 179. How a company depreciates its assets can have a major impact on how much that company pays in taxes.

REMEMBER

Although you won't know how a company depreciated its assets by looking at its cash-flow statement, you'll know the adjustment made for depreciation for cash purposes. Note that depreciation is an expense that must be reported on an income statement and is not a cash outlay.

Financing activities

The financing activities section of a cash-flow statement shows any common stock that was issued or repurchased during the period the report reflects, and any new loan activity. The financial activities section gives you a good idea whether the company is having trouble meeting its daily operating needs and, as a result, is seeking outside cash. You won't, however, find that new financing always is bad. A company may be in the process of a major growth initiative and may be financing that growth by issuing new debt or common stock.

The bottom line: This section of the cash-flow statement shows a company's total cash flow from financing activities. Table 6-11 compares three successive years of cash flow totals from financing activities at Home Depot and Lowe's.

TABLE 6-11 **Total Cash Flow from Financing Activities***

Fiscal Year Ending	2016	2015	2014
Home Depot	(5,787,000)	(7,071,000)	(6,652,000)
Lowe's	(3,493,000)	(3,761,000)	(2,969,000)

All numbers are in thousands.

A negative cash flow from financing activities usually means that a company has either paid off debt or repurchased stock. In this case both Home Depot and Lowe's repurchased stock in 2016. A positive cash flow here usually means new stock or debt was issued. Both companies issued new debt during this period as well. Obviously, many combinations of various financing activities can affect the bottom line, but the key for traders is to gain an understanding of why the change occurred and whether the company's reason for making the change was solid enough to improve its profit and growth picture.

Investment activities

This section of the cash-flow statement shows you how a company spends its money for growing long-term assets, such as new buildings or other new acquisitions, including major purchases of property, equipment, and other companies. It also shows you a company's sales of major assets or equity investments in other companies. Tracking investment activities gives investors a good idea of what major long-term capital planning activities have taken place during the period.

The bottom line: This section shows a company's total cash flow from investing activities. Comparing three successive years of investment activities by Home Depot and Lowe's, Table 6-12 indicates that both companies increased capital outlays in 2016 from 2015. Home Depot increased them at a faster pace. You would need to look closer at the notes to the cash-flow statement to determine exactly how each company is investing its money.

TABLE 6-12 **Total Cash Flow from Investing Activities***

Fiscal Year Ending	2016	2015	2014
Home Depot	(2,982,000)	(1,271,000)	(1,507,000)
Lowe's	(1,343,000)	(1,088,000)	(1,286,000)

All numbers are in thousands.

Scouring the Balance Sheet

The balance sheet gives you a snapshot of a company's assets and liabilities at a particular point in time. This differs from the income statement, which gives you operating results of a company during a particular period of time. A *balance sheet* has three sections, including

>> An *assets* section that details everything the company owns

>> A *liabilities* section that details the company's debt or any other claims on the company's assets made by debtors

>> A *shareholder's equity* (also called *owner's equity*) section that lists all the claims made by owners or investors

The balance sheet gets its name because the total assets of the company are supposed to equal the total claims against it — total liabilities plus total equity.

Assets and liabilities are listed on the balance sheet according to their *liquidity*, or how quickly and easily they can be converted into cash. Assets or liabilities that are more liquid appear first on the list, while the ones that are increasingly more difficult to convert to cash — long-term assets or liabilities — appear later. The assets section is divided into *current assets* (the ones that are used up in one year) and *long-term assets* (the ones whose life spans are longer than a year), as is the liabilities section — current liabilities and long-term liabilities.

Current assets include cash and other assets that can quickly and easily be converted into cash — marketable securities, money market mutual funds, accounts receivables, and inventories. Long-term assets include holdings such as buildings, land, and equipment. Similarly, on the liabilities side, current liabilities include any claims against assets that are due during the next 12 months, such as accounts payable and notes payable. Long-term liabilities are claims due in more than 12 months, such as mortgage or lease payables.

Equity accounts include outstanding (remains on the market) preferred and/or common stocks and retained earnings. Retained earnings reflect the profits that are reinvested in the company rather than paid out to owners or shareholders.

Analyzing assets

In analyzing assets, two key ratios to look at are how quickly a company is collecting on its accounts receivable — the *accounts receivable turnover* — and how quickly inventory is sold — the *inventory turnover.*

You use a two-step process to find the accounts receivable turnover. First you must find out how quickly a company turns its accounts receivables into cash, using this formula:

Accounts receivable turnover = Sales on account ÷ Average accounts receivable balance

Then you need to find out how quickly a company collects on its accounts by dividing the accounts receivable turnover into 365 to find out the average number of days it takes to collect on accounts.

Testing for inventory turnover uses a similar two-step process. First you must find out how quickly inventory turns over during the year, using this formula:

Inventory turnover ratio = Cost of goods sold ÷ Average inventory balance

Then you need to divide the inventory turnover ratio into 365 to find out the average number of days it takes a company to turn over its inventory. Comparing these results for the companies you're considering can help you determine how well each company is handling the collection of its accounts receivable and the sale of its inventory. Obviously, the faster a company collects on accounts or sells its inventory, the better that company is doing in managing its assets. You should compare companies in the same industry to determine how well a company is doing.

WARNING

Whenever you see accounts receivable rising rapidly, and the number of days to collect on those accounts also is rising, that signals a red flag that indicates cash problems likely lie ahead. Whenever you see inventory numbers rising, a company can be having a hard time selling its product, which also raises a red flag, indicating problems ahead.

We're summarizing these two common ratios so you know what they mean whenever you see them mentioned by analysts. As a trader, you aren't likely to take the time to do these calculations yourself.

Looking at debt

When considering debt, or what a company owes, the two primary ratios you want to look at are the current ratio and acid or quick ratio. You can quickly calculate the *current ratio*, which tests whether a company can make its payments, by looking at the balance sheet and using this formula:

Current ratio = Current assets ÷ Current liabilities

REMEMBER

Again, like the other ratios in this chapter, you must compare the ratio of one company to that of other companies in the same industry. A current ratio that's lower than most other companies in the industry can indicate the company is having a problem paying its short-term debts, which, in turn, is a strong sign that bankruptcy may be just around the corner. A current ratio that's significantly higher can be a bad sign too, because it can mean the company isn't using its assets efficiently. For these reasons, traders like to see companies with current ratios that are close to the industry average.

TIP

Luckily, you won't have to calculate current ratios, because they're easily found on any website that includes fundamental statistics. Using Yahoo! Finance, we found that Home Depot's current ratio is 1.30 and Lowe's is 1.01.

The *acid test*, or *quick ratio,* is almost the same as the current ratio; however, the key difference is that inventory value amounts are subtracted from current assets before dividing that result by current liabilities. Many financial institutions take this extra step because inventories aren't as easy to convert to cash. You calculate the acid test ratio by:

$$\text{Acid test ratio} = \left(\text{Current assets} - \text{Inventory}\right) \div \text{Current liabilities}$$

The acid test ratio is primarily of interest to financial institutions thinking about making a short-term loan to a company. They look for an acid test ratio of at least 1 to 1 before considering a company a good credit risk. Even though as a trader you're not likely to be in the business of making loans, a company that has problems getting short-term debt is likely to have problems meeting its short-term obligations in the near future. As the market recognizes the problem, the company's share price is likely to drop.

Reviewing goodwill

Goodwill is not a tangible asset but rather is usually collected through the years as companies are bought and sold. Goodwill reflects a competitive advantage, such as a strong brand or reputation. When one company buys another and pays more than the tangible assets are worth, the difference is added to the acquirer's balance sheet as goodwill. In other words, it's the premium in price that one company pays for another.

Determining Stock Valuations

By now the key question you're probably asking is, "How do I use all this data to decide how much I should pay for a stock?" Basically, a stock's *value* is the amount buyers are willing to pay for the stock and the amount for which sellers are willing to sell the stock under current business conditions. A stock's actual value shifts throughout the day and usually in a matter of seconds when the trading volume is high.

Fundamental analysis is one of the tools that investors and some traders use to analyze earnings, revenue growth, market share, and future business plans so they can determine a stock's value and the price for which they're willing to pay or sell. Earnings and earnings growth are key factors and are considered a part of fundamental analysis. Common ratios used to determine a stock's value or performance include the price to earnings multiple, or P/E ratio; price to book multiple, or price/book ratio; return on assets (ROA); and return on equity (ROE). We talk more about how these ratios are calculated in the sections that follow.

After considering all this data, investors decide whether a company's stock is undervalued or overvalued. Although past performance is no guarantee about a company's or stock's future success, fundamental analysts believe collecting and analyzing the appropriate data enables investors to make more-educated guesses about a stock's value.

Earnings

Using the income statement, we've talked extensively about a company's earnings. Remember, the three types of earnings figures to consider are

>> **Gross profit,** which is calculated after considering the direct costs related to sales

>> **Operating income,** which shows a company's profit after subtracting operating expenses

>> **Net income,** which is the bottom-line earnings after all expenses, taxes, and interest are subtracted

WARNING

When you encounter discussions about earnings figures, be certain that you know which types of earnings are being discussed for the stock you're eyeing. To be able to compare apples with apples, you must know that you're using the same type of earnings figures.

Earnings growth rate

The *earnings growth rate,* which shows how quickly the company is expected to grow, isn't something you calculate. What you'll find in the fundamental-analysis statistics for stocks are earnings growth rate projections made by industry analysts based on their analysis of a company's potential earnings. The earnings growth rate is included on all the websites that we mention in Chapter 4 that provide fundamental statistics. When looking for this data, be sure to check out the earnings growth rate potential at a number of those sites.

Continuing the comparison of Home Depot and Lowe's, Yahoo! Finance projected

>> Home Depot's earnings growth rate for 2017 to be 4.5 percent

>> Lowe's earnings growth rate for 2017 to be 5.2 percent

Clearly, at this point in time, analysts believe Lowe's will grow at a slightly faster pace than Home Depot in 2017.

EYEING THE MOST FUNDAMENTAL DATA OF ALL

If we were allowed to choose only one piece of fundamental data to guide our trading, we'd choose the earnings growth rate (you'll sometimes see this called the *EPS growth rate* — EPS stands for *earnings per share*). You can use it as a quick summary of a company's performance. Evaluating the entire financial condition of a company isn't necessary when its earnings aren't up to par.

We don't put much faith in analysts' estimates and don't use them when evaluating trading candidates. We're much more interested in actual earnings reported than we are in the analysts' estimates for future earnings. And we're interested only in companies whose earnings are growing and growing at a faster rate than most other companies. Those companies typically outperform the broad market.

Investor's Business Daily is an excellent source for EPS growth rate data. It publishes a proprietary ranking that shows which companies are growing earnings fastest.

As much as we like this tool, we don't follow the rankings blindly. (And we don't believe the good folks at *IBD* recommend that you do so, either.) *IBD* doesn't distinguish between companies that are earning more and companies that are losing less. That companies can and do turn from losing money to making money is a fact, and that situation can be lucrative for the knowledgeable trader. Call us old-fashioned, but we prefer companies that actually have a history of reporting real, positive earnings.

Figuring Your Ratios: Comparing One Company's Stock to Another

In this section, we show you how to calculate four key ratios — P/E, price/book, ROE, and ROA — but luckily you can find all these where fundamental statistics are reported (newspapers, websites, and so on — see Chapter 4 for more). Each of these ratios gives you just one more piece in the puzzle of determining how much you want to pay for a stock. By comparing each of the ratios for each of the companies you're considering, you can make a more educated case about the price you want to pay for any stock.

Price/earnings ratio

The *P/E ratio* is probably the one that's quoted most often in news stories. This ratio reflects a comparison of a stock's earnings with its share price. You calculate this ratio using this formula:

$$P/E \text{ ratio} = \text{Stock price} \div \text{Earnings per share}$$

You'll probably find two types of P/E ratios for a stock. The *trailing P/E* is based on earnings reported in previous quarters, and the *forward P/E* is based on projected earnings.

At Yahoo! Finance as of market close on March 28, 2017, the trailing P/E for Home Depot was 22.82, and its forward P/E was 18.08. Lowe's trailing P/E was 23.75, and its forward P/E was 15.61. There isn't much difference in the trailing P/E ratios for Home Depot and Lowe's, but analysts seem to favor Home Depot with a higher forward P/E.

Historically, market analysts believed a P/E ratio of 10 to 15 was reasonable. For a while, much higher P/Es were tolerated, and current market conditions appear to be trending back to the higher P/Es, but many people expect that a market correction is coming.

When comparing companies, you can get a good idea of how the market values each stock by looking at its P/E ratio. Although the P/E ratio is actually a percent, it's rarely stated that way. However, you'll sometimes hear it called a *price multiple* because the P/E ratio represents how much you're paying for each dollar of a company's earnings.

Price/book ratio

The *price/book ratio* compares the market's valuation of a company to the value that the company shows on its financial statements. The higher the ratio, the more the market is willing to pay for a company above its hard assets, which include its buildings, inventory, accounts receivable, and other clearly measurable assets. Companies are more than their measurable assets. Customer loyalty, the value of their locations, and other intangible assets add value to a company. Investors looking to buy based on value rather than growth are more likely to check out the price/book ratio. You calculate price/book ratios using this formula:

$$\text{Price/book ratio} = \text{Stock price} \div (\text{Book value} - \text{Total liabilities})$$

Lowe's price/book ratio at Yahoo! Finance was 8.54, and Home Depot's was 23.27. Based on price/book ratio, the market is willing to pay a higher premium for Home Depot's stock.

Return on assets

Return on assets (ROA) shows you how efficiently management uses the company's resources. ROA, however, doesn't show you how well the company is performing for its stockholders. To calculate return on assets, use this formula:

$$\text{Return on assets} = \text{Earnings after taxes} \div \text{Total assets}$$

Home Depot's ROA at Yahoo! Finance was 17.94 percent; Lowe's was 10.8 percent. Home Depot is doing a more efficient job using its resources based on those two ROA numbers.

Return on equity

Investors are more interested in *return on equity* (ROE), which measures how well a company is doing for its shareholders. This ratio measures how much profit management generates from resources provided by its shareholders. Investors look for companies with high ROEs that show signs of growth. You calculate ROE by using this formula:

$$\text{Return on equity} = \text{Earnings after taxes} \div \text{Shareholder equity}$$

Home Depot's ROE was 97.29 percent, and Lowe's was 35.62 percent.

The ROEs show that Home Depot is doing a better job for its shareholders, which, again, is reflected in the price investors are willing to pay for its shares. As of November 16, 2016, Home Depot's stock price was $125.33, and Lowe's was $67.02.

REMEMBER

As a trader, you may not make your buy and sell decisions based on fundamental analysis, but collecting and having access to this information as part of your arsenal certainly helps you make better and more informed stock choices. Knowing a company has strong fundamentals helps to back up what you're seeing in the technical analysis (see Part 3). If you're trying to decide between two stocks whose technical charts are positive, you can use the fundamental analysis to tip the scale toward your best trading opportunity.

Chapter **7**

Listening to Analyst Calls

S tock analysts are supposed to be independent oracles who help mere mortal traders understand a company's financial future. Don't count on them, however, because they're not always looking to protect the small investor's pocketbook.

Scandals exposed by then–New York Attorney General Eliot Spitzer in the early 2000s showed how analysts recommended stocks to the public to help their companies land lucrative investment banking deals, while at the same time privately writing and sending emails calling those same stocks junk. (This is the same Spitzer who, after becoming governor of New York, was exposed on an FBI wiretap for patronizing high-priced prostitutes. He should have stuck with the high-priced stock analysts.) Whenever you read recommendations from an analyst, you must determine whether that analyst is a buy-side analyst, sell-side analyst, or independent analyst before you ever consider using the information he or she is providing.

Analysts get much of their information from conference calls sponsored by companies when they report their earnings or make other key financial announcements. Today, individual investors are invited to listen in on most of these calls. You can find out a great deal about a company's prospects by listening in on analyst calls, but the language of these calls can be confusing. This chapter explains the types of analysts, their importance, and the language unique to what they do. We also introduce you to resources on the Internet that can make listening in on analyst calls easier.

Getting to Know Your Analysts

If you watch any of the financial news cable television stations, you've probably seen numerous industry analysts touting certain stocks and panning others. Do you know who those analysts represent? Do you know whether they're independent analysts, buy-side analysts, or sell-side analysts? Before deciding whether to follow analysts' recommendations, be sure that you understand who pays their salary and what's in it for them.

Buy-side analysts: You won't see them

You rarely come in contact with a *buy-side analyst* because they work primarily for large institutional investment firms that manage mutual funds or private accounts. Their primary role is analyzing stocks that are bought by the firm for which they work and not necessarily the ones bought by individual investors. Their research is rarely available outside the firm that hired them. Buy-side analysts focus on whether an investment that's under consideration is a good match for the firm's investment strategy and portfolio. In fact, buy-side analysts frequently include information from sell-side analysts as part of their overall research on an investment. You're most likely to hear from a buy-side analyst if you listen to analyst conference calls. They tend to be much harsher on the company officials.

Sell-side analysts: Watch for conflicts

When you read stock analyses from brokerage houses, you're more than likely reading information from *sell-side analysts*. These analysts work primarily for brokerage houses and other financial distribution sources where salespeople sell securities based on the analysts' recommendations.

The primary purpose of sell-side analysts is providing brokerage salespeople with information to help make sales. As long as the interests of the investor, the broker, and the brokerage house are the same, sell-side analysts' reports can be useful sources of information. A conflict arises, however, when sell-side analysts also are responsible for helping their brokerage houses win investment-banking business.

New York State Attorney General Spitzer exposed why this conflict is a primary reason for all the scandals you've read about regarding star analysts, such as Henry Blodget of Merrill Lynch, whose emails privately called stocks *dogs, toast,* or *junk* at the same time he and his team were publicly recommending that their customers buy the same stocks. Why do this? Well, according to Spitzer's charges,

Blodget's recommendations brought in $115 million in investment banking fees for Merrill Lynch, and Blodget took home $12 million in compensation.

Merrill Lynch was only the first to be exposed. Similar charges were raised against many other firms, including Morgan Stanley and Credit Suisse. Few firms that sell stocks and have an investment banking division avoided the scandal. These companies didn't learn much from the scandals. Merrill Lynch was taken over by Bank of America because of errors made during the mortgage crisis. At one time in the distant past, analysts were separated from investment banks by what companies called a *Chinese Wall*. Analysts' work supposedly was kept completely separate from deals that were being generated in a company's investment-banking business. At some point, the lines between the two broke down, and analysts were included in the process of generating deals for mergers, acquisitions, and new stock offerings. By writing glowing reports, analysts helped their companies sign more lucrative investment banking deals, all the while putting their small investors at great risk of losing all their money by buying the recommended stocks. When the market bubble burst in 2000, many of the stocks that were recommended because of these deals (particularly in the Internet, telecommunications, and other high-tech industries) dropped to being worthless, and investors lost billions.

Ratings companies, such as Standard & Poor's and Moody's, were exposed for similar weaknesses when the subprime mortgage crises imploded in 2008. Rather than protect the investors of mortgage securities, the ratings companies put making money first. They failed to warn investors of the dangers of these mortgage securities and instead gave these securities top ratings. They later proved to be junk.

The U.S. Securities and Exchange Commission (SEC) finally stepped into the fray in April 2002 and announced it was broadening the investigation into analysts' roles and was developing new regulations regarding analyst disclosure. The SEC ultimately endorsed rulemaking changes recommended by the New York Stock Exchange and the Financial Industry Regulatory Authority (FINRA), including the following:

>> **Cannot promise favorable research:** Analysts are prohibited from offering a favorable rating or specific price target to encourage investment-banking business from companies. Firms also must abide by a *quiet period,* meaning they can't issue a report on a company within 40 days after an initial public offering (IPO) or within 10 days after a secondary offering if the firm acted as manager or co-manager of that offering. *IPOs* are offerings made for a company selling its first shares to the public. *Secondary offerings* are for companies that already have stock sold on the open market but are issuing new stock.

>> **Limitations on relationships and communications:** Research analysts can't be supervised by the investment banking department. Investment-banking personnel are even prohibited from discussing research reports with analysts prior to distribution, unless staff for the legal or compliance department is present. Analysts also are prohibited from sharing drafts of their research reports with companies that they are writing about unless they're just checking facts.

>> **Analyst compensation:** Analysts' compensation can no longer be tied to a specific investment-banking transaction. If analysts' compensation is based on general investment-banking revenues, that must be disclosed in the firm's research reports. You can review these disclosures and determine how much weight you want to give an analyst's recommendations.

>> **Restrictions on personal trading by analysts:** Analysts and members of their households can't invest in a company's securities prior to the IPO if the company is in the business sector the analyst covers. They also can't trade securities in the companies they follow for 30 days before and 5 days after they issue a research report about a company.

>> **Disclosures of financial interests in covered companies:** Analysts must disclose if they own shares in recommended companies. Firms must also disclose if they own 1 percent or more of a company's securities. You can determine whether the analyst or his or her company stand to gain from the reports they issue.

>> **Disclosures about ratings given:** Firms must clearly explain in their research reports the meaning of any ratings given. They must also provide the percentage of each type of rating given, such as buy, sell, or hold. You can assess how reliable their ratings are. For example, if a firm gives a very high percentage of buy or sell recommendations, you may want to more carefully compare its ratings to others or ignore it completely.

>> **Disclosures during public appearances:** If you've seen analysts on TV or heard them on the radio recently, you may notice that they disclose whether their firm is an investment-banking client of (or has any other direct connection to) the firm they're discussing. This too is a new rule that was implemented in 2002.

REMEMBER

These rule changes helped investors identify conflicts of interest that can compromise the objectivity of the sell-side analyst's report. Pay close attention to the disclosures and the relationships between the brokerage houses and the companies that their analysts' reports cover. Take these connections into consideration when including their buy or sell recommendations in your plans for future stock transactions.

Independent analysts: Where are they?

You're probably wondering where *independent analysts* — people who you can trust who don't have investment banking connections — really are. Although they do exist, most work for wealthy individuals or institutional investors and provide research for people who manage portfolios of much more than a million dollars and pay fees of at least $25,000 per year.

No one really knows exactly how many independent analysts are out there. Estimates range from 100 to several hundred, but their ranks may grow now that independent research is a required part of selling to individual investors.

TIP

In addition to independent research that you probably see distributed by your brokerage house, as a small investor you can turn to some of the major investment research firms such as Morningstar (www.morningstar.com) and Standard & Poor's (www.standardandpoors.com). They offer services to individual investors through their publications and Internet sites at more reasonable fees than many of the small independent analyst firms. Nevertheless, you need to bear in mind that even these analysts are answering to the companies or wealthy individuals that pay the greatest share of their costs.

The Importance of Analysts

No matter which analyst's report you're reading, you must remember that the analyst's primary income is coming either from the brokerage house or the large institutional clients that he or she serves. Analysts rate stocks on whether you should consider purchasing them, but no standardized rating system exists. The three most common breakdowns that you can expect to see are shown in Table 7-1.

TABLE 7-1   **Common Stock Recommendations from Analysts**

Analysis by Company A	Analysis by Company B	Analysis by Company C
Buy	Strong buy	Recommended list
Outperform	Buy	Trading buy
Neutral	Hold	Market outperformer
Underperform	Sell	Market perform
Avoid		Market underperformer

You can see from this table that you must understand how a company's analysts rate stocks for that company's recommendations to have any value. Company A's *Buy* recommendation is its highest, but Company B uses *Strong buy* for its highest rating, and Company C uses *Recommended list* for its top choice. Merely seeing that a stock is recommended as a Buy by a particular analyst means little if you don't know which rating system the analyst is using.

WARNING

Unfortunately, when it comes to stock analysts, if the information is free, it's probably no better than that free lunch you're always looking to find. Someone has to pay the analyst, and if it isn't you, you must find out who is footing the bill before you use that advice to make decisions.

REMEMBER

The best way to use analysts' reports is to think of them as just one tool in your bucket of trading tools. Analysts are one good way to find out about an industry or a stock, but they're not the final word about what you need to do. Only your own research using fundamental and technical analysis can help you make your investment decisions. We discuss fundamental analysis tools in Chapters 5 and 6 and technical analysis tools in Part 3.

Tracking how a company's doing

Analysts are good resources for finding historical data about how a company or industry is doing. Their reports usually summarize at least five years of data and frequently provide a historical perspective for the industry and the company that goes back many more years. In addition, analysts make projections about the earnings potential of the company they're analyzing and indicate why they believe those projections by including information about new products being developed or currently being tested at various stages of market development.

TIP

These reports help you track how a company is doing so you can find the gems that may indicate when to expect a company to break out of a current trading trend. For example, if an analyst covering a pharmaceutical company mentions that a new drug is under consideration by the Food and Drug Administration, you may look for news stories about the status of that drug and monitor the stock for indications that drug approval may soon be announced. Watching the technical charts may help you jump in at just the right time and catch the upward trend as positive news is announced. Stocks usually start to move in advance of news.

Providing access to analyst calls

In addition to reading reports, you can track companies by listening in on *analyst calls.* Some calls are sponsored by the companies themselves to review annual or quarterly results, and others are sponsored by independent analysts.

Company-sponsored calls

Analyst calls sponsored by companies more often are earnings conference calls primarily for institutional investors and Wall Street analysts. They occur on either a quarterly, semiannual, or annual basis and can be the richest sources of information concerning a company's fundamentals and future prospects.

Senior management, which usually includes the chief executive officer (CEO), president, and chief financial officer (CFO), talks about their financial reports and then answers questions during these calls. The calls sometimes are scheduled to coincide with announcements of major changes in a company's leadership or other breaking news about the company. After a formal statement, senior management answers questions from analysts. That's when you usually can get the most up-to-date information about the company and how management views its financial performance and projections. We discuss how to read between these lines and get the most out of these calls in the next section.

Access to these calls used to be limited to professional analysts and institutional investors, but today more than 97 percent of companies that sponsor analyst calls open them to the media and individual investors, according to a survey conducted by the National Investor Relations Institute. This change primarily is credited to the SEC's Fair Disclosure (FD) Regulation, which requires companies to make public all major announcements that can impact the value of the stock within 24 hours of informing any company outsiders. This rule helps level the information playing field for individual investors.

Analysts no longer can count on getting two or three days of lead time on major announcements, which heretofore helped them inform major investors about company news. Often that amount of lead time enabled analysts to recommend buy or sell decisions to their key clients, but that same practice hurt small investors and traders who weren't privy to the news. Some complain this new rule actually hurt the flow of information because companies clammed up in private conversations with analysts, making it harder for the analysts to write their investigative reports. Since the regulation first took effect in 2000, the fair disclosure rule has helped to level the information playing field.

Independent analyst–sponsored calls

Firms that provide independent analysis also sponsor calls primarily for their wealthy and institutional clients. During these calls, analysts often discuss breaking news about a company or an industry that they follow. Doing so gives their clients an opportunity to discuss key concerns directly with the analysts. Unless you're a client, opportunities for listening in on these calls are rare.

SEEKING INSIDER INFORMATION

Investors began seeking insider information about companies long before the scandals that you now read about almost daily. In fact, one of the first stories ever told about trading on insider information involved the startup of one of today's leading financial information services — Reuters. Julius Reuter started his news service in response to the desire investors had for insider information and how it could impact stock prices. In 1849, Reuter used trained homing pigeons to fly information about closing stock prices from Europe's mainland across the English Channel to England, thus giving his subscribers a jump on news about a stock so they'd be able to react before other, less-informed investors received the information. This story highlights a simple but powerful secret of investing: *Information is power.* Investors with privileged access to information hold a distinct advantage over other investors who don't have the same access.

Just to give you an idea of how analysts used insider information more recently, here are a couple of examples.

- In February 1999, during a tour of the headquarters of Compaq Computer Corporation, the company's treasurer told a group of big-time investors that he was concerned about softness in the software industry. Compaq shares dropped 14 percent before most individual investors ever discovered such a concern existed.

- In September 1999, executives at Apple Computer, Inc., called analysts to alert them that an earthquake in Taiwan disrupted the production of iBook and Powerbook notebook computers. The Apple execs wanted to warn analysts that the company would not meet its numbers for the quarter. The stock fell 7 percent in four days, and again, by the time most investors found out, it was too late.

The SEC fair disclosure rule prevents this kind of favored treatment for insiders.

Pointers for Listening to Analyst Calls

Most company conference calls start with a welcome to all call participants, followed by a discussion of the financial results being released or the purpose the company has designated for the call. After the CEO, president, and CFO make their statements, other key managers may comment on the results before the call is opened to questions from the listening audience.

The question-and-answer portion of the call usually is the most revealing and enables you to judge just how confident senior managers are with their reporting. The Q&A period is when you're most likely to hear information that hasn't been revealed in press releases or formal annual or quarterly reports. Analysts and institutional investors are usually given the first shot at asking questions, meaning before other listeners, the press, or individual investors get their turn. Not all companies permit individual investors to ask questions. Even when you can't ask any questions, listening to responses to the questions posed by analysts, institutional investors, and the media is still worthwhile.

TIP

Be sure to listen closely to how the company's senior managers answer those questions. Chances are good that any question you may have will be answered during the Q&A period. If not, you can always write or call the company's investor-relations division to get an answer to your specific question.

WARNING

Analyst conference calls are best used as a research tool and not for taking an immediate action based solely on the information you gather from them. You need to consider them as just one more way of gaining knowledge about a stock that you're thinking about buying, or of tracking stocks after you've already bought them. Day traders and swing traders sometimes use the information from analyst calls to trade after hours, but such trades can be highly risky. We talk more about these two trading strategies in Chapters 17 and 18.

Understanding the analysts' language

Before ever listening to your first call, you must familiarize yourself with the language used during calls. Most of the common terminology is discussed in Chapter 6, including earnings per share (EPS), EPS growth, net income, cash, and cash equivalents, but other terms that are unique to the analyst call world include the following:

>> **Hockey stick:** When company officials say their revenues come in like a hockey stick, they're not exactly talking about getting hit with a puck. Instead, they're talking about the shape of a hockey stick. What they mean is that because most of their revenues are booked in the final days of the quarter, revenue charts take on the appearance of a hockey stick. Most companies, in fact, book revenues this way, because sales incentives are designed to encourage the sales force to close their contracts before the end of a quarter. Salespeople have to meet their quotas, and companies that are planning purchases frequently delay those decisions until near the end of a quarter so they can negotiate the best deals when the salespeople are most desperate to make a deal. You've probably done the same thing yourself when buying a car or other major item.

>> **Lumpy:** Nope, the CEO isn't talking about poorly cooked oatmeal whenever he or she says revenues or orders were lumpy. This term means that sales were uneven during the quarter, with some weeks having low order rates and

others having high order rates. The key is finding out why sales were lumpy and whether lumpy sales are normal for the company.

>> **Run-rate:** Don't worry, you won't be asked how fast you can run a race. The run-rate is the way senior management talks about how its current performance can be projected over a period of time. For example, if the current quarter's revenues show a $1 million monthly run-rate, then you can expect annual revenues to total close to $12 million. This concept may work for companies with steady earnings but not for companies whose products primarily are seasonal. For example, if a retail company reports a run-rate of $1 million per month during the fourth quarter, which of course includes holiday sales, you won't expect that performance to be indicative of a full 12-month performance. You must be certain that you understand a company's revenue picture before counting on run-rate numbers.

TIP

If you hear other terminology that you don't understand, write it down so you can research it and understand it the next time you hear it.

Developing your listening skills

In addition to *what* senior management is saying, you also need to listen to *how* they're saying it. If management is happy with the results, they'll probably be upbeat and talking about a rosy future for the company. On the other hand, if management isn't so happy with the results, the mood probably will be downbeat and apologetic as they try to explain why the company didn't perform as expected and, of course, make excuses for their failure to meet expectations.

Learn to listen and read between the company lines. Try to listen in on every earnings call. The first one you hear may not mean much unless you know how the results differ from previous reports and projections. Before that first call, you need to read analysts' reports and become as familiar as possible with the company's earnings history. After you've followed a certain company's calls for a while, the information presented will mean much more to you. Among the many indicators that may help you determine your trading activity are signs relating to earnings expectations, revenue growth, analysts' moods, company facts, future projections, and employee satisfaction.

Earnings expectations

Whether a company is meeting its own projections and analysts' expectations is the most important clue about how a company is doing and how the stock market will react to its periodic reports. If the company fails to meet expectations, the market will likely punish the stock by driving the price down, and that can point to a good trading opportunity. If you believe the setback is temporary and the company's long-term prospects look good, you may want to wait for the stock to bottom out before buying it. If you think failing periodic expectations is a sign of long-term bad news, and you hold a position in the stock, you may want to sell it as soon as possible. If you don't own it, you may want to consider shorting the stock. We discuss shorting a stock at length in Chapter 15.

Revenue growth

Listen for information that indicates whether revenue growth kept pace with earnings growth. This factor becomes even more critical whenever the economy slows down because a company may play with or manipulate the numbers in a practice that's known as *window dressing*, or making sure that earnings meet expectations. However, manipulating revenues is much more difficult. Growth in revenues is the key to continued earnings growth in the future.

Although manipulating earnings may be difficult, we've seen companies do it successfully for at least a few quarters and, in some cases, a few years. A number of companies caught in recent Wall Street scandals successfully manipulated these numbers with creative methods of booking revenue. One account that you may want to watch for signs of revenue manipulation is accounts receivable. If receivables rise dramatically above historical balances, one of two things are likely — the company is having a hard time collecting on its accounts or the company is booking fictitious revenue. Manipulation may also be detected when a company reports revenue for items sold that is actually greater than the company has the capacity to produce.

WARNING

You may notice analysts questioning revenue-growth figures in great detail. This examination by analysts can be a sign that they may suspect problems with the numbers. Detecting any of these signs while listening to a call can be a sign of possible trouble ahead, and you need to take a closer look before buying the stock or holding what you already have.

Analysts' moods

You can find out a great deal about how analysts are responding to a company's report by merely listening to the tone of their questions. By listening to how analysts are asking questions and what questions they're asking, you can judge whether the analysts are downbeat on company prospects, especially if they're asking increasingly probing questions. On the other hand, you may notice that analysts are upbeat and encourage senior management to talk even more positively about their results and future plans. When you've followed the analysts' calls for a company during several quarters, recognizing whether the mood has changed isn't difficult. When analysts receive news positively, they often start their questions with some kind of congratulatory remark.

Be sure to jot down the names of analysts, especially the ones making positive remarks. The positive remarks from analysts with sell-side orientation may not be as good a sign as the positive remarks from buy-side analysts. If you don't know what type of analyst is commenting, research his or her affiliations and leanings after the call.

TIP

Buy-side analysts carry the most weight whenever they're indicating a positive reaction to the company's financial news. Many buy-side analysts who attend analyst calls already have a stake in the company, so they have a vested interest in putting a positive spin on the news. If they're positive, they'll likely revise their earnings estimates upward, which can be the first indication that they'll recommend additional buys, and the stock may be getting ready to enter an upward trend. This positive spin can give you the first sign of a good trading opportunity, so watch your technical analysis for any signals of a potential breakout. We discuss more about breakouts in Chapter 10.

Just the facts, ma'am

TIP

The best way to judge whether senior managers are confident in their reporting is determining how quickly they respond to questions. If senior managers are confident with their numbers, they respond to questions quickly, taking little time to think their responses through. If senior managers are unsure of their reports, they're more likely to take a good deal of time checking through their papers to answer even the simplest questions. You definitely need to think twice about buying or holding stock in a company whose management shows a lack of confidence in reporting their numbers.

The future

You're likely to get a good reading about how senior managers view the company's future prospects by listening to their vision for the company and whether the results actually demonstrate that they're fulfilling that vision. When managers are successfully fulfilling their vision, they clearly articulate their view of the company's future and how they plan to get there. Ask yourself whether management inspires you with its vision. If not, managers most likely are not inspiring their employees, which can be an early sign that the company is heading on a downward trend.

Employee satisfaction

Happy employees are a good sign that a company will be able to meet its future expectations. If, during the call, you hear that the company is having trouble attracting new employees or retaining its existing staff, you may be looking at a sign of trouble on the horizon. High employee turnover is bad for future growth, and so is having trouble finding and recruiting qualified employees.

Locating Company Calls

Many companies list information about their upcoming earnings reports and analyst calls on their company websites, while others simply post an audio version after the event. Some companies offer their investors a service that alerts them to upcoming events. If these services are not available for the companies you plan to follow, your best way of tracking upcoming calls is at RTT News (`http://www.rttnews.com/corpinfo/conferencecalls.aspx`). You can sign up to get a daily market update for free from RTT News to keep track of upcoming calls.

Yahoo Finance is another good source for finding earnings calls. You can access its calendar of calls at `http://biz.yahoo.com/research/earncal/today.html`.

TIP

If you happen to miss a call, Morningstar (`http://www.morningstar.com`) posts transcripts of analyst calls for many companies. On its website, search for "earnings calls."

Identifying Trends in the Stock-Analyst Community

The regulatory climate in Washington now drives changes in the stock-analyst community following disclosures of the abuses exposed after the stock bubble that ended in 2000. The Financial Disclosure Regulation of 2001 (Regulation FD) controls the flow of information between companies and analysts and ultimately what information makes its way to you as an outside investor or trader.

Some traders believe that the restrictions that ban selective disclosure to friendly analysts or key investors actually hurt the flow of information to the general public. Regulation FD requires that any information disclosed to analysts or key investors that can affect a company's value must be disclosed to the general public within 24 hours, even if the information wasn't part of a planned report.

The preference is for making announcements about material information at the same time for everyone, but sometimes during meetings with an analyst or institutional investor, information is shared inadvertently. For example, if analysts find out information during a company tour, the company then is required to put out a press release disclosing the same information to the general public. Some analysts believe this is making the preparation of their reports much more difficult than it needs to be.

Regulation FD, however, halted some commonplace industry practices, including closed meetings with analysts and institutional investors. Lawyers for many companies warn senior managers to be careful about responding to calls from individual analysts. Some companies require that any contact with analysts first be evaluated and approved through their legal advisors.

Regulations also impact *roadshows,* which are marketing tours that introduce a company's new securities offerings. The SEC permits these events but gives clear guidance that they now need to be more like oral offers that are designed to avoid the prohibition against written or broadcast offers made outside the official prospectus of the offering. The SEC believes these roadshows are best conducted in the open to all investors and has voiced objections to having two separate roadshows, one for institutional investors and another, more sanitized version, for retail investors. Some legal experts also advise companies to be careful about whether they include outside analysts, those not employed by the underwriter of the offering, as part of the roadshow. Including outside analysts, some believe, can be viewed as selective disclosure, which violates Regulation FD.

TIP

The biggest regulatory changes you'll see as an individual investor or trader relate to disclosures that must be made in research reports, including a requirement that securities firms must disclose any compensation they receive for investment banking services they provide during the three months following the public offering for a covered company. In addition, firms that are members of the New York Stock Exchange or the National Association of Securities Dealers must disclose when they stop coverage of a public company. Many times this type of news generates unfavorable publicity for the company and can result in a drop in stock prices. In addition to these big disclosures, analysts' research reports now must include information about the relationships among the analysts, underwriters, and stock issuer.

Operating in this type of fish bowl may make companies and analysts nervous, but it nevertheless leveled the playing field for individual investors. Look carefully for these disclosures as you read analysts' reports, and take advantage of your newfound access to information by attending analysts' earnings conferences and being part of the insider pool rather than a passive outsider waiting to be fed information by the financial media or professional analysts.

3
Reading the Charts: Technical Analysis

Chapter **8**

Seeing Is Believing: An Introduction to Technical Analysis

Anticipating where the markets are heading is a tough thing to do. Still, the challenge doesn't stop folks from trying.

For many investors, the method of choice is *fundamental analysis,* which we describe in Part 2 (Chapters 5, 6, and 7). For traders, *technical analysis,* as described in this chapter and in Chapters 9, 10, and 11, is the go-to. No matter what the strategy, one thing is certain: Investors and traders alike are always looking for an edge to more accurately — and consistently — forecast price movements and improve their trading results.

Although some overlap exists between fundamental and technical analyses, you find dyed-in-the-wool, true believers in both camps, and they argue that their way is best. Some even go so far as to say the other method is worse than useless. For our money, the truth lies between these two extremes. Both have their strengths; both have their weaknesses. We argue that when you adopt elements from both methodologies, you'll find that there's a sweet spot somewhere in the middle.

In this chapter, we begin to introduce the methodology behind technical analysis, dispel some common misconceptions, and set the stage for further exploration into the analysis of charts.

Understanding the Methodology

Technical analysis is the forecasting of future financial price movements based on strategic analysis of past financial data, charted in a variety of visual formats. A *technician* — that's someone who reads stock charts — uses price charts and market statistics (such as trading volume) to develop a profitable trading plan. Some technicians even say that price charts indicate where a stock's price is heading simply by showing where it has been. Detractors liken technical analysis to fortune-telling. However, it's important to remember that whether you're a numbers-driven fundamentalist or a charts-focused technician, both strategies are attempting to accomplish the same goal: use reliable analysis methods to make informed investing decisions.

At its core, the objective of technical analysis is to analyze how the forces of supply and demand affect market prices. A constant tug of war takes place between the buyers and sellers of a stock, and technicians watch it all unfold by analyzing the charts. Market price is the end result of that battle, so technicians uncover insights into which camp is winning by answering two important questions: What is the current price, and how have past prices changed over time to lead to that current price?

REMEMBER

Technicians try to anticipate what is likely to happen in the future and make trading plans based on price-chart indicators. Technical analysis isn't about predicting the future. Its real purpose is to identify probable events that are most likely to occur and to make trading plans in case they do occur and alternative plans in case they don't. Technicians use a logical framework to identify price trends, turning points, trading ranges, and breakouts. These important trading concepts are covered in Chapters 9, 10, and 11.

Understanding technical analysis methods requires familiarity with a few key concepts:

>> Everything about a company is reflected in its price.

>> Price movements are sometimes random.

>> Price changes are caused by an imbalance between supply and demand.

In the following sections we dig into these three concepts. We also discuss exactly how technicians analyze where things have been and make informed forecasts about where they're headed. You need to know how to read price movements and how they're impacted by the basics of supply and demand, so we explore these topics here.

Finding everything in the price

The stock market is a remarkably efficient information-processing machine. So efficient, in fact, that every bit of information currently known about a company is immediately priced into its stock. In other words, the current price reflects the combined wisdom of everyone in the market, including corporate insiders, pension and mutual fund managers, individual investors, stock analysts, fundamental analysts, technicians, and you.

The charts used in technical analysis provide a synopsis of all the fundamental, economic, and psychological factors that affect the price of a stock. Although we personally think putting all your eggs in the price basket is taking the point to an extreme, that's why some technicians don't even try to evaluate the fundamentals. Why bother trying to outsmart the smartest when everything's already reflected in the price?

Technicians are more concerned with understanding *what* is happening than they are with understanding *why* it's happening. The technician's understanding of why a stock's price moves is not important. Technicians don't necessarily care whether the price movement was caused by the most recent analyst's report or by a CEO's resignation. They are concerned only with

>> What the price is now

>> What the price history is

Technical analysts examine current prices relative to the histories of price movements to understand and plan for what is most likely to happen next. Fundamental analysts ask why, trying to understand what piece of news causes a particular rise in price or what bit of insider knowledge causes a sell off. Technicians try to visualize everything the price represents and base their trades only on what they see.

REMEMBER

The stream of news is endless and ever-changing. You can't know what causes every ripple in the price continuum. So why try? Focus on first determining what is happening and how to act on it, and then worry about why it happened.

Seeing that price movements are not always random

Sometimes prices move higher. Sometimes prices move lower. And sometimes prices bounce up and down within a tight trading range. When prices move higher or lower, we say prices are *trending.* The trading periods often appear to be random price movements, and at times, they may actually be random. But when you zoom in to view the price movements within those seemingly random trading-range periods, you find that the trading range is made up of many mini trends. The closer you look, the less random these price movements appear. That pattern is the crux of technical analysis. These concepts are important for trading and are covered more fully in Chapter 10.

At its core, technical analysis is used to identify the periods of time during which trends occur. In general, technicians want to base their trades on trending markets. The idea is to determine when trends begin and when they end. But which trend? Are you the type of trader who is interested in the little mini trends that make up a trading range? Or are you most interested in trading longer-lasting trends?

TIP

The key to technical trading, therefore, is identifying a stock's price trend within the time frame during which you want to trade. Depending on the length of time you plan to hold the stock, you should base your trades on analyses done in the corresponding time frame. If you're primarily concerned with long-lasting trends that span many weeks, months, or even years, you want to analyze charts showing daily, weekly, and/or monthly prices. If, instead, you plan to hold your stock for no more than a few hours or a few days, you want to analyze intraday charts showing one-minute, five-minute, or one-hour prices. When looking at intraday price charts, you see many examples of mini trends and trading ranges. However, if you're buying a stock and holding your position for weeks or months, those mini intraday trends and trading ranges are meaningless. We cover these concepts more fully in Chapter 9.

Balancing supply and demand

If you've ever watched the nightly business news, you've probably heard reporters claim that prices rose because more buyers were looking for stocks than sellers were willing to part with them. But of course, even novice investors realize that every trade must have a buyer and a seller.

What the reporter really means is that supply and demand in the market were out of balance. Price is a function of supply and demand, so an imbalance between the two leads to a movement in one direction. In macroeconomics, this concept is illustrated using a freely traded commodity like wheat. When farmers grow more wheat than bakers need, the price of wheat falls because farmers have to attract customers by selling at lower prices. When bakers need more wheat than farmers grow, bakers bid higher prices to get the wheat they need.

REMEMBER

In many ways, the price of a stock works just like the price of wheat. When buyers want to buy more shares of a stock than sellers are willing or able to sell, buyers bid the stock price higher until they find sellers willing to part with their shares. Conversely, when sellers can't find enough buyers, they offer their shares at lower and lower prices until enough buyers can be found.

Changes in a company's business plan, a new competitor, or any number of other factors can throw the balance between supply and demand out of whack. Realizing that imbalances cause prices to move — and not the news itself — is the point where technical analysis is concerned.

Understanding where you've been

Technicians examine price history, trading volume, and additional market statistics to evaluate the balance between supply and demand. The conceptual framework is easy to understand. If prices are rising, then demand exceeds supply, and buyers are more interested in buying than sellers are in selling. The reverse is equally true. Falling prices mean that supply exceeds demand, and sellers are more interested in selling than buyers are in buying. When a stock trades within a tight range of prices, neither the buyers nor the sellers are dominant in the marketplace. A balance between supply and demand has been achieved, so prices simply bounce up and down. This situation is evident on the price chart when a stock trades within a clear trading range. Examples are shown in Chapter 9.

REMEMBER

Technical analysis uses past and present price data, trading volume, and other important market statistics. Technicians examine charts in search of the price levels where buying pressure stops a stock's price from falling further or where selling pressure squashes a rally.

Here's a hypothetical scenario to illustrate finding the right point to buy. A high-profile investment advisor issues a recommendation to buy shares of XYZ, which closed at $18.50 the day before and has traded in a tight price range of $17 to $18.75 during the past four months. The recommendation to buy is in effect only if the stock trades for less than $19 a share. The idea is not necessarily to buy the instant that a recommendation is made, but rather to buy at a good price.

Taking the hypothetical example a step further, say that the advisor has a devoted following of active investors. Invariably, the recommendation is quickly followed by a surge in the volume of buyers purchasing shares of XYZ, even as the price of the stock rises to $21 due to increased demand.

Buying surges based on these kinds of recommendations have a tendency to stall out and return to the buy-under price (in this case, $19) after all the early buyers make their trades. Patient subscribers of this advisor have seen this movie many times before, so they wait for the pullback and place a limit order near the $19 price (limit orders are discussed in Chapter 2). Enough patient investors are usually in the market for the stock to keep its price from falling further. When the price falls back to the target level recommended by the advisor, the patient subscribers will jump in and buy. That activity supports the price from declining further.

Now imagine that you're watching this stock without knowledge of the investment advisor's recommendation. You'd likely see the price of XYZ shares take the following steps during the course of a week or two:

1. **XYZ breaks out of its trading range and rallies on higher-than-normal volume.**

2. **Buying of XYZ drops off, and the price pulls back.**

3. **High-volume buying of XYZ resumes as the price falls near $19.**

This type of market activity is what intelligent technicians wait patiently for. You see this scenario play out over and over again, in individual stocks, in exchange-traded funds (ETFs), and in the general market indexes. Chapter 9 discusses how to recognize and trade this scenario, but for now, know that it's a textbook example of a *trading-range breakout* defined by the following:

>> A high-volume breakout after a long period of range-bound trading

>> A low-volume pullback

>> A high-volume rally to new highs

If you were interested in this stock, you may have taken a position. In fact, given this setup, the three logical places where a technician takes a position are

>> **At the breakout:** Buy as soon as the stock breaks through the resistance level at the upper end of the trading range.

>> **After the pullback:** Buy immediately as the stock begins trading higher after its price pulls back on low volume.

>> **At the double top:** When the stock retraces the move from the pullback to its high price, it's called a *double top*. Buy on strength as the stock makes a new high for the move.

Of these three alternatives, our favorite is the second. Buying immediately after the pullback is a relatively low-risk, high-reward trade. By trading at pretested prices, you have a better understanding of how the forces of supply and demand for the stock will play out. Our least favorite trade is the last one. Trading the double top as the stock makes a new high is the riskiest of the three alternatives. Both the breakout and the pullback trades are covered in much more detail, including example charts, in Chapter 9.

Technical analysis can allow you to find shrewd entry prices on your trades while also helping keep your losses small. When understood and implemented properly, it is a powerful trading tool to have at your disposal.

Understanding where you're headed

Stock prices move in a never-ending series of upward rallies and downward reactions. Technical analysis helps you discover and analyze where buyers took action throughout those past rallies and reactions. If you recognize where buyers have stepped in before, you can reasonably expect that they will do so again in the future. When they do as you expect, you need to be able to trade on that information profitably.

If they don't act as you expect, you may have to exit your trade, and yet you've still discovered a great deal of valuable information. You hope that the price you pay for that knowledge isn't too great, but you nevertheless know more than you did before. You know that the last wave of buying exhausts demand, and thus you need to begin looking for further evidence of a reversal.

You don't have to adhere to arguments that technical analysis is a good forecasting tool merely to recognize that it is a useful trading tool.

Answering the Detractors

A few arguments against technical analysis may actually make some sense, but the irrelevant complaints far outweigh the legitimate. For example, some people wrongly assert that no technicians have been successful over the long run and that no technician has mustered the stature or success of illustrious market moguls like Warren Buffett, Benjamin Graham, or Peter Lynch.

As if to further this argument, they point to some infamous technician who blew up his portfolio in spectacular fashion. Then a few years later, they harp on another well-known technician who made a boneheaded call, and then it happened again, and they therefore claim technical analysis is useless. Detractors usually leave out the fact that many high-profile fundamental analysts have also blown client portfolios.

In fact, many successful technicians have long, profitable trading careers. While most toil in self-imposed obscurity, some are prominent and outspoken. For example, John W. Henry, who owns the Boston Red Sox, made his fortune as a trend-following technician. Additional examples include Ed Seykota, a trader with 35 years of experience and one of the people profiled in the book *Market Wizards*, and Bill Dunn of Dunn Capital Management, Inc. This is just a tiny sample of the many successful independent traders and fund managers who employ technical-analysis tools to make trading decisions.

Another argument about the alleged ineffectiveness of technical analysis is a chart-reading challenge that no technician has ever attempted (or would even consider). It works like this: The technical analyst is given the first half of a price chart with all identifying information removed. From that information, the technician is supposed to tell whether the stock's price was higher or lower at any point in the second half of the chart.

Of course, nobody ever claims the prize for having accomplished this feat, and that, therefore, is supposed to be proof that no technician ever has enough confidence in technical analysis to even try. Accomplished technicians aren't any better at telling the future than a tarot-card reader — and neither, for that matter, are fundamental analysts. Technical analysis is not fortune-telling; it's simply a trading tool.

In the following sections we present and examine arguments against a couple of the more common theories about why technical analysis doesn't work. We review the random walk theory and questions raised about trading signals.

Walking randomly

The *random walk theory* has nothing to do with hiking without a map, but instead is an academic theory that says stock prices are completely random. What happened to a stock yesterday has nothing to do with what happens to its price tomorrow.

Furthermore, this theory claims that the market is so efficient that consistently outperforming broad-based market indexes is impossible. In other words, any edge that you may gain from fundamental analysis, technical analysis, or any other strategy is useless and expensive. After all, transaction costs far outweigh any performance improvement that your analysis provides.

Armed with computer models and reams of study results, academic experts cling to these efficient-market hypotheses as gospel. Several challenges oppose their argument. No less an authority than the Federal Reserve Bank of New York published a study showing that using support and resistance levels (see Chapter 9) improved trading results for several firms. Additionally, articles published in the *Journal of Finance* suggest that trading based on moving averages and head and shoulder reversal patterns outperformed the market averages. (We discuss reversal patterns in Chapter 9 and moving averages in Chapter 11.)

REMEMBER

Of course, these studies don't prove that technical analysis is effective all the time. But they cast doubt on the validity of the random walk theory, especially the assertion that technical analysis can't be used to consistently improve results compared to the market averages.

Debating these arguments to a logical conclusion is nearly impossible. Even when you use technical analysis successfully, random walkers claim your performance is the result of random chance — nothing more than good luck. Don't believe them. Instead, believe that luck favors the prepared mind.

Trading signals known to all

Anyone who cares to look can see exactly the same patterns and has access to the same indicators as every other trader. So one argument against technical analysis is that there's nothing new under the sun — or in the markets — for analysts to find.

Although some traders create proprietary indicators to gain a trading edge, many more use well-known, off-the-shelf trading tools. The patterns and indicators described in Chapters 9, 10, and 11 are all well known. Some are freely available on the Internet for anyone to use. Thus, if everyone sees the same thing, how can you use those trading signals profitably? The question is perfectly legitimate.

As we show these tools, we also show you how to develop these charts at StockCharts.com.

Although everyone can see the same patterns and indicators, this equality is a strength rather than a weakness. Technical analysis gives you insight into what future actions you can expect from your fellow market participants. With practice, you can use that information to construct a consistently profitable trading plan.

REMEMBER

After you become familiar with traditional patterns and indicators, you can incorporate your experience and market knowledge into your trading plans and thus come to an understanding of when to use specific tools and when results are meaningless. From these plans, you can find out when a trading signal works and when it fails. You can make trades based on indicators and patterns that help and ignore the rest.

Many widely known indicators and trading patterns exist, but personally, we use only a handful of the simplest ones. Your results will differ from ours. You may trade in a different time frame than we do, or you may choose a different set of tools altogether. As long as your tools improve your trading, continue using them. Ultimately, your trading system should be like a fine suit, custom tailored to fit one specific person: you.

Executing Your Trading Plan

As any experienced investor will tell you, there's no single magic tool guaranteed to make you a profitable trader. Finding success in the market is about discovering, learning, and committing to the strategies and techniques that fit your trading style best. Technical analysis is a useful trading tool that can help you decide what action to take when stocks trend a certain way. Incorporating chart analysis into your investing alongside other proven fundamental analysis methods is simply a smart way to strengthen your trading system.

REMEMBER

Successful trading doesn't mean that you have to be right all the time or even half the time. Instead, successful trading is about creating and consistently executing a reliable trading system. First, you must find the right tools to help you achieve those objectives. Technical analysis is an excellent tool for managing your money, controlling your losses, and enabling your profits to run (see Chapter 12 for more money management information).

Even people who base their trades solely on fundamental factors can use chart analysis to help them time market entry and exit points and gauge price volatility and risk. When it comes time to place a trade, even pure fundamentalists must become temporary technicians. It's tough to buy or sell a stock without first taking a glance at its chart to help determine exactly where to place a limit order, for example. Using technical analysis successfully means

>> Being patient

>> Learning how to identify and properly use a manageable number of patterns and indicators

>> Becoming proficient at finding these patterns and profitably trading them

>> Adding methodically to your tool kit to improve your trading results

Remember that no method is foolproof. Nothing ever ensures successful trades 100 percent of the time. But technical analysis is an excellent tool for improving your trading results.

Using StockCharts.com

Before you can read charts, you need to create them. To help you get started creating and reading financial charts, we have partnered with StockCharts.com, one of the web's premier charting platforms. We've even arranged a 20 percent discount especially for *Trading For Dummies* readers toward a subscription on the website. Sign up today and a get a free one-month trial of their advanced charting tools, resources, and more. The coupon code is SCC-DUMMIES-17. Access that trial as a *Trading For Dummies* reader at `http://stockcharts.com/sales/index.html`. If you're already a StockCharts member, use the discount code to renew your existing subscription.

Where you see charts throughout this book, you also find explanations of how to create them on StockCharts.com.

Creating a stock chart involves picking many variables and customizing it to fit your specific trading profile. Figure 8-1 shows you the interface below a chart that enables you to customize it to your individual needs.

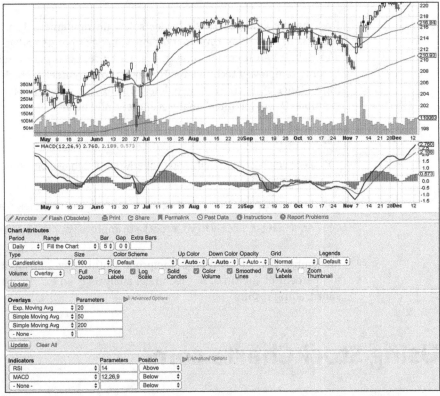

FIGURE 8-1:
To create charts, you set numerous chart attributes, overlays, and indicators.

Among the most valuable data points for your chart are these variables:

>> **Periods:** You can choose daily, weekly, or monthly depending on the time frame of your trading. For shorter time frames, intraday charts are also available in multiple periods, including one-minute, five-minute, and one-hour increments.

>> **Range:** You can set the range as one, three, or six months; one, two, or three years; or year-to-date. Or you can customize your charts using a specific date range of your choosing.

>> **Type:** The type pictured in Figure 8-1 is candlesticks, which is a common option that we use in this book, but you can also use various types of bars, lines, dots, and others.

>> **Size:** You can set the size as well as choose between portrait and landscape.

>> **Overlays:** You can pick numerous types of overlays. The most commonly used are shown in Figure 8-1: 50-day and 200-day moving averages. We talk about other options traders use as we discuss charting techniques.

>> **Indicators:** StockCharts.com allows you to create charts using over 50 different indicators. We discuss them as we discuss trading techniques.

Knowing which settings or indicators to use to produce charts that meet your needs is a key part of technical analysis. So practice charting as you read about each technique.

TIP

We tell you throughout this book about the overlays and indicators that we use regularly, but StockCharts.com also provides an excellent educational resource, ChartSchool, that goes into careful detail about each type of charting tool, overlay, and indicator the site offers and how to use them successfully. To explore ChartSchool, go to StockCharts.com and click the tab labeled ChartSchool at the top of any web page.

Chapter **9**

Reading Bar Charts Is Easy (Really)

Stock charts come in many flavors. Some prominent ones include candlestick charts, point-and-figure charts, and the ever-popular bar charts, which are used throughout this book.

Bar charts are easy to create, interpret, and track over time. Furthermore, charting tools and analysis techniques for bar charts apply to stocks, bonds, exchange-traded funds (ETFs), options, indexes, and futures, and they're applicable across any time frame in which you may want to trade. In addition, most chart patterns work for both *long trades* (buy first, sell later) and *short trades* (sell first, buy later).

This chapter shows you how to draw price charts for a single stock, for an index such as the S&P 500 or NASDAQ Composite, or for an ETF, and how to recognize simple single-day trading patterns. In addition, you find out how to identify trends and trading ranges and how to look for key transition points that often lead to good trading opportunities. Charting is a visual methodology, so you'll find many example charts used throughout this chapter. Examine them carefully. You want to quickly identify the patterns we describe here when evaluating charts in your own trading.

Creating a Price Chart

In the decades before computers, traders followed and carefully documented stock prices to create their charts by hand. Today, however, powerful software has eliminated that need. In the modern, tech-driven world, a seemingly endless supply of charting tools and analysis platforms is available. For instance, you'll find a wide array of online charting services that can be quickly and easily accessed from any Internet-enabled device. Many of those tools can even be securely connected to your brokerage, further streamlining your trading practices. Downloadable software is also available. These resources are discussed in greater detail in Chapter 4.

Even though you no longer need to create your own charts by hand, it's still valuable to understand the basic elements of a stock chart. The basic characteristics of a chart of stock prices are the same as those of the common charts with which you're probably familiar. Stock charts typically are made up of two axes; the *horizontal axis* represents time, and the *vertical axis* represents price. One unusual feature of a stock chart is that its vertical axis, the price axis, usually is shown on the right, as in Figure 9-1. The most current prices are shown on the far right-hand side of the chart, as are the newest trading signals. You always trade while those signals are on the right edge of a chart, so displaying the price axis closest to the most crucial part of the chart makes sense.

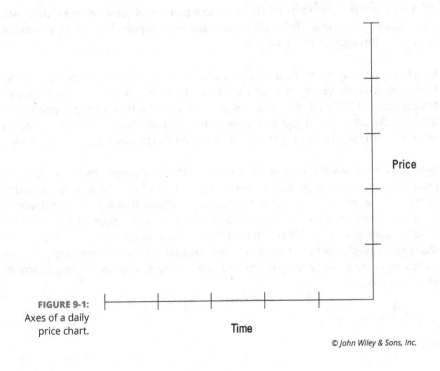

FIGURE 9-1: Axes of a daily price chart.

Price

Time

© *John Wiley & Sons, Inc.*

Looking at a single price bar

Regardless of whether your chart is an *intraday chart* (showing fluctuations throughout a single trading day) or a chart of daily or weekly prices, the format of the price bar is the same. Each bar represents the results for a single trading period. On a chart that provides daily information, for example, each bar represents the results for a single trading day. Alternatively, on a chart that provides intraday data, each bar could represent the results for as little as a single minute of trading activity.

Most stock-price bar charts show four crucial prices on each bar:

>> **Open:** The price recorded for the first trade of the period

>> **High:** The highest price trade at any point in the trading period

>> **Low:** The lowest price trade at any point in the trading period

>> **Close:** The price recorded for the last trade of the period

By convention, a daily bar chart shows trades for the standard New York Stock Exchange (NYSE) trading day — from 9:30 a.m. to 4:00 p.m. ET — but some charting packages include optional after-hours results (prices from trades that occur after the market closes) as part of each daily bar. Likewise, some charting packages omit the opening prices on intraday charts. The opening price on an intraday chart (almost) always is the same as the closing price for the previous bar, so omitting it is of little consequence. However, omitting the opening price on daily, weekly, and monthly charts diminishes a chart's usefulness, so avoid charts that don't provide all four prices.

Figure 9-2 shows a single OHLC price bar. The name *OHLC price bar* is derived from the four prices the bar represents: the open, the high, the low, and the close. The full range of prices traded throughout the period is shown by the vertical bar, with the bottom point representing the lowest price and the top point representing the highest price. The opening price is shown as a small line on the left-hand side of the bar, and the closing price is shown by a similar line on the right-hand side of the bar.

High

Close

Open

FIGURE 9-2:
A single price bar.

Low

© John Wiley & Sons, Inc.

This identical format is used for all time periods. For example, an intraday chart may use 1-minute bars, where each bar spans all the prices for your stock that occur during trades over a single minute. Common time frames for stock price charts are

>> **1-minute bars:** Each bar represents 1 minute of trading.

>> **5-minute bars:** Each bar represents 5 minutes of trading.

>> **10-minute bars:** Each bar represents 10 minutes of trading.

>> **15-minute bars:** Each bar represents 15 minutes of trading.

>> **60-minute bars:** Each bar represents 60 minutes of trading.

>> **Daily bars:** Each bar represents one full day of trading.

>> **Weekly bars:** Each bar represents one full week of trading.

>> **Monthly bars:** Each bar represents one full month of trading.

In our own trading, we typically monitor weekly charts, daily charts, and one or two intraday charts, generally 60-minute and 1-minute bars for stocks and ETFs. We cover our chart selection and methodology more fully in Chapter 13.

Measuring volume

In addition to prices, stock charts often show the *volume* (the number of shares traded) during the given time period represented by each bar. On a daily chart, trading volume shows the total number of shares traded throughout the day. By convention, the volume is shown as a separate bar graph and usually is shown directly underneath the price chart. Figure 9-3 shows an example.

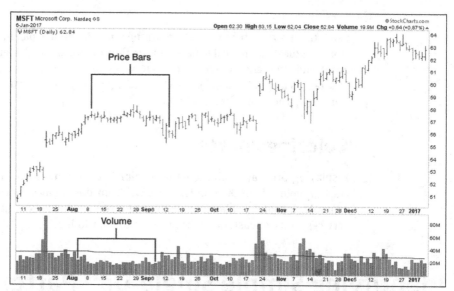

FIGURE 9-3:
A daily chart shows price and volume.

Chart courtesy of StockCharts.com

REMEMBER

Volume is used as a confirming indicator. In other words, if a price bar shows bullish activity (which is discussed later in the section "Identifying Simple Single-Day Patterns"), that bullishness is confirmed by a higher-than-average trading volume. However, that bullish indication may diminish if trading volume is lower than average.

Volume also is used to gauge institutional participation in a stock. Significant trading volume often signals that large institutional investors — mutual funds, pension funds, insurance companies, hedge funds, and others — are placing orders to buy or sell a stock. When prices rise and volume is strong, you usually can infer that institutions are accumulating positions in the stock. The reverse is also true. When prices fall and trading volume is high, large institutions may be liquidating positions, which is considered a bearish development.

Because volume effectively signals demand, low-volume price changes are less meaningful, from a technical perspective, than high-volume changes. That's why technicians say, "Volume confirms price." Ask yourself this: Would you want to buy a stock that 10,000 traders are bullish about, or would you prefer a stock that 10 million traders are bullish about?

TIP

StockCharts.com makes it easy to start using OHLC bar charts like the one shown in Figure 9-3. Click the tab for Free Charts at the top of the site, and then look for the SharpCharts box in the upper-left portion of the page. Enter the symbol you want to view in the box labeled Create a SharpChart, and then click Go. You'll be directed to a SharpChart of your symbol, and you can then customize its attributes using the interface below the chart. In the Chart Attributes panel, change the Type from Candlesticks to OHLC Bars (either thin or thick, whichever is your preference) and then click Update. You can also change the Volume from Overlay to Separate to match the look of the chart in Figure 9-3. We use this same configuration for all the charts in this chapter.

Coloring charts

Displaying price and volume bars in color is common on financial charts. Contrasting colors help distinguish up days from down days. StockCharts.com, for example, defaults to black for up days and red for down, but, like most charting services, you can customize these colors to your liking.

Identifying Simple Single-Day Patterns

The goal of chart reading is to determine whether buyers or sellers are in control of the price. In a bull market, stockowners may be willing to sell, but only if they can coax higher prices from buyers. That cycle drives prices up. In a bear market, buyers are able to negotiate a better price when sellers are more eager to sell than buyers are to buy. That cycle drives prices down.

REMEMBER

You're trying to infer the market's underlying psychology by looking at the history of price movements. You can fairly infer that as prices rise, buyers are more interested in buying than sellers are in selling. In a rising market, buyers must continue bidding prices higher to convince sellers to part with their shares. Rising prices attract additional buyers, who must continue to bid prices higher to convince even more reluctant sellers to part with their shares. Understanding the psychology behind these market movements is the first step to profiting from them.

Single-bar patterns

The most bullish thing that a market can do is go higher. Although technicians typically view each bar within the context of its neighboring bars, each individual bar has something to tell the careful observer. Figure 9-4, for example, shows a *bullish single-bar pattern.*

In the example in the figure, buyers bid prices higher throughout the day. The opening price of $10 also is the lowest trade for the day. The daily range shown on the bar is $2, and the stock closed at $12, the high for the day.

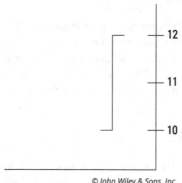

FIGURE 9-4:
A single
bullish bar.

© John Wiley & Sons, Inc.

If you were to keep score, the bulls gained ground and clearly are ahead for the day. Bears holding short positions were hurt where it hurts the most — in their pocketbooks. A trader takes a *short position* by borrowing shares of stock and selling them in the hope of making money if the stock price falls. Short trades lose money if the stock's price rises. The mechanics of selling short are described in Chapter 15. The example in Figure 9-4 shows the stock opening at the absolute low and closing at its absolute high, but the pattern nevertheless is just as bullish when the stock opens near its low and then closes near its high.

Figure 9-5 shows a *bearish single-bar pattern.* The stock opened at $11.75; traded to $12, the high for the day; fell to $10, the daily low; and then closed at $10.25. The stock doesn't have to close at its absolute low for the day for it to be bearish. Closing near the low is close enough.

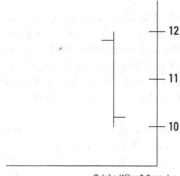

FIGURE 9-5:
A single
bearish bar.

© John Wiley & Sons, Inc.

These single-day patterns are helpful to the trader who's trying to understand the market's underpinnings. Whether these patterns present a trading opportunity depends on the stock's recent history and whether its trading volume confirms the pattern (see the earlier section "Measuring volume"). For example, if a bullish bar like the one in Figure 9-4 shows at a key technical level (perhaps breaking through a well-tested resistance point) and is confirmed by high volume, its bullishness sends a very meaningful signal that prices are likely to continue rising. We give you several examples later in this chapter, in the section "Searching for Transitions," where a bullish single-bar pattern triggers a buy signal.

Reversal patterns

A *reversal bar* is another single-bar pattern that shows a stock opening and closing at the same end of its trading range. Figure 9-6 shows a *bullish single-bar reversal* where the stock opens at the high, trades lower through part of the day, but by the close regains all its losses and closes at its highest intraday price.

FIGURE 9-6:
A bullish reversal pattern.

© John Wiley & Sons, Inc.

During the early part of the trading sessions depicted in the bullish reversal pattern, buyers were willing to buy only if sellers lowered their offering (asking) prices. By the end of the day, the tide had turned and roles were reversed, with sellers willing to sell but only at higher prices. This situation is another win for the bulls because they were able to stop the price slide and recover all the intraday losses, finishing the day back near the stock's opening price.

Figure 9-7 shows a *bearish reversal pattern.* In this case, the stock opens at $10.25, rallies during the day to $12, but closes at the $10 low.

TIP

Reversal patterns often represent a powerful single-bar trading pattern. Whenever a bullish reversal bar is preceded by several periods of falling prices, for example, its pattern can represent a promising buying opportunity. On the other hand, a bearish reversal bar preceded by a rising trend may be a signal to close a long trade or initiate a short position. Selling short is described in Chapter 15.

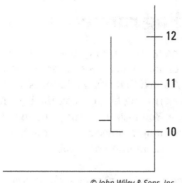

© John Wiley & Sons, Inc.

FIGURE 9-7:
A bearish reversal pattern.

Not all price bars, however, present specific trading opportunities. Some bars are neutral by themselves but add to a stock's history when viewed in context. It's important to learn and recognize important single-bar patterns and also crucial to be able to distinguish the neutral price bars from more significant ones. Through charts, you can use a stock's visual historical record to develop your trading plan, as you see in the following sections.

Recognizing Trends and Trading Ranges

Technical analysis helps you identify trends, allowing you to determine when one begins and ends. Our style of trading, *position trading*, looks for the persistent trend, one that lasts for at least several weeks to several months, possibly even longer. Day traders and swing traders who buy and sell in the shortest of terms also look for trends to trade. Those trends simply play out over a shorter period, whether it's a few minutes, a few hours, or a couple of days. In fact, the primary distinction between a day trader, a swing trader, and a position trader is the length of the trend that each is hoping to identify. Swing trading and day trading are discussed in Chapters 17 and 18, respectively. If you're really interested, check out *Swing Trading For Dummies*, by Omar Bassal, CFA, and *Day Trading For Dummies*, by Ann C. Logue, MBA (both published by Wiley).

REMEMBER

Following trends is an effective trading strategy, especially for new traders. To follow trends successfully, you first need to identify and distinguish between stocks, funds, and market indexes exhibiting trends and their counterparts, trading within specific price ranges. Stocks are either trending up or down or bouncing within a range. Your job is to determine which phase it's currently in and recognize when it begins to transition from one phase to another.

Discerning a trading range

Ultimately, a stock, fund, or index can do only one of three things: rise in an uptrend, fall in a downtrend, or move sideways as prices bounce up and down within a confined price range. A stock that fits the latter is said to be *range bound* or stuck in a trading range, never trading higher than the high nor lower than the low during a specific time frame. You also hear range-bound stocks described as *consolidating* or *building a base.* Although some subtle distinctions may exist among these terms, we nevertheless use them interchangeably.

In general, we're not interested in trading range-bound stocks. Trading ranges can persist for long periods of time. Some may even last for years. For a position trader, having money in a range-bound stock represents wasted opportunity. You won't lose money, but you won't make any either. Although they may not be great trading opportunities, range-bound stocks do make fantastic watch list candidates. Traders are interested in identifying range-bound stocks because they have the potential to begin trending in either direction, up or down. We patiently watch these stocks for a signal indicating the trading range may end and a trend may begin, whether it's to the upside or the downside. Stocks that break out of a long-lasting trading range often begin trends that can be traded profitably.

REMEMBER

Trading ranges are easy to spot after the fact, but anticipating when a stock is about to enter or exit a trading range is nearly impossible. For this and other reasons, range-bound stocks are difficult to trade, especially for new traders. Some short-term traders are able to trade range-bound stocks successfully, so it isn't impossible, but we encourage you first to become a proficient trend trader before attempting to trade stocks stuck in trading ranges. Tools you can use in trading-range situations are described in Chapter 11. In Chapter 10, we discuss what to do if a stock you own stops trending and becomes range bound.

Identifying a trading range is best done visually. Figure 9-8 shows a chart of Wynn Resorts Ltd. (WYNN) moving sideways in a range-bound pattern after an initial run up.

Wynn Resorts spent more than nine months trading between $82.00 and $109.00. Notice how the price moves up and down but always between those levels, never making much progress one way or the other. The closing price for the final trading day on this chart is $92.43, right in the middle of the stock's range. As we discuss more later in this chapter, the upper and lower bounds that define Wynn's trading range represent support and resistance levels.

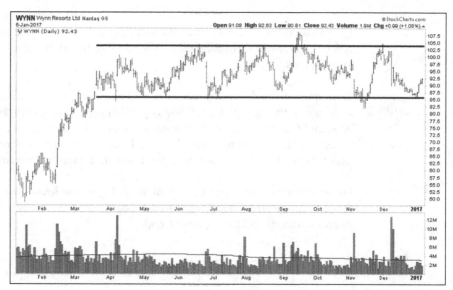

FIGURE 9-8:
Wynn gets stuck in a trading range after an initial run up.

Spotting a trend

Now contrast the Wynn Resorts chart in Figure 9-8 with the chart of Micron Technology, Inc. (MU), in Figure 9-9. MU is clearly quite different from the range-bound stock. Notice the steady stair-step march upward as the stock rises higher and higher.

FIGURE 9-9:
Micron Technology, Inc., is in a distinct uptrend.

Even in a strong upward trend, stocks rarely go straight up. You often see some reversals and mini-consolidations throughout the trend that cause the stair-stepped look.

That stair-stepped upward march is an identifying characteristic of an *uptrend*. Although defining it quantitatively is possible, spotting an uptrend on a chart is easy, and that's the way it often is done. As long as a stock price continues to trade at higher highs and its new lows don't fall below previous lows, the uptrend remains intact. Chapter 10 discusses trends and these stair-step patterns in more detail.

Stocks can also *downtrend*; a series of lower highs and lower lows is as much of a trend as its upward-bound counterpart. See Figure 9-10, a chart showing Valeant Pharmaceuticals (VRX) in a downtrend.

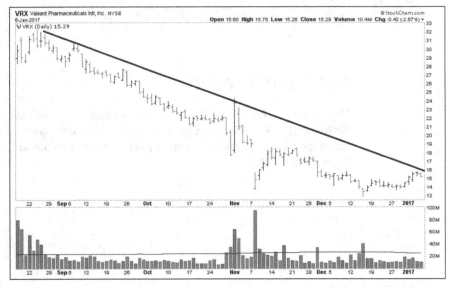

FIGURE 9-10: Valeant's stock is shown here in a clear downtrend.

Chart courtesy of StockCharts.com

Paying attention to time frame

The time frame of your chart determines your trading perspective.

You may notice that the price history of a range-bound stock is made up of many small trends. If you look at an intraday chart of Wynn Resorts stock (WYNN) that spanned the 25 days of trading from May 19, 2016, through June 23, 2016, WYNN appears to be in a strong uptrend. Then again later in the year, between November 15 and November 30, 2016, WYNN was on a tear in a seemingly unstoppable uptrend.

Yet, when you step back and observe a broader historical record of WYNN's trading pattern on the daily and weekly charts, you can easily see that these multiday trends are actually confined within the prevailing trading range during the year.

WARNING

Although short-term swing traders and day traders make a living basing their trading on these mini- and/or microtrends, doing so isn't our cup of tea. Consistently trading range-bound stocks profitably by focusing on much shorter time frames is very difficult to do, and even more difficult to do consistently.

Searching for Transitions

A stock can transition from a downtrend to an uptrend in a wide variety of fashions. It can, for example, fall precipitously, turn on a dime, and begin heading higher. In an alternate scenario, a stock can fall, bounce around in a trading range for a while, and begin a new trend — up or down — as it breaks out of the trading range.

It's enticing when you see a stock turn on a dime from down trending to up trending, and this scenario can sometimes present profitable trading opportunities. However, this sort of V-shaped chart pattern is also difficult to identify and even more difficult to base a trade on. Still, additional tools of technical analysis designed to unearth these transitions are explained in Chapters 10 and 11.

In our trading, we're looking for promising opportunities based on proven patterns, seeking consistent, repeatable results instead of occasional jackpots. Rather than trying to score big on sharp transitions, we recommend searching for stocks that are developing strong new trends after a well-defined period of range-bound trading, preferably lasting at least six to eight weeks or more. This is simply a more reliable strategy with a higher probability of success.

Support and resistance: The keys to trend transitions

The transition from sideways, range-bound trading to defined up or down trending is relatively easy to identify visually. It's also the easiest to trade profitably. To find the transition, you must be familiar with the concept of support and resistance.

REMEMBER

Support is always the lower trading-range boundary. Think of support as the floor. *Resistance* is always the upper trading-range boundary. Think of resistance as the ceiling. Once a resistance level has been broken, it often turns into a future support level. On the flip side, once a support level has been broken, it's likely to turn into a future resistance level.

You'll see support and resistance used in many contexts. For example, these levels are used to identify a trading range, as discussed in this section. They're also used to help identify when a trend has reached its end, as we discuss in Chapter 10.

For an example of how support and resistance levels are shown on a chart, refer to Figure 9-8, the chart showing WYNN stuck in a trading range. The support line shown on this chart is at roughly $86.00; the resistance line is shown near $104.00.

When technicians talk about support, they mean the price where buyers are willing to purchase enough stock to stop the price from falling. Framed another way, when sellers recognize enough buying interest at the support price, they grow less willing to sell and will do so only if they can coax buyers to raise their bids. Buyers are now more eager to buy than the sellers are to sell; thus, the buyers are willing to bid a little more to complete the transaction. The result: Prices end their descent and begin heading higher.

The reverse is true as the stock's price approaches the resistance level. Buyers begin losing interest as the stock reaches elevated prices. Eager sellers must lower their offer (asking) price to complete the transaction, which causes prices to stop rising and begin falling.

TIP

Support levels and resistance levels often are determined visually by looking back at a stock's price history. Knowing the specific price where levels of support and resistance need to be drawn is difficult, and traders may differ on exactly where to draw these lines. Some choose the extreme, plotting intraday highs and lows of a trading range during a specific time frame to establish those levels. Others prefer to use closing prices on a daily or weekly bar chart to define the upper and lower boundaries within the trading range. If you're analyzing an intraday chart, use the last trade price on each bar when drawing the support and resistance levels. The choice is ultimately yours, but in our opinion, closing prices (or last prices) have more significance and better represent the consensus of traders and investors. The majority of the market's trading volume occurs in the first and last hours of the trading day; therefore, opening and closing prices generally paint a truer picture of how the majority of buyers and sellers are pricing the stock.

REMEMBER

Technical analysis should never be taken as an exact science. As such, it's often better to think of support and resistance as areas rather than specific price points down to the penny. Many technicians actually define support and resistance zones on their charts as narrow ranges rather than single lines. It's important to remember what support and resistance represent: key technical levels where buying and selling pressures have caused interesting things to happen in the past. When current prices approach those levels again, smart traders watch closely for new signals to appear once more.

Finding a breakout

A stock remains stuck in its trading range as long as it bounces between zones of support and resistance. Short-term traders may be interested in these back-and-forth movements, but as a position trader, you're looking for a more substantial trend. You must therefore wait for something to change the status quo and cause the stock to break out of its trading range.

TIP

A *breakout* signals the transition of a stock trading within a range to a new uptrend or downtrend. When breaking out to the upside, you want to see the stock trade above resistance at the top of its trading range by a significant amount, certainly more than 5 or 10 cents. More important, you want the resistance zone to be broken on substantially higher volume than the average. Ideally, volume needs to be at least 50 percent higher than average. The greater the volume of the breakout, the stronger the signal.

Figure 9-11 shows a chart of Northern Trust Corp. (NTRS) and is a textbook example of a stock breaking out of a trading range. NTRS had been trading within a range from early 2016 to the beginning of November. We drew the support line at roughly $62.00 and the resistance line near $73.00. The support and resistance levels were tested several times in 2016.

On November 9, 2016, NTRS opened above its previous close, traded through the zone of resistance, and closed near its high of the day at $76.79. Trading volume was almost 2.5 million shares, nearly double the average daily volume of 1.3 million shares. As the breakout continued, volume kept increasing, with as many as 3.6 million shares traded on the fourth day of the move.

Waiting patiently for winning patterns

We can hear the gears grinding from here. Yes, it's a nice trade . . . but you're probably saying to yourself, "Couldn't I have bought NTRS for about $61.00 several times back in June or July? Why wait until the breakout drives my entry price up?"

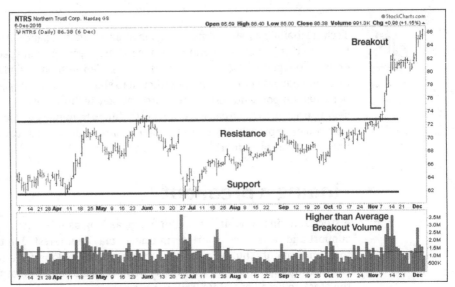

NTRS Northern Trust Corp. Nasdaq GS
6-Dec-2016
Open 85.59 High 86.40 Low 85.00 Close 86.38 Volume 991.3K Chg +0.98 (+1.15%) ▲
© StockCharts.com

Breakout

Resistance

Support

Higher than Average
Breakout Volume

Chart courtesy of StockCharts.com

FIGURE 9-11:
Northern Trust stock breaks out of its trading range.

REMEMBER

The answer: Finding a good trading signal is important; avoiding bad trading signals is more important. A stock trader can endure two losses: capital and opportunity. If you fall for bad trading signals, let your losses build, and fail to protect your capital, there can be no opportunity. Without cash to invest, you have no options. However, if your first objective is to protect your capital, you'll always have another opportunity.

Foretelling the future is hard. Of course hindsight tells you that buying NTRS at $61.00 would've earned you more money than buying it above $75. But when the price was $61.00, how could you know that NTRS wouldn't stay in its trading range for many more months or years? Or how could you tell that NTRS wasn't going to break out of its trading range to the downside and start trending lower?

It happens. In fact, if the stock had traded below its zone of support, technical analysis would've suggested a potential opportunity to sell NTRS short.

Fine-tuning your trading-range breakout strategy

No two trading ranges are created equal, and it's important to respect the differences between stronger trading-range breakouts and weaker ones. To help improve your breakout trading strategies, consider the following:

» Breakouts from long trading ranges tend to produce more profitable buying and selling than breakouts from shorter trading ranges.

>> Breakouts from tight trading ranges, where price fluctuations are confined to a relatively narrow price range, usually result in better trades than breakouts from wider trading ranges.

>> Wait for a short while — at least one day, possibly two or three — to confirm the trading range breakout. Waiting to see whether the stock falls back into its trading range before you take a position can save you from suffering a loss in a false breakout. It isn't uncommon to see a wave of selling immediately after a breakout. The stock's reaction to that selling is often just as important as the breakout itself.

REMEMBER

Consistently catching the lowest price is nearly impossible, regardless of whether you use technical analysis, fundamental analysis, or your magic 8-ball. Technical analysis can help you find transitions, but it can't predict the future. No financial analysis tool can. As a technician, you rarely buy stocks at their lowest prices, and you rarely exit your positions at the highest prices. Fortunately, you don't need to perfectly time your entry and exit points to trade profitably.

TIP

If you wait for a solid and reliable trading signal, you can ride the middle part of the trend for a large portion of the move. Try not to be greedy. The middle part of the trend is a very profitable place to trade.

Trading stocks isn't about hitting home runs every time. Instead, the key is to design and commit to a consistent investment system based on proven methods that will allow you to repeatedly achieve positive returns. Take a long-term view and keep the bigger picture in mind without over-focusing on one specific trade.

Sipping from a cup and handle

Another widely followed transitional formation is called a cup and handle. In a *cup and handle formation*, a stock's price levels form a rounded curving bottom that looks a bit like a cup or a saucer, which often is followed by a modest shakeout formation that, if you use your imagination, looks a bit like the handle on a coffee cup.

Figure 9-12 shows a chart of Prudential Financial (PRU) that illustrates the cup and handle formation.

The entry strategy for this pattern is similar to that used for the trading range breakout. The trigger occurs when the stock price breaks above the handle on high volume. In the Prudential example, it occurs in the final trading days of September. The stock makes a strong move above resistance, takes another brief pause, and then continues upwards once more through the end of the year.

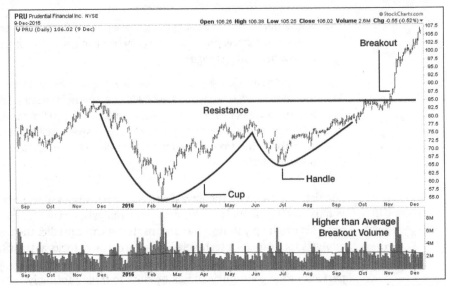

Chart courtesy of StockCharts.com

FIGURE 9-12:
Prudential stock prices show a cup and handle pattern.

WARNING

The cup and handle is a reliable trading pattern, but that doesn't mean the pattern never fails. Nothing is ever guaranteed in the stock market, and you need an exit strategy in case the pattern you're trading fails, just like every other trade. Exit strategies are discussed in Chapter 12.

Deciding what to do with a double bottom

Another transition pattern that often leads to profitable trading opportunities is the double bottom. Visually, a *double bottom* looks like a *W* on the chart, so it's very easy to recognize. However, a double bottom doesn't need to form a perfect *W* to be valid. In fact, we actually prefer the right-hand trough to be a little lower than the left-hand trough. When a minor new low forms, it tends to shake out the stock's weakest owners, thus making it much easier for bulls to drive the price higher when the stock begins to rally.

Figure 9-13 shows a well-formed double bottom on the chart of Capital One Financial (COF). The left-hand trough occurred in the early months of 2016; the right-hand trough formed shortly after in the summer months of that year.

The entry criteria for this pattern are again similar to that of the trading-range breakout. In this case, the trigger point occurs when the stock breaks above the midpoint peak between the two troughs. This peak is sometimes called the *pivot point*. Ideally, higher-than-average volume confirms the trigger.

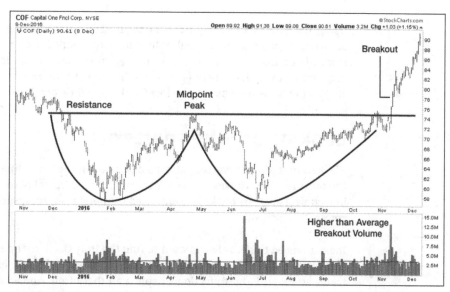

FIGURE 9-13: Capital One Financial (COF) shows a well-defined double bottom.

The trigger price on the chart is right around $75.00, which corresponds to the price levels the stock traded at during late April. The stock does stumble across its resistance level in a false breakout in late October, but after a short pullback it rockets up across the $75.00 range on November 9. Notice that the stock trades over 13 million shares that day, well above its average daily trading volume of around 3.5 million.

An alternative double-bottom strategy

One scenario where aggressive traders may want to anticipate the formation of a double-bottom pattern is when the W is particularly deep and the pivot is many points away from the trough. When that happens, taking a position as the stock is forming the right-hand trough sometimes makes sense.

If the price holds near or just below the left-hand trough and volume confirms the reversal, then aggressive traders can enter a position. You may also want to enter a position if signals from other single-day patterns confirm the reversal. The risk is relatively small, and the potential reward is relatively large. If the stock falls below the lowest low, you'll know your trade has failed and you must exit. Otherwise, hold the position until the stock tests the pivot point (see the preceding section).

Using the COF chart in Figure 9-13 to illustrate this strategy, the buy trigger occurred on July 6 after COF fell, rallied upwards, pulled back again, but was then stopped at a higher low. The stock climbed from there for a nice gain into mid-July. In this case, your entry point could be the next trading day, July 7, and your stop would be below $58.98, the low for the July 6 reversal bar.

Looking at other patterns

We believe that the reversal patterns described in the preceding few sections are the most reliable. However, many other common reversal patterns are published in technical analysis books and online educational resources, such as StockCharts.com's ChartSchool.

WARNING

Inexperienced traders always want to find the Holy Grail, that pattern or indicator that enables them to profitably trade the turn-on-a-dime *V-bottom* pattern. In truth, however, V-bottoms don't happen all that often. And when they do, many reasons express why it's probably not the best trading opportunity available to you. If you talk shop with other traders, you're certain to hear them discuss many esoteric patterns. We know them, but we rarely trade them. The simple techniques we've shown you in this chapter enable you to trade profitably. It doesn't hurt to learn other patterns, even if only to satisfy your curiosity, but be careful. There's no need to look for the obscure when the simple does the job just as well.

IN THIS CHAPTER

» **Spotting uptrends and downtrends**

» **Finding areas of support and resistance within a trend**

» **Identifying different kinds of gaps**

» **Understanding continuation and retracement patterns**

» **Planning for failed trading signals**

Chapter **10**

Following Trends to Boost Your Probability of Success

Technical analysis helps you identify emerging price trends and anticipate the end of existing trends. Being able to identify those two extreme end points means you can develop a consistently profitable trend-following trading system. Technical analysis can also help you evaluate the persistence of a trend, which is useful for finding secondary entry points and generating short-term trading signals.

In this chapter, we discuss trading strategies for several trend-following techniques. In addition, you discover methods for identifying continuation patterns, retracement patterns, and reversal patterns, as well as strategies for dealing with the inevitable failed trading signal.

Identifying Trends

Identifying a trend is relatively straightforward. Instinctively, you know it when you see it. Remember, a stock can be in only one of three states: an uptrend, a downtrend, or a sideways trading range. Don't overthink it!

You can use visual techniques and calculated indicators to identify trend signals. We discuss visual identification techniques in this chapter. We cover calculated indicators in Chapter 11.

A steadily rising or falling stock is a *trending stock.* But if you watch stocks for any period of time, you know that they rarely go straight up or down. Instead, you see a stair-step effect in which a stock rises several steps and then falls back. Talking about a trend as a series of intermittent highs interrupted by intermittent lows makes good sense. So an *uptrend,* then, is a series of higher intermittent highs and higher intermittent lows. Conversely, a *downtrend* is a series of lower intermittent highs and lower intermittent lows.

Figure 10-1 shows a price chart of Williams Companies, Inc. (WMB), exhibiting a series of higher highs and higher lows as it climbs in a distinct uptrend.

FIGURE 10-1:
Williams' stock reaches higher intermittent highs and higher intermittent lows.

Chart courtesy of StockCharts.com

The first step to successfully recognizing an uptrend is spotting the higher highs and higher lows. You use those points to draw the upper and lower channel lines of the trend's range. We explore how to draw trend lines and trend channels later in this chapter.

Figure 10-2 shows a downtrending price chart of First Solar, Inc. (FSLR), and identifies its series of lower highs and lower lows. As the downtrend continued throughout 2016, the stock lost over half its value. This is a perfect reminder of why it's difficult to call the bottom in a falling stock and goes to show why trend following is a higher-probability practice. If the trend is strong and clear, don't fight it.

Chart courtesy of StockCharts.com

FIGURE 10-2:
FSLR falls to lower intermittent highs and lower intermittent lows.

Supporting and Resisting Trends

You may have noticed in Figure 10-2 that a small double bottom formed in late June/early July (see Chapter 9 for more on double bottoms) and was followed by a nice positive trend until the beginning of August. Although smaller than others you'll find, this is known as a *retracement*. Although the pattern of lower highs and lower lows appeared to be breaking, FSLR fell sharply in early August and resumed its clear downtrend.

TIP

In an uptrend, as long as the pattern of higher highs and higher lows continues, you can say that the trend persists. The converse (lower highs and lower lows) is true in a downtrend. However, it's foolish to conclude that any one break in these patterns represents the end of the existing trend. Even the strongest of trends are bound to see reversals at some point along the way.

As higher prices are reached, for example, old sellers will need to be shaken out of the stock, causing a brief reversal that could (falsely) appear to signal the end of the uptrend. With an educated understanding of trends and the right exit strategies in place, you'll be able to better distinguish the false ends from the real reversals and trade these moves appropriately.

Drawing trend lines to show support

Similar to the support and resistance lines covered in Chapter 9, trend lines can be drawn across a price chart to help clearly identify the trend's direction and slope. Trend lines can also uncover key price points that are likely to trigger short-term trading signals as you monitor the progress of a trend.

You need only two points to define a trend line, but the more price points that touch the trend line, the better.

>> In an uptrend, the line is formed by connecting at least two price lows. This results in a trend line that follows the bottom of the uptrend.

>> In a downtrend, the line is formed by connecting at least two price highs. This results in a trend line that follows the top of the downtrend.

REMEMBER

If you're stuck, remember this simple line: bottoms up, tops down. To see an uptrend in action, take a look at Figure 10-3.

Trend Line

FIGURE 10-3:
Drawing a trend line in an uptrend along the price lows.

Chart courtesy of StockCharts.com

Unfortunately, drawing trend lines is not a precise discipline, and no universal consensus exists for where and how to draw them. In fact, you're not likely to find any two traders drawing trend lines in exactly the same place for the same stock. Furthermore, you'll drive yourself crazy trying to touch all the important price points with your trend line.

Despite the ambiguity, don't lose sight of the overall purpose of a trend line. What's important is that each trend line you draw strengthens your interpretation of the stock's present state. It's not about the exact position of the trend line itself.

Instead, it's about the question that the trend line is meant to answer: In what direction are prices currently moving?

Watching the price bar cross below the trend line can be disturbing, because doing so can signal the end of the trend, or it may mean that you need to redraw the trend lines. Unfortunately, when the stock price closes below the trend line, you can't know whether the break represents the end of the trend or just another opportunity to redraw the trend line to conform to the newest price data.

One alternative technique for drawing a trend line reduces the ambiguity just a bit. Instead of drawing the trend line from left to right, the way most people instinctively do, draw the trend line backward, or from right to left. For instance, if the stock is in an uptrend, connect the two most recent lows in the trend by drawing a trend line backward as long as it's meaningful, and then project the trend line toward the right. This approach has a couple of benefits:

>> The slope of the trend line is more closely aligned with the most recent trading data, which is more relevant to your trading decisions.

>> You'll resign yourself to the necessity of continually redrawing your trend lines based on the newest data.

With the online chart annotation tool at StockCharts.com, you can draw trend lines directly on your charts. Click the tab for Free Charts at the top of any web page, and then look for the SharpCharts box in the upper-left portion of the page. Enter the symbol you want to view in the box labeled Create a SharpChart, and then click Go. When you get to the chart, set up the chart attributes at the bottom of the chart, such as HLC Bars and Separate Volume, as we explain in Chapter 9. Then click the Annotate button just below your chart. Select the trend line tool — the second button down in the menu on the left — and then click and drag to begin drawing your trend lines. You can save your annotations directly to your account and even edit them in the future as new price data is added to the chart.

Using channels

Traders use *channels* to identify potential entry and exit points during a trend. You form channel lines by drawing two parallel lines on the chart, one along the trend's price lows and one along the trend's price highs. The two channel lines bound the trading prices to help you visualize the range in which the stock is trading throughout the trend. The *top channel line* is analogous to the resistance line in a trading range, which we discuss in Chapter 9. Similarly, the *bottom channel line* corresponds to the support line in a trading range. Figure 10-4 shows an example of a channel.

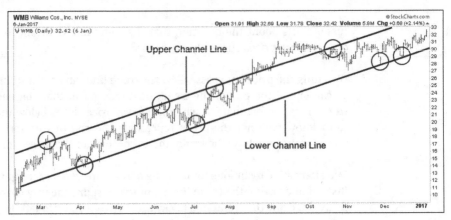

FIGURE 10-4:
A channel.

Trending and channeling strategies

The strategies for using trend lines and channels are similar. When an uptrending stock approaches the trend line or the bottom channel line, short-term traders often see an opportunity to take a position in the direction of the dominant trend. As long as the stock's price doesn't fall through this support level, they will hold the position. Position traders, on the other hand, may use these same conditions to confirm that their existing positions are still in play. If, however, the stock closes below the trend line and remains below it for longer than a day or two, position traders *and* short-term traders must consider the possibility that the trend has reached its end. At this point the stock may enter a new trading range or even reverse into a downtrend.

It may seem surprising, but an uptrending stock breaching the top channel line isn't always good news. After such a move, the stock may become overextended, making it more likely to pull back sharply. At the very least, it's an indication that traders should pay close attention. In Figure 10-4, WMB rose outside of its top channel line several times. In September, the stock hovered above the top of its channel for nearly an entire month. Eventually, however, after a failed retest of its new high around $31.00, the stock reversed back down all the way to the bottom of its channel.

REMEMBER

Trend lines and channels work better across longer periods of time. A stock price that violates a long-running, persistent trend or channel line on a weekly chart provides more meaningful guidance than when it breaches a support line on a daily chart or an intraday chart.

When a stock breaks a short-term trend line, we believe the best practice is to step back one time increment to evaluate the situation. For example, if you're trading based primarily on daily chart data, pull up a weekly chart and examine its trend.

If the march of higher highs and higher lows remains intact on the weekly chart, you may want to give your trade a little more room to work itself out. However, if a longer time frame shows a break in the trend of higher highs and higher lows, a reversal is much more likely. This dual-chart signal should cause you to consider exiting your position right away.

We use trend lines for guidance while trading, but rarely do we make decisions solely on the basis of a trend-line penetration. Although initiating short-term positions in the direction of the dominant trend is possible by using channels to enter and exit the position, doing so is very difficult, and few traders are able to engage in that practice profitably. Some traders even take this concept one step further by trying to take positions in opposition to the dominant trend as the stock price approaches the upper channel line. We believe trading in the direction opposite that of a dominant trend is simply foolish. Doing so is an excellent way to lose a substantial portion of your trading capital. If a trend is clear and strong, why fight it?

Bottom line: Trend lines and channels are additional tools that you can use to monitor the progress of a stock price trend. You can use them to help identify trading opportunities and make informed decisions about the likely future direction of a stock or fund. Still, we recommend they not be your primary method of determining entry and exit points. Instead, combine trend lines and channels with other tools and strategies to form a robust technical system.

Seeing Gaps

A *price gap* forms on a bar chart when the opening price of the current bar is above or below the closing price of the previous bar. Gaps occur mostly on daily charts, sometimes on weekly charts, and rarely on intraday charts. Depending on the circumstances, gaps can show continuation and reversal patterns, and they can signal an opportunity to enter or exit a position.

Some gaps are obvious and some are subtle. For example, if the opening price is above the previous close but the low of the current bar is below the previous high, then those bars overlap and the gap is hard to spot. Many traders simply ignore that type of gap. If, however, the low of the current bar is obviously higher than the high of the previous bar, that gap is clear and will draw the attention of most traders. In reality, traders only focus on these obvious gaps that immediately stand out. Examples of clear gaps are shown in the following sections.

Gaps are divided into several broad categories based on where the gap occurs. These categories determine your trading strategy and are discussed in the sections that follow.

Common gap

Gaps that occur within a trading range, as described in Chapter 9, can be either a *common gap* or a *breakout gap*. If the gap occurs in the middle of the trading range, far from either its support or resistance level, it's a common gap. Common gaps occur frequently and are, well, rather common. They rarely provide meaningful trading opportunities. Ignoring them is usually the best policy. Figure 10-5 shows several common gaps in addition to a breakout gap.

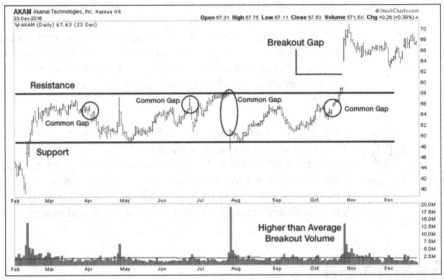

FIGURE 10-5:
A breakout gap and common gaps.

Chart courtesy of StockCharts.com

Breakout or breakaway gap

When a stock gaps above or below the resistance or support levels, respectively, or a well-established trading range, traders classify the gap as either a *breakout* or *breakaway gap*. A breakout gap often provides excellent trading signals to enter a new position, in the direction of the gap. Figure 10-5 shows an example of a breakout gap from a longstanding trading range. We discuss trading strategies for trading range breakouts in Chapter 9.

Continuation gap

A *continuation gap* is also known as a *runaway gap* or an *acceleration gap.* This type of gap occurs within an uptrend when the open price of the current bar is higher than the close price of the previous bar. If the low of the current bar is also obviously above the high of the previous bar, this gap usually indicates that the trend is very strong. Continuation gaps may also occur in downtrends. The defining characteristics are opposite those of a continuation gap in an uptrend.

Figure 10-6 shows several examples of continuation gaps in an uptrend. Some short-term traders may use a continuation gap as a signal to enter a position in the direction of the gap. Position traders may use this same signal to confirm that a current trade remains in play. You sometimes see a series of continuation gaps occur in close proximity to each other, and these gaps usually provide strong confirmation of the prevailing trend. However, continuation gaps also warrant caution, because they can turn into what is known as an *exhaustion gap.*

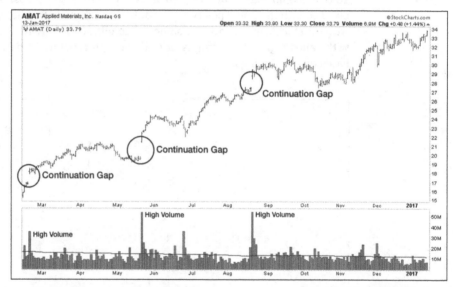

Chart courtesy of StockCharts.com

FIGURE 10-6: Continuation gaps.

Exhaustion gap

WARNING

Exhaustion gaps occur at or near the ends of strong trends. Unfortunately, the defining characteristics for an exhaustion gap are virtually identical to those for a continuation gap. Exhaustion gaps are often accompanied by very large volume, which is one clue that the gap may not be a continuation gap. Otherwise, distinguishing an exhaustion gap from a continuation gap is sometimes impossible, until the stock price changes direction. By that time, it's usually obvious that something is wrong with the trade, and you should exit your position.

In Figure 10-6, the third continuation gap could have easily turned out to be an exhaustion gap. Before resuming its climb to the upside, the stock actually filled the initial gap and fell back to its pre-gap price level in early October. At that point, the bulls regained control, and the stock moved higher. However, if that pullback had turned out to be the start of a new downtrend for the stock, the continuation gap would be classified as an exhaustion gap.

Island gap

An *island gap,* or an *island reversal* (shown in Figure 10-7), forms when a trend changes direction. The pattern is actually two gaps that isolate either a single bar or a short series of bars from both the dominant trend and the new trend. An island gap usually is a good indicator that the prior trend has been extinguished. You can use an island gap to signal an exit from an existing position. You may also use it to initiate a new position, but only if the direction of the new trend aligns with the stock's underlying fundamental condition. Be sure to review the "Dealing with Failed Signals" section, later in this chapter, before initiating any positions based on an island gap.

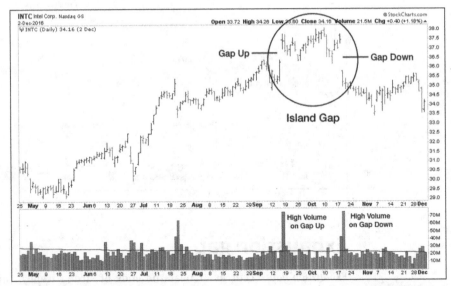

FIGURE 10-7:
An island gap.

Chart courtesy of StockCharts.com

Waving Flags and Pennants

Flag and pennant patterns represent areas of consolidation within a trend. You've already encountered these patterns, just not by name. In a series of higher highs and higher lows, for example, these patterns form the basis for the higher lows. In other words, the higher lows are made of flag and pennant patterns.

A *pennant pattern* looks like, well, a pennant. Support and resistance lines converge into a point forming what looks like a small pennant shape. A *flag pattern*, on the other hand, is bounded by parallel lines. All these patterns almost always fly counter to the prevailing trend, but the direction in which they're flying is not actually a requirement.

Figure 10-8 shows examples of flags and pennants on the chart of a trending stock.

Chart courtesy of StockCharts.com

FIGURE 10-8:
Flags and
pennants.

TIP

The key for each of these patterns is the breakout. If the breakout from the formation is in the direction of the established trend, then the trend continues. If prices break against the dominant trend, then the trend may be over.

Flags and pennants typically are associated with a trend, but you may also see these patterns appear as a stock moves sideways within a trading range. When a flag or pennant forms near the top of a trading range, it hints at an eventual breakout. That pattern shows the stock consolidating near the top of its trading range, which suggests that selling pressure is diminishing and the stock is preparing to test the zone of resistance.

Withstanding Retracements

A *retracement* occurs when a trending stock revisits recent prices. You've already seen many examples. When a stock makes a higher high followed by a higher low, it's considered a retracement. A trading range as discussed in Chapter 9 can also be considered a retracement. You may hear a retracement called a *price consolidation* or a *pullback*, but the concept is the same.

Flags and pennants are relatively simple forms of retracement patterns. More complex retracements can occur within a defined trend, and like their simpler counterparts, they don't actually signal the end of the trend. Unfortunately, when complex retracements occur, they can both confuse and frustrate traders. Besides being difficult to anticipate, they send conflicting signals to traders trying to make sense of which trading-plan adjustments are needed.

Three-step and five-step retracements

In an uptrend, higher highs and higher lows aren't always a given. Sometimes you see breaks in this pattern as the stock fails to reach a new high or makes a lower intermittent low. You may even see several occurrences of these worrisome lower lows and/or lower highs happen one right after the other, but then find that the strong uptrend suddenly resumes.

You'll see a couple of these benign multistep patterns frequently occur in the midst of a strong trend, so it's useful to watch for them. A *three-step retracement* makes at least one lower intermittent high and one lower intermittent low. A *five-step retracement* makes two lower highs and two lower lows. Multistep retracements also occur during downtrends when a falling stock makes a brief, countertrend series of higher highs and higher lows.

Figure 10-9 shows an example of a five-step retracement that ultimately resolves in the direction of the prevailing trend. The five steps are identified, along with the corresponding intermittent highs and lows.

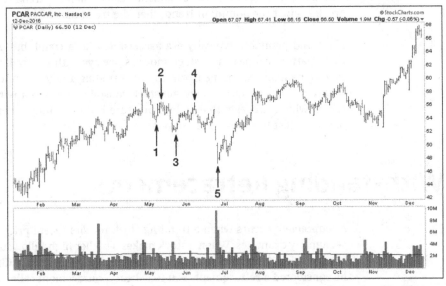

FIGURE 10-9:
A five-step retracement pattern.

Chart courtesy of StockCharts.com

As a trend-following trader, it's natural for these retracement situations to feel disconcerting, even frightening. There can be a fine line between a healthy retracement pattern and true trend reversal. There's no magic tool to signal exactly when a trend has ended, but by closely watching the charts and maintaining a proper exit plan, you'll be ready to take action when the time is right.

TIP

Exactly where the multistep retracement occurs within a trend should have some bearing on your trading plan. If the stock price has just broken out of a long trading range and then falters, you may want to close the position and wait for a subsequent attempt to break out of the trading range. Keep an eye on the stock while you look for additional trading opportunities elsewhere.

If a stock price starts what may be a three-step or a five-step retracement after a long period of strong trending, and your position is profitable, you may want to see how the retracement plays out. Absent any obvious sell signals, such as an island reversal or a downside breakout from a flag, pennant, or trading range formation, you can wait to see how the retracement resolves itself. The risk may be worth the reward in this case.

Checking out a chart that covers a longer time frame can also be helpful here. For example, you can examine a weekly chart when the retracement occurs on the daily chart. If the trend shows no signs of faltering on the weekly chart, hold your position and let the retracement play out. If the stock recovers and heads higher, so much the better, but if it establishes another lower high and trades below its next lower low, it's time to exit.

Finally, considering fundamental factors before making your decision makes good sense. If a company's deteriorating financial situation or weak forward guidance is an underlying cause of the retracement, then you may want to exit your position. You also need to be aware of the cycle the economy is in when making your decision. If the economy is approaching a turning point as your stock's technical situation deteriorates, getting out of the position is usually a smart idea.

Subsequent trading ranges

Trading ranges and cup and handle formations, like the ones described in Chapter 9, also are complex consolidation patterns. A trend that's interrupted by a period of range-bound trading may indicate either a pause before the trend resumes or the end of the trend entirely. The only way to know which direction the trend will go is to watch for the breakout. Unfortunately, you may be in for a long wait.

While we see a clear five-step retracement pattern on the chart in Figure 10-9, some technicians could justifiably argue that the chart's price history actually forms a cup and handle pattern. Remember, technical analysis is an art, not a science, so you may encounter ambiguous situations like this. The results in this case were the same regardless of your interpretation. The stock broke out of its consolidation pattern in early July and resumed its trend to the upside.

TIP

Breakouts that occur in the direction of the prevailing trend may indicate that the trend has further to run, but they may also be a prelude to a failed breakout signal. Trading-range breakouts provide the strongest signals when they result in a change of direction from the previous trend.

Dealing with Failed Signals

All trading signals are subject to failure. Sometimes, things just don't work out as planned. However, even a failed signal provides important information that you can use to revise your trading plans. In fact, sometimes the best trading signals are the direct result of a failed signal.

Trapping bulls and bears

Breakouts from trading ranges and cup and handle patterns sometimes fail. These failures happen to both bullish and bearish signals, and when they fail, it's called a *trap*. The two kinds of traps are

>> **Bull traps:** These traps occur after an upside breakout. The stock breaks out of its trading range to the upside but then reverses back into the trading range and ultimately breaks out to the down side. The bullish traders that took action based on the breakout signal are trapped by the reversal, hence the name *bull trap.*

>> **Bear traps:** These traps occur after a downside breakout. This opposite scenario to the bull trap is often very bullish. The stock reverses course and reenters its trading range. If a bear trap occurs within a trading range that's preceded by an extended period of declining prices, it often represents an excellent buying opportunity because it's a sign that selling pressure has evaporated in the stock, which thus is likely to attempt an upside breakout.

TIP

Whenever you see a potential bear trap taking place and the stock meets all your fundamental criteria, you may want to enter a long position as soon as the stock price reenters the trading range.

Filling the gaps

A developing gap is usually interpreted as a signal that the prevailing trend will continue. If a stock reverses and retraces prices within the gap, we say that the gap has been *filled*. A gap that's filled negates the trading signal that it generated.

WARNING

When dealing with a breakout gap, a stock that reverses, fills the gap, and falls back through the trading range resistance zone is likely to turn bearish. Similarly, when a continuation gap is filled, you need to consider it a failed signal and exit your position. The same is true for an island gap. If prices trade back into the area of the isolated island, the trading signal has failed, and you need to exit your position.

Deciding whether to reverse directions

A bear trap shows an example in which taking a position based on a failed signal makes sense. If, however, you already have a position and the signal fails, it's wise to exit your position. Let the market sort out its psychology without leaving your money at risk.

You also need to consider economic and fundamental factors when deciding how to handle a failed signal. Acting on a contrary signal makes sense only if economic and fundamental conditions support the decision.

For example, if a bullish signal fails and becomes a bearish signal, selling a stock short makes sense only if it's fundamentally weak and the stock's sector is in decline. Conversely, if a bear trap occurs and generates a buy signal, taking a position in the stock makes sense only if its earnings are strong and growing, its sector is performing well, and the economy is on an upswing.

REMEMBER

Many inexperienced traders mistakenly think that the best course of action after exiting a long position is to dive headfirst into a short trade. Just because your analysis says the stock is likely to stop rising doesn't mean that a short position is the smartest option. If other factors confirm that decision, it can be carefully considered. If not, stay patient and trust that another opportunity will come along soon enough.

Chapter **11**

Calculating Indicators and Oscillators

I n today's tech-driven world, computer technology and powerful software developments have ushered in a new era for technical analysts. With greater reliance on Internet-ready computers, tablets, and smartphones, we're constantly connected to the online world. This gives us endless access to a steady stream of financial data, news, analysis tools, and much more, something that was little more than a wild dream only a decade or two ago. Thanks to technology improvements, we have more methods and resources available to us as market participants. In technical analysis specifically, powerful chart indicators have become faster, easier to calculate automatically, and much more accessible to the individual investor.

However, the ease of calculating, modifying, testing, and using computer-generated trading tools is as much a curse as it is a blessing. New traders often shun visual pattern analysis, instead preferring computer-generated indicators (series of data points) and oscillators (which show fluctuations of data points). Doing so is a mistake. Although the perceived precision of these calculations seems to add to their allure, you nevertheless need to be aware that computer-generated analysis tools still have their flaws. These changes give you a combination of visual pattern analysis and calculated indicators and oscillators, such as those we discuss in this chapter.

WARNING

The indicators and oscillators that we describe in this chapter provide you with additional insight into the technical condition of a stock or the market. As with all other financial analysis tools and methods, however, they can't provide faultless trading signals. No indicator works in every situation, finds every opportunity, and generates perfectly accurate trading signals with guaranteed certainty. When used properly, these indicators help increase your probabilities of making profitable trading decisions, but they must be understood thoroughly and integrated into your trading system appropriately.

As a new trader, it's easy to be swept up in the seemingly infinite array of indicators and analysis tools at your disposal. By following too many, you risk what we refer to as *analysis paralysis*. This results when your never-ending analysis and insatiable desire to check one more indicator, chart, or data set freezes you, preventing you from actually making a decision and taking action. You're paralyzed by your unending analysis. At the end of the day, your research means nothing if you fail to pull the trigger and place a trade. However, by narrowing your focus to a specific set of tools and indicators that you're intimately familiar with, you prevent yourself from suffering the unwanted effects of analysis paralysis.

This chapter describes how to create and use a manageable subset of the tools that are available in today's charting platforms. We recommend that you learn how to use a small set of tools that can help you trade profitably rather than worry about how every available tool works. Find out how to trade profitably using this subset of tools before deciding that you need to add to your toolbox.

In this chapter we describe the computer-generated tools that we use every day. We explain two types of moving averages, along with the highly popular moving average convergence divergence indicator (MACD) and the stochastic oscillator. In addition, we discuss the powerful concept of relative strength.

TIP

These indicators and concepts are but a tiny subset of the full collection of technical analysis tools that are available online or in other charting software packages. Although simple, this subset is more than enough to get you started as a profitable trader. Again, try to become familiar with these common and effective tools before branching out into other, more complicated technical indicators. Play around with them using historical data to see when they work and when they fail, and try to understand why. That way, you'll know when the tools can help you and when they can't.

The Ins and Outs of Moving Averages

A *moving average* is a trading indicator that shows the direction and magnitude of a trend over a fixed period of time. Some traders call it a *price overlay* because it's superimposed over the price data in a bar chart. Moving averages visually smooth out the data on a price chart to help make trend identification less subjective. All moving averages follow a stock's price trend but can't predict changes. They report only what has happened.

As its name implies, a moving average shows the average of a stock's up-and-down price movements during a specific period of time. A stock's daily closing price usually is the value being averaged, but any value on a price chart can be displayed as a moving average. Some traders, for example, prefer using the midpoint between daily high and low prices for the moving average calculation, while others prefer to use the opening price, the high, or the low. You can also apply moving averages to other financial data, such as volume.

You'll find that moving averages are used as indicators by themselves or in conjunction with other indicators. They're also the building blocks for other indicators and oscillators such as the moving average convergence divergence (MACD), invented by Gerald Appel in the 1960s. Before discussing how the MACD is used (see the section "Tracking Momentum with the MACD," later in this chapter), we must explain moving averages and how they're calculated. Two important types of moving averages are described in this section.

Simple moving average

A *simple moving average* (SMA) is simple to calculate and simple to use. To calculate it, you add a number of prices together and then divide by the number of prices you added. (We explain how to use an SMA in the later section "Comparing SMAs and EMAs.")

An example makes the SMA clearer. In this example, a nine-day moving average of Bank of America's (BAC) closing price is calculated throughout August 2016 and then is plotted on a price chart. To start the SMA calculation, use the closing prices shown in Table 11-1. Add the first nine closing prices together, from August 1 through August 11, and divide by 9. The resulting value is placed alongside the ninth trading day, August 11. Continue for each subsequent day in the month.

TABLE 11-1

Simple Moving Average of BAC Closing Price

Date	Close	SMA
8/1/2016	14.21	
8/2/2016	14.01	
8/3/2016	14.36	
8/4/2016	14.36	
8/5/2016	14.92	
8/8/2016	15.00	
8/9/2016	15.06	
8/10/2016	14.69	
8/11/2016	14.76	14.59
8/12/2016	14.79	14.66
8/15/2016	14.90	14.76
8/16/2016	15.04	14.83
8/17/2016	15.02	14.90
8/18/2016	15.03	14.92
8/19/2016	15.09	14.93
8/22/2016	15.05	14.93
8/23/2016	15.22	14.98
8/24/2016	15.27	15.04
8/25/2016	15.40	15.11
8/26/2016	15.66	15.19
8/29/2016	15.71	15.27
8/30/2016	16.06	15.38
8/31/2016	16.08	15.50

Figure 11-1 shows a bar chart of Bank of America (BAC) from August 2016 through September 2016. The thick black line superimposed on the chart's price data represents the simple moving average for BAC.

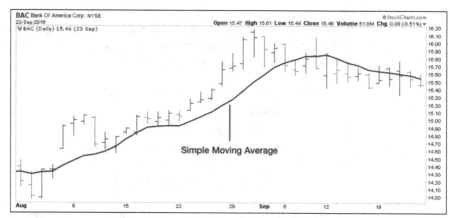

Chart courtesy of StockCharts.com

FIGURE 11-1:
This chart shows a nine-day simple moving average for Bank of America.

To calculate the second SMA point, add the prices from August 2 through August 12 together, divide by 9, and place the result as the SMA data point next to August 12. Another way to think of calculating SMAs is that you drop the oldest price in the calculation and add the closing price from the next price bar. Continue this series by dropping the oldest price, adding the newest price, and dividing by 9 for the remainder of the month.

If you're mathematically inclined, here's what the series looks like as an equation:

$$SMA = \left(P_{[1]} + P_{[2]} + P_{[3]} + \dots P_{[N]} \right) \div N$$

Where: N is the number of periods in the SMA

$P_{[N]}$ is the price being averaged $\left(\text{usually the closing price}\right)$

TIP

Luckily, you don't have to perform these calculations yourself. You can let Stock-Charts.com automatically calculate the SMA for you. Below your chart on the SharpCharts Workbench (`http://stockcharts.com/h-sc/ui`), you find the simple moving average as one of the dropdown menu options in the Overlays panel. Select Simple Moving Avg. from the menu, choose the period over which you want the SMA to be calculated, and then click Update. The simple moving average lines will be automatically generated on your chart. Refer to Figure 11-1 to see an example of a nine-day simple moving average for Bank of America (BAC).

Exponential moving average

Another commonly used moving average is the *exponential moving average* (EMA), which can be superimposed on a bar chart in the same manner as an SMA. The EMA is also used as the basis for other indicators, such as the MACD (moving average convergence divergence) indicator, which we discuss later in this chapter.

Although the calculation for an EMA looks a bit daunting, in practice it's simple. In fact, it's easier to calculate than an SMA, and besides, your charting software will do it for you. Here are the calculations:

$$EMA_{[today]} = \left(Price_{[today]} \times K\right) + \left(EMA_{[yesterday]} \times (1-K)\right)$$

Where: $K = 2 \div (N+1)$

N = the length of the EMA

$Price_{[today]}$ = the current closing price

$EMA_{[yesterday]}$ = the previous EMA value

$EMA_{[today]}$ = the current EMA value

You can handle the start of the calculation in one of two ways. You can begin either by creating a simple average of the first fixed number (N) of periods and use that value to seed the EMA calculation, or you can use the first data point (typically the closing price) as the seed and then calculate the EMA from that point forward. You'll see other traders handling it both ways, but the latter method makes more sense to us. It's the method used in calculating the EMA amounts in Table 11-2, which shows a nine-day EMA calculation for Bank of America throughout August 2016. The EMA value for August 1 is seeded with that day's closing price of $14.21. The actual EMA calculation begins with the August 2 closing price. For comparison, we include the results of the earlier SMA calculation to illustrate the difference between an EMA and an SMA.

TABLE 11-2   **Exponential Moving Average of BAC**

Date	Close	EMA	SMA
8/1/2016	14.21	14.21	
8/2/2016	14.01	14.17	
8/3/2016	14.36	14.20	
8/4/2016	14.36	14.23	
8/5/2016	14.92	14.36	
8/8/2016	15.00	14.48	
8/9/2016	15.06	14.59	
8/10/2016	14.69	14.61	
8/11/2016	14.76	14.64	14.59
8/12/2016	14.79	14.67	14.66
8/15/2016	14.90	14.71	14.76

Date	Close	EMA	SMA
8/16/2016	15.04	14.77	14.83
8/17/2016	15.02	14.82	14.90
8/18/2016	15.03	14.86	14.92
8/19/2016	15.09	14.90	14.93
8/22/2016	15.05	14.93	14.93
8/23/2016	15.22	14.98	14.98
8/24/2016	15.27	15.03	15.04
8/25/2016	15.40	15.10	15.11
8/26/2016	15.66	15.21	15.19
8/29/2016	15.71	15.31	15.27
8/30/2016	16.06	15.46	15.38
8/31/2016	16.08	15.58	15.50

In this example, the EMA doesn't show the same nine-day lag at the beginning of the chart as the SMA. Notice that the results of the moving-average calculations also differ. Figure 11-2 shows the difference between the SMA and the EMA on the Bank of America chart. The EMA data is shown as a solid dark line. For comparison, the SMA data is also plotted using a thinner, lighter line.

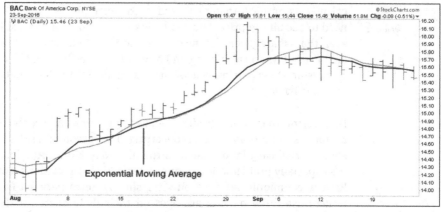

FIGURE 11-2: This chart shows a nine-day exponential moving average for Bank of America.

Chart courtesy of StockCharts.com

TIP

Good news! You don't have to perform the EMA calculation yourself either. You can let StockCharts.com automatically calculate it for you. Below your chart on the SharpCharts Workbench (`http://stockcharts.com/h-sc/ui`), you'll find the exponential moving average as one of the dropdown menu options in the Overlays panel. Select Exp. Moving Avg. from the menu, choose the period over which you want the EMA to be calculated, and click Update. The exponential moving average line will be automatically generated on your chart. Refer to Figure 11-2 to see an example of a nine-day exponential moving average for Bank of America (BAC).

Comparing SMAs and EMAs

Both simple moving averages and exponential moving averages are used regularly by long-term investors, position traders, and short-term traders alike. Each moving average has its strengths and weaknesses. Which you choose can be a matter of personal preference, but one may be better suited than the other depending on the time frame you're trading. As position traders, we use a combination of both SMAs and EMAs.

Consistency

The SMA has the benefit of being consistently calculated from one charting platform to the next. If you ask for a 20-period SMA, you can be certain that the result will be identical to every other 20-period SMA for the same stock during the same time period (assuming there are no errors in the price data).

WARNING

Unfortunately, EMAs are not always as consistent as SMAs because of the way the EMA is calculated. The starting point matters. You actually need more data when calculating an EMA than was used in the example in Table 11-2. In theory, you need to use all the price data available for any individual stock. In practice, however, that is rarely done. Some charting software enables you to specify how much data is used when calculating an EMA, but most web-based charting sites do not. The result: One charting vendor may calculate EMA values that differ from those provided by another.

Discovering that you're basing your trading decisions on an inaccurate moving average is more than a bit disconcerting. This problem has less of an effect with short-period calculations such as the nine-day EMA example in Table 11-2, but it's especially problematic for longer-term EMA calculations. For this reason, the EMA is commonly reserved only for shorter-term periods. For example, many traders use three moving averages on their daily charts: a short-term 20-day EMA, an intermediate-term 50-day SMA, and a longer-term 200-day SMA.

Reaction time

In general, short-term traders are more likely to employ EMAs, but position traders are more inclined to use SMAs. The EMA is usually closer to the current closing price, which tends to make it change direction faster than the SMA. As a result, an EMA is likely to be quicker in signaling short-term trend changes. One of the most common EMA durations is the 20-period. This is a popular moving average on daily charts.

TIP

The SMA is probably the better indicator for identifying long-term changes in a trend. Unfortunately, those signals are likely to take more time to appear than the ones generated by a comparable EMA. The method used to calculate the SMA causes it to react to price changes a bit more slowly, and that's the trade-off for getting a signal that is potentially more reliable.

Sensitivity

An unfortunate result of the method of calculating an SMA is that every time you add a price, another price falls off the back end of the equation. In other words, each new SMA data point is affected by two prices, the most recent closing price and the oldest closing price in the calculation. Ideally, you want the most recent data to have a greater influence on your indicators than the older data. But with an SMA, the oldest price affects the newest SMA point with the same weight as the newest price.

EMA calculations eliminate that concern. Each data point affects the EMA only once. You never have to drop the oldest price as a new price is added. For that reason, the EMA has a much longer memory than the SMA. Every price ever used in calculating the EMA has some small effect. As an added benefit, EMA calculations place additional weight on the most recent price.

Interpreting and using moving averages

Traders use moving averages to better visualize the trend of a stock and to trigger buy and sell signals. In general, when a moving average slopes upward, you can infer that the trend is up, and when the moving average slopes downward, the trend is down. When prices cross over the chart's moving averages, signals are generated and trends are likely to change.

One simple mechanical strategy that some traders employ works like this:

>> Buy when the moving average slopes upward *and* the closing price crosses above the moving average.

>> Close the position when the price closes below the moving average.

>> Sell short when the moving average slopes downward *and* the closing price crosses below the moving average.

>> Close the short position when the price closes above the moving average.

Although simple crossover strategies like this are remarkably effective in some trending situations, they're ineffective in others. As with all other strategies we've covered, nothing is certain. There's no holy grail system that's guaranteed to return profitable trades 100 percent of the time. Many variables must be in alignment for this approach to work, just like any other system. For example, the stock must be trending (see Chapter 10), and the period for the moving average must be chosen carefully for the indicator to be effective. These trend-following systems break down when a stock is stuck moving sideways in a trading range (see Chapter 9).

Figure 11-3 shows an example of this simple mechanical strategy on a chart of the SPDR S&P 500 ETF (SPY), an exchange-traded fund (ETF) that mirrors the S&P 500 Index. The chart is shown with a 50-period SMA.

FIGURE 11-3: A chart of SPY, an ETF that mirrors the S&P 500, with a 50-period SMA.

Chart courtesy of StockCharts.com

After bottoming in early June, SPY began climbing to the upside. Using the trading rules of this simple mechanical strategy, the first buy signal occurred shortly after in late July, when the stock closed above its SMA as the moving average turned higher. Notice that SPY traded above its 50-period SMA until late October, when it closed below its moving average. According to our simple mechanical strategy, this generated a sell signal for the position.

As it turns out, this sell signal indicated the beginning of a relatively brief retracement (see Chapter 10). Notice that the SMA rolled over and began to slope downward during the pullback. However, on the final trading day of the year, December 31, SPY closed well above its 50-period SMA just as the moving average was beginning to reverse its downtrend. This signals a buy according to the simple mechanical system and ultimately marked the start of a strong uptrend for multiple months. Notice that the price of SPY seemed to bounce off of its 50-period SMA multiple times during the course of that uptrend.

We normally want some sort of confirmation signal before entering or exiting any position in a stock or ETF. For example, we may temper the buy signal in the simple mechanical strategy described earlier with a requirement that the stock price remain above its SMA for several days after the initial signal before entering a position. The same is true for the sell, or close, signal. You want the stock to close below the SMA for several days, or you'd like to see another coincident sell signal — perhaps one of the visual patterns we discuss in Chapter 10 — before exiting your position. We use a long-period SMA to provide one of several signals to exit from existing positions. For example, if the price closes below a relatively long-term moving average and remains below it for a couple of days, we use that signal to exit our position.

TIP

When your trading strategy is based on just one moving average or a simple trend-following model, your ability to analyze a stock or fund during a period of range-bound trading can be limited. When a stock is stuck in a trading range or pulls back in a retracement, it's difficult to know whether the buy and sell signals that the moving averages generate are truly good entry or exit points. Using multiple moving averages and thoroughly understanding the implications of their crossovers is a good way to prevent falling for false signals, but ultimately, the smartest strategy is to combine these tools with other indicators, chart pattern analysis, fundamentals, and more. This helps you either confirm or reject the signals you're receiving from the moving averages.

Support and resistance factors

In addition to their trend-following abilities, moving averages also tend to provide support and resistance in stock prices that are trending up or down. When a price is trending higher, you often see the stock bounce off its moving average during its inevitable pullbacks, only to reverse course and head higher. The same is true in reverse for stock prices that are trending lower. You often see a down-trending stock rally up toward its moving average and seemingly bounce off that price before heading lower. The moving average acts as an area of resistance.

Back in Figure 11-3, the uptrending SPY approached its 50-period moving average in mid-December (2012), early 2013, late February 2013, and mid-April 2013.

In each small retracement within the broader uptrend, SPY pulled back very close to its moving average before recovering back to the upside. Short-term traders use these opportunities to enter positions in the direction of the dominant trend. When moving averages show a stock trending higher by sloping upward, for example, short-term traders buy into a position when the stock price closes near or just below the moving average so they can ride the trend to sell at a higher price later on. Position traders also can use these signals as second-chance entry points, whenever they miss the first breakout. This strategy is called *buying on a pullback.*

Deciding the moving average time frame

Perhaps the most difficult decision you have to make when creating a moving average is determining the length or period that best fits the situation. Regardless of whether you select an EMA or an SMA, shorter periods yield more signals, but a greater percentage of those signals are false. Longer moving average periods yield fewer signals, but a greater percentage of those signals are true. One hitch: Longer-term moving averages react slower to new price changes, and thus the signals they generate take more time to appear and occur later than they do in shorter-term moving averages.

TIP

In general, the shorter your trading horizon, the shorter the moving averages you want to select. For us, a nine-period moving average is nearly useless. It generates too many signals that we have no intention of following. More isn't always better. We want our technical analysis tools to provide better signals, not more, because although getting good signals is important, avoiding bad signals is paramount.

To reiterate, we rarely use ultra short-term moving averages to generate buy signals. Instead, we use a combination of short-, intermediate-, and long-period moving averages to monitor the health of a trend on daily charts. Typically, we select a 20-day EMA (for the short term), a 50-day SMA (for the intermediate term), and a 200-day SMA (for the long term). These can change, however, depending on the duration of the existing trend and prevailing economic conditions. If a trend has existed for a relatively long period of time, the 50-day SMA can provide good signals as an exit indicator. However, if the economy appears to be nearing a peak, as described in Chapter 5, then we tend to tighten our exit procedures and look more toward the 20-day EMA for indications of a trend change. See Chapter 13 for more on trading strategies and exit procedures.

WARNING

Traders can fall into a trap when trying to fine-tune the moving average — or any indicator, for that matter — for a specific stock or situation. Logically, it seems right to test many different moving average periods using historical data to find the one that generates the most profitable trades and the fewest losing trades, and modern charting software enables you to do just that to your heart's content. However, you'll soon discover that what worked when using historical data often fails miserably when trading real money in real time. This problem is well-known to statisticians and economists who build mathematic models to forecast future events. It's called *curve fitting* because you're molding your model to fit the historical data. We talk about this problem more in Chapter 16. For now, know that fine-tuning an indicator for a specific stock or index rarely results in consistent predictive value, and you must avoid it. You simply can't trade using historical data. You're better off settling on a moving average period that satisfies the requirements for a great many situations, rather than trying to fine-tune the time frame of a moving average to fit each stock.

Understanding Buy and Sell Pressure through Stochastic Oscillators

The *stochastic oscillator* indicates momentum and is intended to help show buying and selling pressure. This indicator compares current closing prices with the recent range of high to low prices and displays the results on a chart. Stochastic oscillator values cycle, or oscillate, between 0 and 100 percent.

Calculating stochastic oscillators

The typical stochastic oscillator is measured across a 14-day period, but a different time frame can be specified. Here's the calculation:

$$\%K = 100 \times \left(\text{closing price} - \text{lowest low}\left(N\right)\right) \div \left(\text{highest high}\left(N\right) - \text{lowest low}\left(N\right)\right)$$

$\%D = 3$-period moving average of %K

Where: N is the number of periods used in the calculation (usually 14)

This calculation describes a fast stochastic. The names %K and %D, respectively, identify the stochastic oscillator and the signal line. We typically use a variation of this indicator that's called a *slow stochastic*. The slow stochastic oscillator calculation is

$$\%K = 3\text{-period moving average of } 100 \times \left(\text{closing price} - \text{lowest low}\left(N\right)\right)$$

$$\div \left(\text{highest high}\left(N\right) - \text{lowest low}\left(N\right)\right)$$

$\%D = 3$-period moving average of %K

Where: N is the number of periods used in the calculation (usually 14)

In effect, the slow stochastic uses the %D value from the fast stochastic calculation as its starting point. While the fast and slow stochastics look similar when plotted on a chart, the slow stochastic is smoother and less jumpy. It generates fewer and more reliable trading signals, but the signals appear more slowly than with the fast stochastic. *Note:* Some charting platforms permit you to specify different values for the moving average period, and some even permit you to change from an SMA to an EMA.

Again, this calculation is done for you at StockCharts.com. Below your chart on the SharpCharts Workbench (`http://stockcharts.com/h-sc/ui`), you find the fast and slow stochastics in the dropdown menu of the Indicators panel. Select whichever indicator you prefer, set the parameters that fit your needs, and then click Update. The stochastics indicator automatically appears on your chart. The default settings are the most common, but you can apply custom parameters if you please. You can also choose whether you want the indicator displayed above or below the primary price chart.

Interpreting stochastic oscillators

As we mention earlier, the stochastic oscillator cycles between 0 and 100 percent. Readings of more than 80 percent imply an overbought condition. Readings of less than 20 percent are interpreted as an oversold condition. As with most indicators, an overbought condition can be resolved if a stock trades lower or enters a period of consolidation. Similarly, an oversold condition can be resolved if a stock trades higher or enters a period of consolidation.

Overbought and oversold conditions can persist for extended periods of time, so when the indicator line crosses above the 80 percent threshold or below the 20 percent level, it's not an immediate signal to sell or buy. Although this move should tell you to keep a close eye on things in case a sudden reversal is initiated, the real stochastic oscillator signals are generated in the following circumstances:

>> When the stochastic oscillator moves from below to above 20 percent, triggering a buy signal

>> When the stochastic oscillator moves from above to below 80 percent, triggering a sell signal

Figure 11-4 shows a slow stochastic oscillator on a price chart for Alaska Air (ALK). Note the transitions from below to above 20 percent that occurred in June, September, and November 2016. All three represented good entry opportunities for this uptrend, particularly in June after the stock had remained below the 20 percent level for multiple weeks. Also, note that few of the indicator's sell signals, where the stochastic oscillator crosses below 80 percent, represented good selling or shorting opportunities while Alaska was trending higher. (*Note:* Figure 11-4 shows a slow stochastic oscillator with the parameters 14, 3 positioned below the chart.)

Some traders use a *stochastic oscillator crossover strategy*, where buy signals are triggered when %K crosses above %D, and sell signals are triggered when %K crosses below %D. For our style of trading, that generates too many signals, a very high percentage of which are false, as you can see in Figure 11-4.

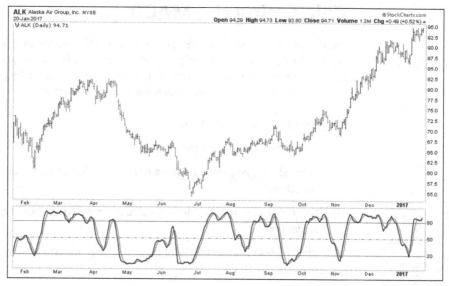

FIGURE 11-4:
A chart of Alaska Air with the slow stochastic oscillator below the price chart.

Chart courtesy of StockCharts.com

TIP

The stochastic oscillator is most effective when used in conjunction with other technical indicators. When a stock is trending, the stochastic oscillator is useful in finding entry points within a dominant trend. In an uptrend, for example, a buy signal that's generated when the stochastic oscillator moves from below to above 20 percent is likely to be a reliable one. At the same time, however, the stochastic oscillator signals many overbought conditions within an uptrend and rarely generates useful sell signals. For this reason, it's wise to pair the stochastic oscillator with other indicators to help generate useful sell signals in an uptrend.

The stochastic oscillator also works well in trading-range situations. Many short-term traders use it to trigger buy and sell signals when a stock is in a trading range.

Tracking Momentum with the MACD

The *moving average convergence divergence* (MACD) *indicator* is one of the most popular trend-following momentum indicators. The MACD is designed to generate trend-following trading signals based on moving-average crossovers while overcoming problems associated with many other trend-following indicators. The MACD also acts as a momentum oscillator, showing when a trend is gaining strength or losing momentum as it cycles above and below a center zero line. The MACD is an excellent indicator and an integral part of our trading tool set.

Calculating the MACD

As with other technical indicators, today's charting software calculates the MACD for you. Still, knowing how this indicator is created helps you gain a better understanding of how it works. Based on just three moving averages of different periods, the MACD isn't complex to calculate. Here are the steps:

1. **Calculate a 12-period EMA.**

2. **Calculate a 26-period EMA.**

3. **Subtract the 26-period EMA from the 12-period EMA to create the MACD line.**

4. **Use the resulting MACD line to calculate a 9-period EMA to create the signal line.**

5. **Plot the MACD as a solid line; plot the signal line as either a dashed or lighter-colored line.**

An additional indicator, the MACD *histogram*, is often shown as part of the MACD. It uses a histogram to show the difference between the MACD line and the signal line:

>> When the MACD line is above the signal line, the histogram is plotted above zero.

>> When the MACD line is below the signal line, the histogram is plotted below zero.

>> When the MACD line and the signal line cross, the histogram is plotted at zero.

Figure 11-5 shows a daily chart of Bank of America (BAC) along with the MACD indicator (including the MACD histogram), shown below the primary price chart.

BAC traded sideways for the first few months of 2016, consolidating within a trading range. In early July, the stock began to rally to the upside. It continued its bullish climb throughout the last half of the year, turning on the jets in November and rocketing up in the last few months of 2016. Notice the corresponding periods on the MACD. The MACD line (the solid line) crosses over the zero center line in mid-July, just after the stock begins what would eventually become a strong uptrend. This was a buy signal for this stock. You may also notice that the MACD line crossed the signal line earlier in the month at the start of July. This MACD crossover signal is another early indication suggesting a possible new uptrend. See Chapter 13 for more about how we use this signal.

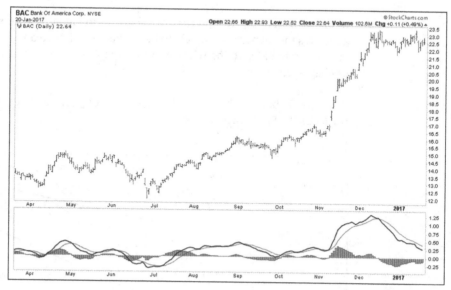

FIGURE 11-5:
A daily chart of
Bank of America
with the MACD
and an MACD
histogram.

TIP

You can easily add the MACD indicator to your charts on StockCharts.com. Below your chart on the SharpCharts Workbench (http://stockcharts.com/h-sc/ui), use the dropdown menu in the Indicators panel to select MACD. Use the default settings (12, 26, and 9) or customize the moving average parameters to your liking. Click Update and the MACD will automatically appear on your chart. As with other indicators, you can choose to position the MACD either above or below the primary price chart, whichever is your preference. In Figure 11-5, you see that we set the MACD below the chart.

Using the MACD

The MACD provides a remarkable amount of information in a concise format. As you can see in Figure 11-5, the MACD oscillates above and below a center zero line and serves as a good indicator for showing the direction of the dominant trend. It signals

» An uptrend when the MACD line crosses above the center line

» A downtrend when the MACD line crosses below the center line

Some short-term traders use the signal line to trigger

>> Buy signals when the MACD line crosses above the signal line

>> Sell signals when the MACD line crosses below the signal line

In our own trading, we find that the short-term signal line crossover technique generates too many false signals to be a reliable tool. Instead, we prefer using the position of the MACD line relative to the zero line as an indication that the stock has begun trending.

Figure 11-6 shows a chart of daily prices for QQQ, an exchange-traded fund that tracks the NASDAQ Index.

FIGURE 11-6: The chart of QQQ shows a bearish divergence between price and the MACD.

Chart courtesy of StockCharts.com

Notice how QQQ establishes a series of higher highs and higher lows beginning in late June, but the MACD line establishes a series of lower highs between early August and the start of November. This creates what's known as a *divergence pattern*. This particular example of a divergence pattern is a bearish or negative divergence. In a bearish divergence, the stock establishes a series of higher highs and higher lows in an uptrend, but the MACD establishes a series of lower highs and shows a downtrend. A bullish divergence is the reverse: The stock establishes a series of lower highs and lower lows, while the MACD establishes a series of higher highs and shows an uptrend.

TIP

Divergences that occur in the same direction as the dominant trend are often useful for entering positions. However, a divergence that is counter to the dominant trend is less likely to be a reliable trading signal. For example, a bearish divergence in a dominant uptrend is rarely a good signal to enter a short position. During a strong uptrend, the MACD is likely to show a bearish divergence simply because the pace of the uptrend is likely to slow. As the uptrend slows, the longer-term moving average catches up to the shorter-term moving average, resulting in a bearish divergence on the MACD. While this type of bearish divergence may not be a great signal to enter a short position, it may indicate that the stock has entered, or is about to enter, a period of retracement.

The bearish divergence on QQQ in Figure 11-6 is best interpreted as a sign that the momentum of the strong July rally was slowing. The slope of the fund's uptrend during that month was remarkably strong, which simply can't continue forever. As the stock entered a new month, the uptrend continued, but not at such a steep slope. This allowed the moving averages used in the calculation of the MACD to converge, resulting in a negative divergence.

Each time the MACD line crosses above or below the signal line, it suggests a potential change in the direction of the dominant trend. Although it's not an outright buy signal or sell signal, it does suggest that a change may be in the wind. In the case of a bearish divergence, the best way to utilize that information is to monitor individual stocks and ETFs for weakness and either close long positions when they deteriorate or initiate new short positions as they present themselves. In Chapter 13, we provide additional ideas to help integrate the information generated by the MACD indicator into a useful trading strategy.

REMEMBER

Nothing in the stock market is ever guaranteed. There's no magic indicator that will send perfectly reliable buy and sell signals 100 percent of the time. Instead, indicators such as the MACD can help increase your probability of making smarter, more-informed trading decisions. Your goal is to act rationally based on the information available to you. Indicators such as the MACD can help you achieve that very objective.

WARNING

Most charting platforms enable you to fine-tune the MACD calculation, customizing the moving average parameters to your liking. Many traders adjust the 12-, 26-, and 9-period values in an attempt to better fit the MACD to their trading needs. Although nothing is inherently wrong with this approach, you nevertheless run the risk of inadvertently curve-fitting whenever you try to find parameters that give you better results for a specific stock. That said, Gerald Appel, the man who developed the MACD, uses values different from the original 12, 26, and 9. He also uses different values to generate buy signals than he does to generate sell signals.

It's perfectly fine to experiment with various MACD settings, but we recommend first establishing some solid experience using the default parameters. The 12-, 26-, and 9-period settings are the most common for a reason. Learn how to use the indicator with the standard parameters before attempting to modify and improve it.

Revealing Relative Strength

Relative strength measures the performance of one security — a stock, ETF, index fund, and so on — against another, or against the performance of a benchmark index such as the S&P 500. The idea is to determine how the stock is performing compared with, for example, the broader total market. By focusing your attention on the strongest stocks or funds that are outperforming the rest of the pack, you increase your probability of successful, profitable results.

WARNING

Unfortunately, you may run across another indicator with a similar name when working with your charting software. The other indicator is called the *relative strength index* (RSI), and it's completely different from the relative strength discussed here. RSI is an oscillator that is used in a way similar to the stochastic oscillator described earlier. To keep the two separate, we suggest you call the RSI by its initials and use the phrase *relative strength* when you mean to compare the performance of a stock or ETF against a broad-based index or another security.

Calculating relative strength

There are multiple ways to calculate relative strength, but one of the simplest and most effective is to simply divide the stock price by the index value and plot the result, like this:

Relative strength No. 1 = Stock price ÷ Index value

Another technique compares the price of the stock during a given period of time against the index during the same period. Our preference is comparing percentage changes during the same period. The calculation looks like this:

Relative strength No. 2 = Percentage change in stock price
÷ Percentage change in index value

You can plot both of these approaches on a stock chart. Some online resources provide powerful relative strength tools that allow you to visualize the performance of one stock or fund against another security. The PerfCharts tool at

StockCharts.com, for example, allows you to simultaneously chart the performance of multiple stocks or ETFs within a group to see how they perform against a benchmark (typically the S&P 500). See www.stockcharts.com/charts/performance for an example.

TIP

StockCharts.com lets you create your own performance charts using any stocks, ETFs, or indexes of your choice. This unique relative strength tool is called a PerfChart. You can customize your PerfCharts with up to ten different symbols. To get started, visit www.stockcharts.com/freecharts and look for the PerfCharts box on the left side of the page. Select from one of the predefined groups or enter your own list of symbols in the box labeled Create a PerfChart. Once your PerfChart has loaded, you can adjust the date range and time frame using the slider below the chart. You can also change the PerfChart's mode from line to histogram view using the buttons in the bottom-left corner.

Putting relative strength to work

TIP

At its core, relative strength allows you to strategically determine which stocks or ETFs are outperforming others. This allows you to zero in on the best trading candidates and, most importantly, helps you avoid stocks or funds that are underperforming the rest of the pack. If you're consistently investing in average or below-average stocks, you're bound to keep placing losing trades. By narrowing your focus to the top performers, relative strength improves your probabilities of making profitable trading decisions.

Relative strength is one of the final pieces of the technical-analysis puzzle. The strongest trading candidates fit the following criteria:

» Exhibits solid fundamentals as a strong company

» Has earnings that are growing faster than average

» Is a leading stock in a strong sector of the market

» Operates in a growing economy

» Is approaching a technical buy signal on its price chart

» Performs better than the average stock

These characteristics favor a long position, of course. For short position candidates, the criteria are reversed.

4

Developing Strategies for When to Buy and Sell Stocks

Manage your money and successfully trade by protecting your principal and minimizing your risks.

Use both fundamental analysis and technical analysis to maximize your trading success.

Consider exchange-traded funds (ETFs) for trading to minimize risk.

Discover how to enter and exit your trades with precision.

Explore the secrets of developing your own trading system.

Chapter **12**

Money Management Techniques: Building a More Robust Portfolio

You may find this hard to believe, but many successful traders actually book more losing trades than winning trades. How? Simple: Their profits from winning trades overwhelm the losses from losing trades. The key to this success is disciplined money management, knowing when to let a trade run, and, more importantly, when to cut your losses and move on. You must develop the discipline to keep your losses under control by quickly closing losing positions. The trick is to consistently follow the rules and routines you set.

Good money management minimizes your trading losses when they occur and helps you secure a profit when a good trade goes your way. Recognizing winners and losers — and setting your target prices before ever entering a position — is crucial to your money management strategies. In this chapter, we give you a set of rules to follow to get you started.

Achieving Your Trading Goals with Smart Money Management

Successful traders share a common trait: They all successfully manage their money. The critical points of successful money management may be difficult to implement, but they're easy to identify. They include

>> Planning your trades carefully by identifying entry and exit points

>> Minimizing losses by ruthlessly adhering to your stop-loss points

>> Protecting your profits by setting trailing stops on your trades and adjusting them over time to lock in gains

>> Being objective about your positions and quickly exiting your trades when the trend ends

REMEMBER

When using technical analysis to make your trades, you may not always get the lowest entry price or the highest exit price. Most of the time, you'll end up leaving something on the table. Perfect timing is simply impossible. Instead, the idea is to identify when a trend has begun, enter the position, and ride the trend until it ends.

The secret to profitable trading is disciplined money management, and it all starts with trade planning. The key to success is to develop a plan for your trades and stick to that plan, even if it goes against what your gut tells you. Once you're an experienced trader with years of profitable investing under your belt, your gut can become a useful tool. Until then, stick to your trading plan, watch the charts, and follow the data. The more objective you can be about your trades, the better.

Before entering any trade, you need to set an *entry point,* the price at which you'll enter the position, and an *exit point* where you'll close out of the trade if it goes poorly. Don't deviate from your plan, even if it means accepting the fact that you made a mistake. We discuss setting entry and exit points in the later section "Protecting Your Principal." For more info about entering and exiting positions, check out Chapters 10 and 11.

REMEMBER

Experienced traders make rational decisions based on what they see, not what they wish to see. They cut their losses short on the bad trades and let their profits run on the good ones. Most importantly, they don't let their emotions get the best of them. No matter how excited you are about a current position or how high your hopes were for the stock, if the trade starts to go against you, get out.

TIP

Your most important money management goal is to get out of losing positions as quickly as possible. After taking into consideration normal up and down price fluctuations (as discussed in Chapters 9 and 10), you must develop a method of recognizing when a stock is not behaving the way you expected. Be prepared to close a losing position before it consumes too much of your trading capital. Try to keep losses below 5 or 6 percent for any position. Alternatively, you can think in terms of your total trading capital and try to keep the loss from any single position below 1 or 2 percent. Just remember that there's always another trading opportunity. If you close out of a position too quickly and miss out on a potential gain, don't dwell on what could have been. Learn from the experience and move on to your next trade.

Managing Your Portfolio

To be successful, you need to treat your trading as a business. Think of the stocks in your portfolio as your inventory. Just like any other business, you must carefully manage your inventory to succeed. The following factors are paramount to successful trading:

>> **Viewing trading as a business:** You trade to make money. Sometimes you pick the wrong stock and have to accept a loss. Losses are a part of any business. Good business planning is about minimizing losses and making sure that you don't repeat the same mistakes in the future.

>> **Overcoming the most common trader's dilemma:** Many new traders struggle to control their emotions. They get emotionally attached to a stock and refuse to accept a loss, even as the trade moves in the wrong direction. Alternatively, they hold on to a winning stock too long, convinced that it's only going higher, and end up squandering good profits. When your choices no longer make good business sense, you must quickly make cold, hard decisions and act decisively to cut your losses short.

>> **Approaching the solution to your trading dilemma as if it's a business problem to solve:** Sell when you've booked a healthy profit on paper or when you must accept that a trade has gone wrong and it's time to move on. Don't be greedy with your profits, and don't be in denial about your losses. Simply figure out the most logical and appropriate solution and take action.

Thinking of trading as a business

So how do you start thinking of trading as a business? Conceptually, it's simple. Like any other business, traders have fixed costs; variable costs; finite amounts of working capital, assets, and liabilities; and inventory. Managing these business factors results either in profits or losses. Your primary objective, of course, is to maximize profits and minimize losses. The most important step you can take in treating trading as a business is thinking of the contents of your portfolio as your inventory.

REMEMBER

Psychologically, it's important to approach your trading with a sense of professionalism. When your investing capital is the same as your personal capital, it's easy to let your emotions get the best of you. Unfortunately, putting your hard-earned cash on the line often leads to biased thinking and clouded judgment. To combat this, think of your trading as a job, not a hobby, and manage your portfolio with the same clear-eyed, cold-hearted detachment as any successful business owner. In doing so, you'll be more likely to make rational decisions based on objective observations.

Recognizing the trader's dilemma

WARNING

No matter how experienced you are, selling is hard. For many of us, it's emotionally more difficult to close a position, especially a losing position, than it is to open it. Traders rationalize holding a losing position by saying to themselves, "I'll give it some room to work out; it's only a paper loss." But that rationalization is foolish. You rarely hear traders describe a winning trade as a paper gain. Losing positions shouldn't be rationalized that way, either.

Falling in love

Traders often fall in love with their stocks. It's easy to do. After all, you work hard to find the right stock. You evaluate the economic conditions, gauge the state of the market, determine the strongest sector, and diligently research the group's top stocks. With a few targets in mind, you carefully analyze the charts, select the most promising, and find the perfect entry point.

No trader ever means to fall in love with a stock. It's simply an example of basic human psychology working against you. You devoted your time and energy to find the position. Naturally, you want the trade to succeed. When it doesn't, it can be a tough pill to swallow.

Still, no matter how frustrating it may be, losing trades are just a part of the game. Acknowledging and accepting that fact allows experienced traders to manage the impact of their emotions. Instead of fixating on individual trades, they take a longer-term view. If a trade goes against them, they exit quickly and move on to the next opportunity. Overall, profitable investing is about extracting more from your winners than your losers extract from you. By minimizing losses, focusing only on trades that turn profitable, and keeping the bigger picture of your total portfolio in mind, you can prevent yourself from falling in love with one specific stock.

Fixating on mistakes

After all the time and energy you invested carefully analyzing the market and finding that losing trade, you may end up asking yourself, "How could I have been so wrong?" The question you should be asking instead is this: "What did I get wrong and how can I learn from this trade to prevent repeating the same mistake in the future?" Don't fixate on your losing trade. Cut your losses, exit the position, and use it as an opportunity to learn.

REMEMBER

After you've taken a position, it's obviously natural to want to be right. In reality, though, being right about every trade is impossible. Unfortunately, many new investors struggle to overcome the desire to be right. Their frustration over a losing trade becomes destructive when they foolishly allow results in the past to negatively affect new trading opportunities in the future. If a trade goes against you, don't panic. Think of it as paying tuition to the market. You've paid the market to teach you a lesson. Take it to heart, and that payment can produce positive returns in the form of future profits. Ignore the chance to learn, however, and the losing trade is truly a loss.

Finding a better plan

Approaching the trader's dilemma as though it were a business problem for you to solve can be helpful. The fashion industry provides an analogy that will do so nicely. The fashion industry works in obvious cycles. For example, you see long-term cycles at work as hemlines rise and fall and even longer cycles as you witness periodic mysteries that cause capri pants and bell-bottom trousers to appear and just as easily disappear. You also see shorter cycles as clothing for the current season is discounted to make way for the next season's fashions. These shorter seasonal cycles illustrate the day-to-day issues that traders face.

Dealing with seasonal stock

As spring approaches, retailers stock up on colorful, lightweight merchandise. You may even see swimsuits. Fall clothes start showing up in stores as summer heats up. Before summer is over, heavier-weight clothes, including a selection of winter coats, begin appearing on clothing racks.

Ideally, retailers try to sell all their winter coats — and all their bathing suits and spring outfits — before the next season arrives, but that rarely happens. Retailers often have unsold inventory as the end of the season approaches.

Retailers can use a couple of alternatives for handling unsold seasonal inventory, but neither is pleasant. The retailer can store the merchandise until next year, but storage costs carry charges that eat into capital. The greatest cost of storing merchandise is the lost opportunity. The retailer's capital gets locked up in unsold merchandise and thus can't be used to buy current-season inventory that's more in demand.

Another alternative is marking down the price of merchandise beginning relatively early in the season and continuing to do so until all the merchandise is sold. This approach quickly

>> Frees up capital that the retailer then can use to buy newer inventory

>> Stops the accrual of carrying charges

>> Clears out storage and display space

>> Avoids the risk that the merchandise will become worthless in the future

This solution is better, even though it sometimes means selling the merchandise below cost.

Clothiers buy inventory to sell it at a profit. They know their costs, and they determine the profits they want to earn from the sale of each item. Retailers try to earn as much profit as possible but start cutting prices whenever sales don't happen quickly enough. Retailers can't afford to fall in love with their winter coats. They need the space and capital for spring merchandise. They don't get choked up when it's time to sell.

Keeping your inventory current

Managing your trading business as if you were a retail merchant is a good idea. The cycle of economic expansion, peak, recession, and trough, as described in Chapter 5, is somewhat akin to the four seasons. Your stocks are your inventory. Their prices rise and are discounted in anticipation of the changing economic cycles, as we describe in Chapter 13. And your trading account is your working capital. Just like the retail merchant, your goal is to protect your principal, your working capital, so you can stay in business.

However, you may find that some factors differ. The stock market is, of course, a much more efficient pricing mechanism than the retail clothing industry. You can't set the price of merchandise; the market does it for you. You can take several approaches to keep your trading inventory current. Many traders use trend analysis and relative strength analysis, as described in Chapters 10 and 11, to try to take positions in the best-performing stocks and sectors. Some traders also track general market conditions, quarterly and annual SEC filings, company announcements, and key analysts' reports, as described in Chapters 5, 6, and 7.

We tend to combine both approaches in the ways we trade. We want to own strong stocks in strong sectors, and we want to know how well the companies manage their businesses. Although any changes in these elements are worth a look, we don't have immediate hair-trigger reactions. We do sometimes replace positions that begin to underperform (relative to the market) with emerging leaders, and yet we show a little extra patience with positions that are profitable but are beginning to slightly underperform. If, however, a stock position starts losing money, then we quickly close the position without a second thought. The goal is to protect your trading capital, and we show you some techniques and examples to accomplish this in the next section.

Protecting Your Principal

In the same way that retail merchants face the possibility of holding on to their stock of winter coats that may fall out of style, you must avoid the risk of owning a stock that falls out of favor with other investors and loses its value. By acting fast when you see changes in the market, you can avoid losing a large chunk of your trading capital (or *principal*). Exiting out of a position quickly prevents your trading capital from being tied up in a losing stock position. This allows you to escape a losing trade with minimal loss of capital. Your principal remains protected and, most importantly, you'll be able to trade another day.

REMEMBER

It makes sense, of course, to hold on to a stock as long as its price is appreciating. However, being mindful of when your stock price begins to fall is important. You must have a detailed plan for dealing with losing trades or deteriorating profits. Most importantly, you must have the emotional control to remain objective when the time comes to sell. Don't let your losses build by being stubborn and unwilling to accept a weakening stock.

REMEMBER

If your goal is to keep trading for a long time, the only way to do that is to not lose too much money. This fact may seem patently obvious, but you would be surprised by how many investors, and even some traders, fail to make capital preservation their highest priority. To keep from making that mistake, remember these important goals as you trade:

>> Protect your principal first.

>> Don't let a large profit turn into a small profit.

>> Don't let a small profit turn into a loss.

>> Don't let a small loss turn into a large loss.

Recovering from a large loss: It ain't easy

REMEMBER

When thinking about protecting your principal, you need to accept that taking a small loss is better than risking a larger one. You need to understand how badly (and quickly) things can go wrong, and how that can result in a loss of a huge chunk of your capital with little chance of recovering it. To illustrate, check out an example of the impact that large losses can have on your money.

Imagine that you purchase XYZ stock for $10 per share. The stock falls to $9, representing a $1 loss. You've lost 10 percent of the original price of the stock. To recover from that loss, the stock price must rise from $9 to $10, but notice that 10 percent of $9 is only 90 cents. In other words, your stock must gain more than 10 percent to recover from the initial 10 percent loss. Let's take a quick look at the math using percentages.

To determine the exact percentage gain required to recover the initial $1 loss, divide $1 by $9 and multiply by 100:

$$(1 \div 9) \times 100 = 0.1111 \times 100 = 11.11\%$$

In other words, your $9 stock now needs to gain a little more than 11 percent to get back to even.

For losses of less than 10 percent, the required gain isn't significantly greater than the loss you've just experienced. However, for larger losses, the problem grows unmanageably. Check out Table 12-1 to see what we mean.

TABLE 12-1

Percentage Gain Required to Recover Loss

Loss of	Percentage Gain Required to Recover Loss
5%	5.2%
10%	11.1%
25%	33.3%
50%	100%
75%	300%
100%	Game over

Getting a stock to go up 5 or even 10 percent is hard enough. It seems irrational to hope for a stock that's fallen by 50 percent to quickly recover 100 percent, or for one that's fallen by 75 percent to ever recover 300 percent.

WHY TRADERS TALK IN TERMS OF PERCENTAGES

Why do traders use percentages to describe their results? The use of percentages is a simple way of accurately comparing the results of one trade with the results of another — as a percentage, a $1 gain on a $10 stock is identical to a $10 gain on a $100 stock. The price per share is not as important as the percentage gain (or loss) or the total gain (or loss). Look at it like this: If you have $1,000 in your trading account, you can buy 100 shares of a $10 stock, or you can buy 10 shares of a $100 stock. If the price of either stock rises by 10 percent, your account total is the same in either case — $1,100. A 10 percent rise in a $10 stock is $1. A 10 percent rise in a $100 stock is $10. But the total amount of money earned is the same in either scenario.

If you think in terms of percentage gains or losses, you can directly compare the results of one trade with that of another. The actual price of a stock, and the actual number of points gained or lost, isn't as important as the size of the move in percentage terms. Although you can buy many more shares of the lower-priced stock, it's equally difficult for either stock to move 10 percent. If you think about it like this, you'll see that there is no reason to favor the lower-priced stock, even if you can buy more shares, over the higher-priced stock.

REMEMBER

Selling quickly and avoiding large losses is a better course of action. Otherwise, you'll be out of trading capital, and out of business, faster than you can say "oops."

Setting a target price for handling losses

REMEMBER

The most important step toward protecting your principal is accepting the fact that a trade has turned against you and moving on. You can't afford to hesitate to sell a loser. Hesitation to exit a losing trade allows small losses to quickly become large ones. Before entering a trade, make sure you set a target price that you're willing to initially pay for the stock, and set a lower stop target where you're willing to sell in case the trade results in a loss.

Setting a stop-loss price (or, as traders say, *setting your stop*) has no single formula. You can employ several techniques for determining your stop-loss price. One that many traders follow is to choose a predetermined percentage loss as your stop-loss price. Others set stops at previously established price lows, determined by analyzing the stock's charts. We think using technical analysis (see Chapters 9 and 10) to identify when a trade has failed is a better approach.

Here's an example: Figure 12-1 is a daily price chart of the Select Sector SPDR Industrial Sector ETF (XLI) that shows support and resistance lines, respectively, drawn on the chart at approximately $56.04 and $58.51 and indicates the ETF has just broken out of a long trading range on high volume. Support, resistance, and breakouts are discussed in Chapter 9. The breakout is identified on the chart.

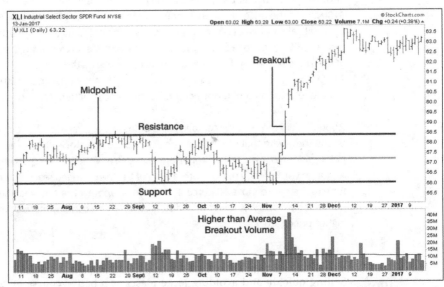

FIGURE 12-1:
A daily chart of XLI, the Industrial Sector ETF.

Chart courtesy of StockCharts.com

Figure 12-1 represents a picture-perfect setup for entering a trade. As discussed in Chapter 9, your entry point for this trade occurs above $58.50 when the ETF breaks through its resistance level. But how do you handle the trade if it doesn't work out? Or perhaps a better question to ask is this: How do you know when the trade has failed?

>> One of several approaches suggests that if the breakout fails (the price pulls back below its resistance level), you need to exit your position immediately. For the XLI example in Figure 12-1, if the ETF were to fall below the resistance line ($58.51) after it breaks out above it, you should exit. The failed breakout may signal that there is some bullish pressure behind the stock and it's worth keeping an eye on, but the trade is off for the time being.

>> Another approach suggests that if the ETF falls below the midpoint of its trading range, in this case somewhere around $57.25, then the breakout buy signal has failed. In that case, you can use any price below $57.25 as the stop-loss price to exit from the position.

In the first scenario, the financial risk is small. As long as both your entry and exit orders are filled at good prices, your risk should be no more than $1.00 per share, which reflects a maximum loss of just over 1.7 percent on the trade. We discuss fills further in Chapter 16.

In the second approach, the risk is greater. The difference between the $58.51 breakout price and the $57.25 stop-loss price is $1.26. However, the strength of the ETF's breakout gap means that your actual fill price will be closer to $60.00 or more, resulting in a greater percentage risk on the trade (closer to 4.5 percent). Poor fills on either entry or exit orders increase the amount of capital at risk.

The trade-off between the two approaches is clear. The first one risks a smaller amount before triggering the exit trade, but it's prone to whipsaws. This means that you may be forced out of a potentially winning trade as it simply makes a healthy retest of its former resistance level. The second approach risks a greater amount but is less prone to whipsaws. Position traders who expect to hold a trade for several weeks or months are more likely to choose the second.

TIP

Either approach is rational, so you need to choose the one that is more closely aligned with your personal risk tolerance. If you start second-guessing your stop-loss points, they're no longer useful, so be sure to use an approach that you'll honor. Using the first approach may make more sense for new position traders because tight stops can serve as educational tools. You'll risk less on each trade, but you'll be subject to a few whipsaws, and you'll get into the habit of selling when you have small losses. And that's a good habit to learn. Ultimately, it's crucial to determine the amount of risk you're willing to take on as a trader. What is comfortable for another trader may be excessive for your own personality, or vice versa. Be honest with yourself and adopt a stop setting system that truly fits your unique investing profile.

Strategies for managing profitable trades

Profitable trades are somewhat easier to manage than losses, but they're not without complications. You must carefully adjust your stops as the price rises in order to lock in some of your gains on paper, and eventually decide when to take profits for real and exit out of the winning trade.

You obviously want to try to keep any profit from turning into a loss. For example, say that you enter the XLI trade in the Figure 12-1 example, and a few days after entering the order it remains in positive territory with a small profit. For this discussion, assume that your original stop price is $57.25, the midpoint of the trading range. Your choice is to leave the stop where it is or move it above the resistance line, to $58.52.

>> If you choose the former, and the stock trades below $57.25, your once profitable trade will be closed for a loss.

>> If you choose the latter, you will be stopped out if XLI trades below $58.52, which could prematurely close the trade if the pullback to the former resistance level turns out to be a retest, not a reversal.

You must decide whether to move your stop-loss order to protect the small profit, or leave the stop where it is to keep from jeopardizing the stock's chances of gaining more. This balancing act is delicate. You're trying to catch the bigger move of the larger trend, which argues for leaving the stop where it is for a little while longer. But sooner rather than later, you'll want to move your stop-loss above your entry price. This decision becomes easier as the position progresses. As your profit grows, you'll want to continue adjusting your exit points upward. This is called a *trailing stop* and is discussed in the later section "Using trailing stops."

Breaking the pattern of higher highs and higher lows

Trends are easy to see on charts. Take one quick look at Figure 12-2 and you can instantly identify the strong uptrend that carried the price of Amazon (AMZN) from $480 per share to more than $840 per share in less than eight months. In this case, the stock climbed to a series of higher highs followed by higher lows, interspersed with only a few small retracements to slightly lower lows. For more on trend trading, higher highs and higher lows, and retracements, see Chapter 10.

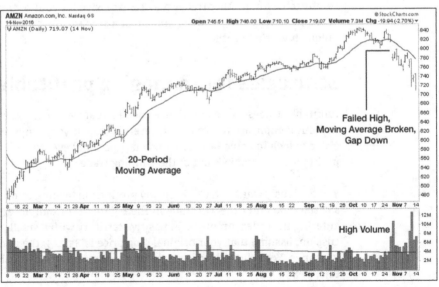

FIGURE 12-2:
A broken pattern of higher highs and higher lows.

Chart courtesy of StockCharts.com

Amazon had a long and impressive run up throughout a good portion of 2016, but after peaking in early October, the charts began sending a few important signals of potential weakness ahead. After a brief retracement, the stock failed to break its high in late October. The failed test of the October high was followed by a few down trading days, then a significant gap lower. A brief rally to the upside was quickly squashed, after which the stock collapsed again in another wave of selling. In addition, these moves against the longstanding uptrend came on higher-than-average volume.

REMEMBER

When a stock clearly breaks its pattern of higher highs and higher lows, the smartest move is to exit the position. Trends resume, and a broken pattern is not always a surefire sign that the uptrend has run out of steam. However, trading is about managing risk. When an uptrend is broken, the risk of a strong move to the downside grows significantly. Your primary objectives at this point should be to limit your risk exposure and protect your capital.

Using trailing stops

After you've entered a position and it becomes profitable, you want to adjust your stop to protect your profits. This is known as a *trailing stop* because you keep moving it higher as your profits grow. In an uptrend, a stock makes a series of higher highs and higher lows (see Chapter 10). Use the higher lows to define your stop points. After the stock has made a higher high, reset the stop to either the most recent higher low or the one just before it. Using Figure 12-2, as AMZN reached new highs in early October, you would have reset your stop using the most recent closing low around $799.16, which occurred during a brief pullback in late September.

Tracking market indexes

Individual stocks and entire sectors of similar stocks regularly fall in and out of favor with the market. Sometimes these changes happen in a grand way, such as when the technology bubble burst in the early 2000s, or when the financial sector crashed in 2007 and 2008.

Look at the weekly chart of the S&P 500 Index in Figure 12-3. Although the S&P 500 peaked in October 2007, by 2008 it had formed a lower high and lower low below its recent intermittent lows. The price also closed well below its 50-period moving average. By the time 2008 rolled around, the vast majority of financial stocks were in worse shape than the broad market index — a prime example of a dramatic shift in market conditions. If you were trading at the time, you could

>> Sell your positions when you saw that prices, market fundamentals, and technical indicators were simultaneously deteriorating.

>> Wait out the market, hoping things would get better.

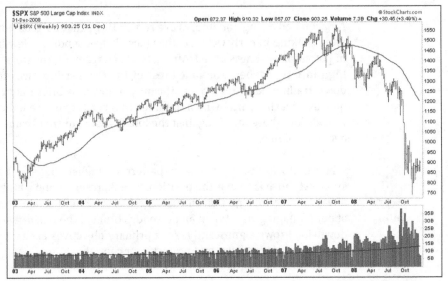

Chart courtesy of StockCharts.com

FIGURE 12-3:
A weekly chart of
the S&P 500
Index, 2003–2008.

If you held financial stocks during that time and chose the second option, you took a much greater loss by selling later. Unfortunately, many buy-and-hold investors unwisely believed that the downturn was a temporary blip and that financial investments would remain viable. In fact, many financial stocks still have not recovered back to their pre-recession highs. Some are no longer even trading. As you can see in Figure 12-4, one of the largest financial sector ETFs (XLF) still has not broken its 2007 high, even after nearly 10 years of trading.

FIGURE 12-4:
A weekly chart of
the Financial
Sector (XLF),
2006–2017.

Chart courtesy of StockCharts.com

The right choice then, as usual, was to close your positions. By following these simple strategies, you'd have had more than enough information to know that things were not going according to plan. Although you wouldn't have sold your stocks at the highest prices, you also would have prevented yourself from riding those stocks down to their extreme lows. By selling, and selling quickly, you protect your profits and your trading capital so you can trade another day. In the stock market, nothing happens in a vacuum. If the market begins to deteriorate or its sector begins to weaken, chances are your stock will soon follow suit, even if it looks stable for the time being. When you see broader signs of a market sell-off or a rotation out of your stock's sector, keep a close eye on the charts and be ready to spring into action if the trade begins to fade.

REMEMBER

Knowing when a trend is complete is just as difficult as knowing when it began. You can't trade with perfect knowledge, and you can't predict the future. No trader can. However, by using the right charting tools, you'll be able to identify when a trend is likely to begin and when it's likely to end. When combined with proper money management strategies, you can dramatically increase your probability of profitable trading.

Understanding Your Risks

It's important to understand the array of risks that traders, investors, and other market participants face. The three general categories are market risks, investment risks, and trading risks.

Market risks

For the most part, market risks are out of your control. Of course you know the risk that the markets are bound to rise and fall, but understanding the risks you face when they do helps you manage your money better. Three key risks that you can manage as a trader are

>> **Inflation risk:** This describes the risk that your money won't grow fast enough to exceed the cost increases caused by inflation. Basic goods and services such as housing, clothing, medical expenses, and food increase in price each year. If you invest in monetary vehicles that don't keep pace with inflation, you actually end up losing money. Although inflation is a risk that stock traders rarely consider, it nevertheless impacts investors who are risk-averse.

>> **Marketability risk:** This risk relates to the liquidity of your investments. If you're restricted from selling an investment when you want to do so,

your target selling point is irrelevant. For most stock traders, this factor isn't an issue, but if, for example, you choose to invest in a small company whose stock isn't traded on one of the major exchanges, you risk not being able to close your position when the time is right. Many small-cap stocks or penny stocks with low trading volume can also suffer from low liquidity that affects your ability to sell.

>> **Currency translation risk:** Currency translation refers to disparities in trading stocks of companies in foreign countries. It's only a factor when you trade foreign stocks because you then must be concerned with fluctuations between the values of your local currency and the currency in the country where the company is located. Even if the stock increases in price, you can still lose money based on the currency exchange rate. If the value of your currency falls against the other currency, your investment can be worth less when you convert it back.

Investment risks

Investment risks relate directly to how you invest your money and manage your entry and exit trades. Two critical risks you must manage are

>> **Opportunity risk:** This kind of risk involves balancing your trade-offs. When you trade, you establish a position that ties up money that otherwise can be used elsewhere. After you choose a stock and buy it, you lose the opportunity to invest that capital in another stock or fund until you trade out of the first position. Essentially, you can miss other opportunities while your money is tied up in another position.

>> **Concentration risk:** This kind of risk happens when you put too many eggs in one basket. You may think you've found the miracle stock that's going to make you a millionaire, so you decide to invest a huge portion of your principal into that one position. By concentrating so much of your money on one investment, you also disproportionally expose yourself to the risks associated with that one specific investment. The less diversified your portfolio, the higher your concentration risk.

Trading risks

Risks that are unique to trading increase simultaneously with increases in trading volume. Day traders and swing traders often see a greater impact caused by these risks than do position traders or long-term investors, but all market participants should be aware of them. (See Chapters 17 and 18 for more information about swing trading and day trading, respectively.) Risks associated with trading are

>> **Slippage risk:** This risk considers the hidden costs associated with every transaction. Each time you enter or exit a position, your account balance shrinks by a small amount due to the stock's bid-ask spread. Buy orders are executed at the ask price (the lowest price available for the stock that you want), while sell orders are executed at the bid price (the highest price someone is willing to pay for shares you own). Unfortunately, the bid price is always less than the ask price. The difference between the two is referred to as the stock's *bid-ask spread*. For example, if the current quote for a stock is $20.50/$20.55, a buyer would pay the ask price of $20.55, while a seller would receive the bid price of $20.50. If you bought one share of the stock and then immediately sold it, you would instantly lose $0.05 on the trade. Although you can mitigate bid-ask problems by using limit orders, doing so subjects you to the risk that your order won't get filled. The amounts for each trade may at first seem small, but as your trading volume increases, so do the amounts you lose to slippage.

>> **Poor execution risk:** This problem occurs whenever your broker has a difficult time filling your order, which can result from any number of factors, including fast market conditions, poor availability of stock, and the absence of other buyers and sellers. The result is always the same: The price you expect differs from the price you actually receive. Although you can mitigate this problem to a degree by using limit orders, you still risk the stock trading through your limit price, preventing your order from being filled at all.

>> **Gap risk:** This risk comes into play whenever a break in trading occurs. Sometimes a stock opens at a price significantly higher or lower than its previous close. When this happens, the stock can trade right through your target exit price or your stop. For example, a stock may close at $25 a share today and open tomorrow morning at $20. If you've entered a stop order to exit you out of the trade at a price of $24, the order is likely to be filled at the $20 opening price or lower, clearing your stop entirely. Price gaps created in this way occur most often at the open. Although more rare, a gap also can occur during the trading day, perhaps if surprising news is reported or after trading has been temporarily halted.

Chapter **13**

Combining Fundamental and Technical Analyses for Optimum Strategy

K nowing the current state of the economy can help you improve your trading results. However, knowing the current state of the market is crucial because you obviously want to buy stocks in a bull market and sell them, or short them, in a bear market. Besides the obvious, you also want a strategy for trading stocks during market transitions and consolidation phases.

As a result, you need a method for identifying and categorizing the various phases of bull and bear markets. We recommend using the six phases described in the list that follows. Doing so enables you to adjust your trading strategies for each phase of the market, regardless of whether you're trading stocks, exchange-traded funds (ETFs), bonds, futures, or options. The six phases of the market are

» **Bullish transition:** A transition from a bear market to a bull market

» **Bull market:** A persistent rising trend in the market

» **Bullish pullback:** A bull market in the midst of a pullback

» **Bearish transition:** A transition from a bull market to a bear market

>> **Bear market:** A persistent downtrend in the market

>> **Bearish pullback:** A bear market in the midst of a consolidation

This chapter shows you how to identify these market phases using the combined techniques of fundamental and technical analyses that we describe throughout this book. Although no single detail or event can enable you to out-and-out declare a bull market or bear market, we address many small details that, when taken together, enable you to make informed trading decisions in a variety of market conditions. Likewise, distinguishing a transition phase from a pullback phase can be difficult. This chapter helps you methodically analyze the economy, the market, the leading and lagging sectors, and individual stocks so you can more accurately and consistently identify the particular phase a market is in. Furthermore, this chapter describes unified trading strategies that are built around these market phases.

Seeing the Big Picture

Identifying the current economic climate is the first step toward identifying the current phase of the markets. Only a tiny fraction of available economic data is required to develop a snapshot of the economy, which you can then factor into your analysis of the current state of the markets. You need to know the following conditions to be able to determine and evaluate the cycle that the economy currently is in:

>> **Where interest rates are headed:** Are they rising, falling, or remaining flat?

>> **What officials of the Federal Reserve Board (the Fed) are doing now:** What is the Fed likely to do in the future?

>> **How business is performing, in general:** Is industrial production rising or falling?

>> **Which sectors are leading and which are lagging:** Are more aggressive, economically sensitive stocks appreciating or declining in value, or are traders currently favoring defensive stocks?

REMEMBER

This information is crucial for determining the cycle in which the economy is currently functioning. (For more about economic cycles, see Chapter 5.) Fortunately, the economic picture doesn't change quickly, so taking the temperature of the economy can be a weekly or monthly exercise. Ultimately, maintaining an ongoing, up-to-date knowledge of the cycles through which the economy is passing helps you identify current phases of the markets, which, in turn, can help you make better trading decisions.

Knowing when the Fed is your friend

Current interest rates and interest-rate trends help determine the current position of the economy within the business cycle. Low interest rates are associated with economic troughs, and high rates with economic peaks. In a nutshell, the Fed lowers rates to stimulate economic activity and raises rates to slow it. But the time lag between the Fed's activity and any reaction by the economy is often a long one, making the Fed's monetary policy an imprecise indicator. Nevertheless, you can use interest rates to get a rough idea about the current economic landscape.

TIP

Interest-rate reductions that the Fed approves are generally good news for the stock market. And when the Fed tightens its monetary policy by raising interest rates, stocks normally react poorly. Either way, stock markets may not react immediately, and unfortunately, many months can pass before either the stock market or the economy responds in either direction to the Fed's action. Although the old stock market saying "three steps and a stumble" doesn't always hold true, markets do often head lower after the Fed raises rates for the third time.

In short, falling interest rates typically lead to a rising economy and to a market that's changing from a bear market to a bull market — in other words, a bullish transition. Ultimately, a bullish transition leads to a new bull market. Conversely, however, rising interest rates sooner or later lead to a market that's changing from a bull market to a bear market — a bearish transition, and ultimately a bear market. The problem: No consistent timetable exists that enables you to anticipate when these changes will occur. You should therefore use interest-rate changes only as a hint that a transition may be coming and wait for an additional confirmation before you act on a trading strategy.

TIP

You can monitor activities of the Federal Reserve Open Market by checking its calendar, statements, and minutes at `www.federalreserve.gov/monetarypolicy/fomccalendars.htm`.

Keeping an eye on industrial production

In addition to interest rates, industrial production is another indicator that provides insight into the health of the economy. New economic growth is suggested when industrial production statistics start inching higher, a sign that usually indicates the market is either entering a bullish transition or will do so soon. Similarly, robust growth numbers often accompany a bull market phase. Conversely, leveling off or falling industrial production data shows that a bearish transition can be expected. And finally, a bear market phase often accompanies falling production data.

TIP

You can monitor industrial production by keeping track of the Federal Reserve's monthly report "Industrial Production and Capacity Utilization" at `www.federalreserve.gov/releases/g17/current`.

Watching sector rotation

Monitoring leading and lagging economic sectors (see Chapter 5) provides direct insight into the current state of the stock market. Some "aggressive" industries tend to perform well at the beginning of an economic expansion, while other "defensive" industries tend to perform relatively well as the economy cools. Traders often try to anticipate changes in the economy by watching specific sectors that they know have tendencies to rise or fall in specific patterns that coincide with one economic or market cycle. These patterned tendencies are called *sector rotation*. Although you won't see picture-perfect sector rotation with every cycle, you'll see enough similarities from cycle to cycle to enable you to gain additional insight into the current phase of the economy and the stock market.

Sectors that perform well during specific economic cycles and market phases are described in the following sections. You can take advantage of sector rotation in your trading by using sector ETFs. We discuss these strategies in Chapter 14.

Anticipating a new bull market

Economic conditions that foster a new bull market include low interest rates and indications that industrial production is beginning to rise. Traders who monitor these economic conditions often respond to them by buying the stocks of cyclical and technology-based companies. Bullish transition phases usually begin in this manner.

TIP

The stocks of companies whose business is sensitive to the economic cycle have traditionally been called *cyclical stocks*. Within the past few decades, technology-based companies have joined these so-called cyclical companies as bellwether economic indicators. In short, think of it this way: In a strong economy, when consumers have more disposable income, they're more likely to spend on superfluous goods such as clothes, cars, a new TV, or a night at a fancy hotel. When the economy contracts, however, and those same consumers have less cash on hand, they're more likely to spend only on the basic essentials, such as toothpaste, food, and their electricity bills.

The stocks of cyclical and technology-based companies perform best when interest rates are low. Increased sales of their products drive industrial production numbers higher. These companies usually lead the market and often rally before an economic trough, or recession, completely bottoms out. Unfortunately, traders jump the gun as often as they get it right, so whenever you see cyclical and tech stocks begin to rally, it pays to be at least slightly skeptical. Rather than immediately commit to the conclusion that a sector rally means a bull market is just around the corner, you need to instead consider that it potentially indicates only a bullish transition.

Industries known for making up cyclical sectors include

>> Automobile and automotive component manufacturers

>> Consumer durable manufacturers that produce products such as appliances and consumer electronics

>> Retailers, such as department stores, big-box discounters, and specialty retailers (excluding food, beverage, pharmaceutical, and other nondurable retailers)

>> Media companies, such as movie studios, radio and television companies, and book publishers

>> Hotels, restaurants, and entertainment and other leisure companies

Technology-sector industries include

>> Semiconductor (computer chip) manufacturers and manufacturers of equipment to produce semiconductors

>> Computer and computer peripheral device manufacturers

>> Software and service companies

>> Telecommunication and Internet service companies

>> Information technology service companies

Watching the economy rebound

Strength in the industrial sectors is a condition that usually indicates the markets may be entering a bull market phase. As the economy begins showing signs of growth, you often see a rally in industrial sectors. Large industrial companies often need to borrow money to increase production, a factor that makes them sensitive to interest-rate changes. These companies tend to perform best in a low-interest-rate environment. Rising industrial production that drives industrial-sector earnings and stock prices higher is no coincidence.

Companies in the industrial sectors include

>> Building products manufacturers

>> Construction and engineering firms

>> Aerospace and defense companies

>> Electrical equipment manufacturers

>> Airlines and air freight, transportation, and infrastructure companies

>> Major manufacturing conglomerates (which are widely diversified companies such as GE, United Technologies, and Honeywell)

Approaching a market top

When the economy is firing on all cylinders, industrial production is robust, and interest rates are beginning to rise. However, the stock market is trying to anticipate what happens next, and it's probably nearing its peak. Basic material stocks, energy stocks, and consumer-staples stocks tend to do well under these conditions. When you begin seeing strength in the consumer-staples sector, you need to begin searching for confirmation of a bearish transitional phase.

Companies in the basic industry and materials sectors include

>> Metals and mining companies

>> Chemical companies

>> Construction material companies

>> Forest-product companies, including paper, packaging, and container companies

The energy sectors include

>> Oil and natural gas exploration and drilling services

>> Coal and coal processing

>> Pipelines

Companies in the consumer-staples sectors include

>> Food and beverage companies

>> Household and personal-care product companies

>> Tobacco companies

>> Retailers, specifically food, beverage, drug, and other nondurable goods retailers

Weathering a bear market

Healthcare and other service-sector stocks often perform better than the average stock as the economy peaks and as bullish market tendencies fade to bearish outlooks. The stocks of utility and financial companies also tend to perform better than average during bear markets because they're considered safe havens from the accompanying tide of falling interest rates and flattening industrial production. As these stocks begin showing higher relative strength, you need to move your indicator from bearish transition to a bear market phase.

Consumer-service sectors include

>> Healthcare equipment and supplies companies

>> Healthcare providers

>> Pharmaceutical and biotechnology companies

The utility sector includes

>> Electric power generation and distribution companies

>> Natural gas distribution companies

>> Water utilities companies

Companies in the financial sectors include

>> Diversified financial-service companies, including banks and brokerage firms

>> Commercial banks

>> Insurance companies

TIP

Taking a longer-term view as you monitor the markets for sector rotation is a good idea. By that we mean you're not interested in the day-by-day ups and downs, but rather you're trying to evaluate sector performance during periods of many weeks and even months. Remembering that bull markets tend to lift prices for all stocks is also important. When you monitor sector performance, try to find the sectors that are outperforming others. In bear markets, stocks that hold their values, for example, outperform all stocks that have falling prices.

Finding the dominant trend

You need to own stocks during bull markets and sell them, or short them (see Chapter 15), during bear markets. In other words, you want to trade with the *dominant trend*, not against it. The stock market tends to lead the economy, so using the market's performance as your primary reference to find the dominant trend makes sense. Combining your analysis of the dominant market trend with the background knowledge you gained from analyzing interest rates, industrial production data, and sector rotation helps you refine the way you categorize the current phase of the market. That kind of refinement means your trading performance will improve when you can make trades with the dominant trend or market phase on your side.

Looking at weekly index charts

You need only a handful of tools to determine the dominant trend or phase of the market. We use two, the weekly charts of broad market indexes and the bullish percent index, which is discussed in the next section. Significant changes in the markets develop more slowly than in individual stocks and thus appear more clearly on weekly charts than on daily charts. Weekly charts help filter out financial noise, allowing you to focus less on the insignificant day-to-day price moves and more on the bigger picture.

We typically monitor charts of the major indexes such as the S&P 500, Dow Jones Industrial Average, and the NASDAQ Composite Index. Doing so makes visually identifying bull markets and bear markets easy. They appear as trends, exactly like the ones shown on the stock charts in Chapter 10. A bull market appears as a series of higher highs and higher lows on weekly index charts. A bear market appears as a series of lower highs and lower lows. These are the dominant trends.

Pullback patterns, such as the flag, pennant, and other retracement patterns discussed in Chapter 10, correspond to the bullish pullback and bearish pullback conditions. And bullish transition and bearish transition phases may signal a trend reversal in much the same way that reversal patterns and trading ranges often lead to a change in direction.

Figure 13-1 shows the phases of a bull market using a weekly chart of the S&P 500 Index. Figure 13-2 shows the phases of a bear market using an earlier weekly chart of the S&P 500 Index from the last major bear market period between 2007 and 2009.

Trend identification tools that we discuss in Chapters 9, 10, and 11 all apply to these weekly charts. For example, you can easily spot the higher highs and higher lows in Figure 13-1 that occurred after the double bottom in February 2016. These higher highs and higher lows correspond to a bull market. You also can easily see the lower highs and lower lows in Figure 13-2; they accompanied the long-running bear market during what we now refer to as the Great Recession.

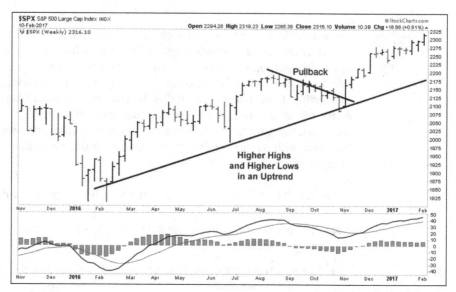

FIGURE 13-1:
Weekly chart of
the S&P 500
Index reflects a
bull market.

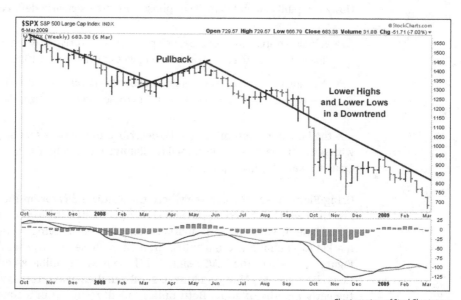

FIGURE 13-2:
Weekly chart of
the S&P 500
Index reflects a
bear market.

You also need to be able to identify the moving average convergence divergence (MACD) crossover points and divergent patterns on these charts. We describe MACD in detail in Chapter 11. MACD signals provide you with additional information to augment the way you categorize current phases of the market.

TIP

You can easily create these index charts at StockCharts.com. Click the tab for Free Charts at the top of any web page, and then look for the SharpCharts box in the upper-left portion of the page. In the box labeled Create a SharpChart, enter the symbol for the NASDAQ Composite ($COMPQ) or any other index you're interested in charting, then click Go. You'll then be directed to a SharpChart of your symbol. At the top of the chart, set the Period to weekly. Then, using the interface below the chart, set the Chart Attributes as follows: HLC Bars, no overlays, and MACD Indicator with parameters 12, 26, 9. Then click Update to update the chart with your criteria.

Using MACD to indicate bull and bear markets is straightforward:

>> A bull market is indicated when the MACD line is greater than the zero line and greater than the signal line.

>> A bear market is indicated when the MACD line is less than the zero line and less than the signal line.

However, pullback and transition phases are not as clearly defined:

>> A bullish transition — or a bearish pullback — is indicated when the MACD line is less than the zero line and it crosses above the signal line.

>> A bearish transition — or a bullish pullback — is indicated when the MACD line is greater than the zero line and it crosses below the signal line.

Use the bullish percent index (BPI), described in the next section, in conjunction with pattern analysis, as described in Chapter 10, to help distinguish between the transition and pullback phases.

Using Figure 13-2, you can see where the MACD indicator on the weekly chart is less than zero but crosses above its signal line. When the MACD crossed above its signal line, it suggested the market may have been trying to turn from a bear market to a bull market in a bullish transition phase. You can see two instances in Figure 13-2 where the MACD signaled these bearish pullbacks or bullish transitions, first in April, May, and June of 2008 and then again from late December into the early months of 2009. Both rallies failed, resulting in a continuation of the bear market.

Using the bullish percent index

You can use the *bullish percent index* (BPI) to fine-tune and confirm trading signals you see on the weekly index charts. The BPI is a powerful indicator that shows the percentage of stocks that have generated buy signals compared with the total number of stocks in a given index. In short, it provides a simple yet effective way to analyze market participation, which can in turn be used to judge the strength of the market's trend. In a strong bull market, for example, a large percentage of stocks participate in the upward rally. The idea here is simple: If every stock in the market is rising, the strength of that trend is more powerful than if only 55 percent of stocks are rising. In a bear market, the opposite is true. The greater the percentage of stocks declining — participating in the downtrend — the weaker the market.

This indicator originally was used to track all the stocks on the NYSE, but it also can be applied to any broad market index, including the S&P 500, the NASDAQ Composite, or even the more narrowly defined NASDAQ 100 and sector indexes. The BPI does, however, provide fewer and better signals when evaluating larger groups of stocks.

TIP

The BPI is based on Point and Figure charts — one of the oldest and simplest stock charting techniques — and helps you evaluate the strength of the market as a whole. Calculating the BPI is a bit daunting, but fortunately, it's published online. For example, you can find BPIs at StockCharts.com, where the current states of this indicator for the major indexes and several sector indexes are displayed and interpreted. You can find more information about creating BPI charts online in the ChartSchool section of StockCharts.com. Visit `http://stockcharts.com/school/doku.php?id=chart_school:technical_indicators:bullish_percent_inde`.

As an indicator, BPI works a bit like an oscillator (see Chapter 11). It displays values ranging from 0 to 100 percent to identify oversold and overbought market conditions. For example, when fewer than 30 percent of all stocks are on a buy signal, the BPI indicates that the market is becoming oversold and is more likely to experience a turnaround. When more than 70 percent of all stocks signal a buy, the BPI shows the market is becoming overbought and is more likely to experience a downturn.

However, like individual stocks, broad market indexes can remain overbought or oversold for extended periods of time, so by themselves, BPI readings below 30 percent or above 70 percent don't necessarily represent immediate buy or sell signals, respectively. The BPI can often show readings well above 70 percent and well below 30 percent for extended periods of time. As with most other financial analysis tools, it is the pairing of the BPI with other technical indicators, market statistics, and fundamental data that makes it a powerful addition to your investing strategy.

Changes in BPI levels are triggered by reversal patterns. A 6 percent change in the stocks of a given index is required to trigger any changes (up or down) in the BPI. These reversal patterns are interpreted to describe the state of the market using six unique conditions that roughly correspond with the six phases of the market described in the introduction to this chapter. Here are the six states of the BPI:

>> **Bull alert:** Corresponds with the bullish transition phase. It's triggered when the BPI is less than 30 percent and reverses direction when 6 percent (or more) of all stocks change to buy signals.

>> **Bull confirmed:** Corresponds with the bull market phase. When the BPI indicator forms a higher high, a bull market is confirmed.

>> **Bull correction:** Corresponds with the bullish pullback phase. This condition occurs only after the BPI confirms a bull market, and a minimum of 6 percent of all stocks change from buy to sell signals. If the BPI is greater than 70 percent, this change may lead to a bear alert.

>> **Bear alert:** Corresponds with the bearish transition phase. It's triggered when the BPI is greater than 70 percent and reverses direction after 6 percent of all stocks change to sell signals.

>> **Bear confirmed:** Corresponds with the bear market phase. When the BPI indicator forms a lower low, a bear market is confirmed.

>> **Bear correction:** Corresponds with the bearish pullback phase. This condition occurs only after the BPI confirms a bear market and at least 6 percent of all stocks change from sell to buy signals. If the BPI is less than 30 percent, this change may lead to a bull alert.

REMEMBER

Although the BPI is not a leading indicator, it gives you a good feel for the market's overall health. When used with broad-based indexes, the BPI doesn't speak often. After all, more than 2,800 stocks are traded on the NYSE. For the BPI to register a reversal, at least 6 percent (or approximately 168) of those stocks must change from a buy signal to a sell signal (or vice versa). Technically, the distinction is a bit more subtle than that. A total of 168 more stocks must change to sell signals than are changing to buy signals for the index to change from bull confirmed to bull correction conditions.

The BPI for smaller stock indexes generates considerably more signals. A 6 percent change on the NASDAQ 100 requires only a balance of six stocks to change from buy to sell signals. Although the BPI provides information about the condition of these smaller indexes, you must use the signals with care. We believe this indicator is best used with broader-based indexes such as the S&P 500, the NASDAQ Composite, and the NYSE.

Selecting Your Trading Stock

After you've identified the dominant trend, the leading and lagging sectors, and the current economic climate, it's time to select the most promising stocks to trade. Beyond general market conditions, two factors drive a stock's price higher or lower:

>> The fundamental condition of the company's business

>> The technical condition of the company's stock

We cover these topics in great detail in Parts 2 and 3 of this book, so in this section, we highlight only a few important factors for you to consider when selecting a stock to trade. On the fundamental side, earnings matter more than any other fundamental data. Traders pay particular attention to the rate of earnings growth as characterized by the earnings per share (EPS) growth rate. In general, the bigger the EPS growth rate, the better the stock price, and vice versa.

WARNING

Stocks without earnings often make very dangerous trading candidates for long-side trades. Although some special situations may merit your consideration, stocks without earnings carry a special risk. Any hint of unfavorable press sends the stock's price crashing. Besides, the downside risk is simply too great for our taste.

You also need to consider the company's size when selecting a trading candidate. Although small companies can and sometimes do return outsized trading profits, they also present problems for traders. Stocks of small companies usually are more lightly traded, which leads to liquidity concerns that make them difficult to buy and even more difficult to sell. You can afford to be patient when entering a trade but not when exiting a position, especially when the stock hits your stop-loss price. Lightly traded stocks (or ETFs) make exiting a position difficult because the price is likely to fall quickly and dramatically when many traders are trying to exit simultaneously. You're bound to lose more of your precious trading capital (when selling) or spend more of it (when buying) than you intended.

On the technical side, you want to trade the strongest stocks in the strongest sectors. You want to enter positions in these high relative-strength stocks as they break out of trading ranges or reversal patterns. And you want to hold them as long as they remain relatively strong compared with other stocks.

Trading Strategies

Categorizing the phases of the market enables you to adjust your trading strategies based on current market conditions. The idea: Trade aggressively when you're confident in your market assessment, but protect your capital when you're uncertain. In this section, we present strategies for dealing with various market phases.

Trading the bullish transition

When you first detect that the market may be entering a bullish transition phase, you must use extreme caution when trading. At this phase of the market, your primary goal is to preserve your capital. Your secondary goal is to catch the bull market, should it truly materialize.

TIP

You may take new positions during a bullish transition, but the situation isn't urgent, so you should be selective. You need to take small, partial positions rather than full positions by

>> Identifying the strongest stocks in the strongest sectors

>> Looking for trading-range breakouts and other reversal signals

We give an example in the later section "A hypothetical trading example."

Keep your stops very tight and honor them rigorously. Consider an ETF if you have difficulty finding individual stocks that meet your fundamental and technical criteria. Trading the sectors or, more narrowly, the smaller industry groups of the market using ETFs is a perfectly acceptable option at this point.

Trading in a bull market

In a bull market, while capital preservation remains paramount, your primary goal is to become fully invested. Focus on establishing long positions in your trading. You shouldn't take on new short positions in this phase. Buy breakouts and take full positions because your goal is to be 100 percent (fully) invested. If you have a margin account for leverage, now is the time to use it. (The mechanics of using margin when trading are discussed in Chapter 15.) You may loosen your stops a bit because doing so allows for more ebb and flow of higher highs and higher lows.

TIP

The most reliable bull market signals occur during the early part of a bull market — after a bullish transition rather than following a bullish pullback. You may want to adjust your strategy to be a bit less aggressive following later-stage bull market signals. For example, you may want to tighten your stops a bit or even take profits altogether, especially when you're using margin for leverage.

Trading the bullish pullback

A bullish pullback is a consolidation phase within a bull market. Here, your trading strategy needs to continue looking for high-quality stocks that are breaking out of new or subsequent trading-range bases. When you decide the market has entered a bullish pullback phase, you may want to tighten your stops and seriously consider hedging your positions by using options, especially if you're using margin for leverage. Hedging is like buying insurance. In this case, you can purchase put options to protect most of your trading capital in case the market moves dramatically against you. The cost of hedging depends on the amount of protection you buy.

WARNING

A bullish pullback is still a bull market, so you can continue taking full positions on breakouts, but you need to be selective. Make sure that your new *and* existing positions are the best-performing stocks in the best-performing sectors. You need to become a bit more cautious when the particular bullish pullback isn't the first to occur during the current bull market. Bullish pullbacks can be a fantastic opportunity to enter new positions while the market cools off, but they can also quickly turn into bearish transitions. Stay vigilant and be quick to pull the trigger should the market turn against you.

Trading the bearish transition

A bearish transition indicates the market may be transitioning from a bull market to a bear market. You react to a bearish transition by

>> Tightening stops on all your open positions

>> Monitoring your positions closely

>> Honoring your stops rigorously

>> Exiting any long position at the first sign of trouble

You also need to consider hedging long positions by using options. If you're using margin for leverage, exiting deteriorating positions quickly is even more important.

If you're so inclined, you can begin looking for short-sale candidates. However, be careful and only nibble at these trades. If you plan to short, take small positions and keep your stops very tight. We discuss the mechanics of selling short in Chapter 15.

Trading in a bear market

When you're certain a bear market has begun, don't enter new long positions. Your open positions are likely to hit their stops and be closed, but for the ones that remain, tighten your stops and exit any existing long positions at the first sign of trouble. Hedge any remaining long positions with put options.

If you're inclined to short stocks, a confirmed bear market is the time to do it. The mechanics of shorting stocks are discussed in Chapter 15. You may want to take full-sized short positions and become fully invested on the short side. (See the upcoming section "A hypothetical trading example" for an example of position sizing.) *Note:* A margin account is required for selling short. We rarely use margin for leverage when trading short, but if you're going to do it, now is the time. Alternatively, you can use inverse ETFs (which use derivatives to profit from declining values of the underlying securities) to trade the short side of the market.

Trading the bearish pullback

A bearish pullback is a consolidation phase within a market that nevertheless remains a bear market. As such, a bearish pullback isn't a good opportunity for taking new long positions. You need to tighten stops on existing short positions and consider hedging these positions using call options, especially when you're using margin for leverage. A bearish pullback is an opportunity to take short-side profits and enter additional short positions when you see new or subsequent downside breakout patterns (see Chapter 9). Confirm that new and existing short positions are the worst-performing stocks in the worst-performing sectors.

A hypothetical trading example

Here's a hypothetical scenario. The market is trying to begin a new bull market by entering a bullish transition phase. At this time, your $100,000 example portfolio is sitting 100 percent in cash. Your goal: Establish ten positions by the height of the bull market, which means that you plan to allocate an average of $10,000 of your initial capital for each position.

When you begin seeing signs of a bullish transition, you're likely to be champing at the bit to start taking positions, even though you haven't yet found stocks that fit your trading criteria. Still, you'd like to participate in the new bull market, and you're willing to risk a small loss if the bull market doesn't materialize.

In this case, you may want to start by taking a small position, perhaps a half-sized $5,000 position, using exchange-traded funds (ETFs) for the broad market indexes and perhaps for a sector fund or two as they break out. For example, you can take a $5,000 half-sized position in the NASDAQ ETF (QQQ), with a similar commitment to the S&P 500 ETF (SPY), and similarly sized positions in the cyclical and technology sector ETFs (XLY and XLK, respectively). In all, you'd have positions totaling $20,000, which is 20 percent of your capital, committed to the market. That kind of commitment is appropriate for a relatively risky bullish transition phase.

As stocks break out of their trading-range patterns, you may add positions, but you need to continue taking small positions until you're certain the market has changed to a bull market. You also need to set an upper limit to the amount of capital that you're willing to commit during a bullish transition phase, perhaps no more than 40 percent or 50 percent of your total trading capital.

If market conditions turn to a bull market, you then can start taking full positions and become fully invested. You may also want to reallocate your positions from the ETFs into leading stocks showing high relative strength. If you plan to use margin as leverage, a bull market is the time to do it. In this case, you could leverage your $100,000 of trading capital into a portfolio of stocks and ETFs worth up to $200,000 or more as your portfolio grows (see Chapter 15 for more about trading on margin). You can either add to existing positions or add new positions in leading stocks as they break out of trading-range patterns. Whatever you decide, keep the number of positions small.

When the market consolidates into a bullish pullback phase, you need to tighten your stops and consider hedging your positions. Doing so enables you to use your stops to get out of underperforming stocks. If you're stopped out of a position, forget about it. If it's a profitable trade, pay your taxes and be pleased with your profits. If you're leveraged, you want to get out of your margined positions quickly whenever they move against you so you don't give up your profits.

During a bullish pullback, you first must decide whether to hedge the portfolio and then decide whether you want to hedge each individual position or the portfolio as a whole. In general, you're probably concerned more about a marketwide downdraft than you are about a major stumble in any single position. If that's the case, then hedging the whole portfolio with index options makes sense. However, the larger the number of stocks in your portfolio, the more sense it makes to hedge your individual positions.

As a bullish pullback reverts back to a bull market, reallocate your capital into the new leaders as they break out. After each bullish pullback, becoming a bit more conservative is prudent. For example, you may tighten your stops, use less leverage, or continue providing a hedge against a significant downdraft.

When the bull market transitions to a bear market, you need to exit your long positions when your stops are hit. You may continue to hold your positions as long as they're not losing money, but don't let your bull market profits evaporate. If you want to sell short, the bear market is the time to do so.

REMEMBER

Making profitable trades is significantly easier if you buy during bull markets and sell or sell short during bear markets. Again, don't try to fight the dominant trend. Of course, subtleties may exist. You may, for example, take long positions in defensive stocks, such as utilities and financial companies, during bear markets. Some traders find it profitable to hold a two-sided portfolio, where the best-performing stocks are purchased and poorly performing stocks are simultaneously shorted, even during a raging bull market, but our advice is to keep it simple. Become proficient by trading with the dominant trend before trying to fine-tune your strategy.

Chapter **14**

Minimizing Trading Risks Using Exchange-Traded Funds

F inding just the right stocks to trade as you build your sector-based portfolio can be time-consuming and risky. You may pick the right sectors but then choose a stock that ends up underperforming in that group, negating the accuracy of your sector analysis. However, you can minimize the risks of individual stock picking by using exchange-traded funds (ETFs) to implement your sector rotation strategy.

In this chapter, we review the basics of ETFs, explore the different family types, and discuss some of the limitations of ETFs. Then we show you how to implement a sector rotation strategy and introduce you to alternatives to stock ETFs.

What Is an ETF?

Exchange-traded funds, or ETFs, are built with a basket of stocks that track a particular index, whether it's a large, traditional index such as the S&P 500 or a smaller, more specific group such as biotechnology stocks within the healthcare sector. When you buy an ETF, you buy an index fund that tries to match the performance of that index. Most ETFs are passive trading tools that try to match rather than beat an index.

In the following sections, we outline the benefits and drawbacks of ETFs so you know what you have to pay attention to if you invest in them.

Examining the advantages

You may wonder why using an ETF is a good thing for sector rotation trading. The key advantage is that these funds allow you to actively manage your portfolio based on your analysis of the current sector rotation environment, but without having to take on extra risk from individual stock picks. Plus, there's no need to worry about an active mutual fund manager making trades that negate the sector rotation analysis because ETFs are passively managed. When you buy a sector ETF, you know exactly what you're getting.

ETFs offer you a number of advantages:

>> **Minimal managerial risk:** The fund manager makes only minor periodic adjustments to keep the fund in line with its index, which mitigates the element of managerial risk. You're harnessing the power of the index you choose, making it easier to control exactly where your money is invested.

>> **Fewer management fees:** Because trading is minimal, the management costs of ETFs are low, so less of your money goes toward fees.

>> **Diversification:** By spreading your investment across a wider number of stocks, ETFs keep your portfolio more diversified. They limit your overexposure to just one or two stocks in a sector that you need to research and then closely monitor.

>> **Trading flexibility:** They're traded just like stocks. You can buy and sell ETFs throughout the trading day. Rapid trading triggers no penalties. You can use market orders, limit orders, stop orders, and stop-limit orders. And, unlike a traditional mutual fund, you can short shares of an ETF. They can also be bought on margin. (Read Chapter 15 for the mechanics of selling short.)

>> **High volumes:** They're often traded at much higher volumes than many individual stocks, which provides greater liquidity. This makes it easy to buy and sell exactly when you want.

REMEMBER

The ETF market has grown substantially in recent years, making it easy to find an ETF to match nearly any group you're interested in. You can find ETFs for any sector you want. You can also find ETFs that match the market cap you want, such as small-, mid-, large-, and mega-cap companies. You can use them to trade commodities or currencies. Although you may not have difficulty finding an ETF that tracks exactly what you want, you do need to understand how that ETF builds its portfolios (check out the later section "Does Family Matter?" for more on this topic).

Avoiding the flaws

WARNING

ETFs can be a great way to minimize risk while effectively implementing a sector rotation trading strategy, but they do have some faults that shouldn't be ignored:

>> **Fees:** Every ETF charges fees. Always be sure you understand the fees and carefully compare the options you're considering.

>> **Volatility:** ETFs can be volatile, particularly as you start trading funds with more specific benchmarks such as industry group ETFs that track gambling stocks or apparel retailers. The narrower the focus of the fund, the more volatility it will bring. For example, an ETF that tracks a broad market index will be less volatile than an ETF that tracks a particular sector or industry group. If you pick an oil and gas ETF, it can fall just as hard as any oil or gas stock when the entire industry takes a sharp downturn.

>> **Liquidity:** While many ETFs offer high volume and high liquidity, the dramatic expansion of the ETF market in recent years has also resulted in a large number of newer, more thinly traded funds with lower liquidity. Watch the trading volume for any ETF you're considering for your portfolio. If the trading volume is small, you may have a hard time finding a buyer when you want to get out. One sure sign of low liquidity is a larger spread between the bid and ask prices than those of other funds you're considering.

>> **Capital gains:** Some ETFs pay capital gains. That means you have to pay taxes on the capital gains you receive. If this is a problem for you, you're better off using only ETFs that reinvest their capital gains.

REMEMBER

You're using ETFs to minimize trading costs and reduce risk. Be sure you don't add volatility or liquidity problems when you pick your ETFs. Also, you want to minimize your tax hit, so avoid those that pay out capital gains.

Does Family Matter?

Major advisor groups create the ETFs. The ETFs from the same advisor are called a *family*. Each family is developed based on a set of sector rules established by the advisor for the family. Families can be developed in three ways: market-weighted, equal-weighted, or fundamentally weighted. In the following sections, we take a look at how each of the weighting options can impact the ETFs you choose.

Market-weighted ETFs

Market-weighted ETFs are based on market capitalization and their underlying sectors. This type of weighting gives you a good exposure to the overall U.S. economy and the sectors in it. They're biased toward large-cap stocks and don't provide much exposure to small-cap stocks (which tend to be more volatile). Because many sectors have only a few companies that are large- or mega-cap stocks, these types of ETFs can be concentrated in only a few companies. ETFs are available for each of the eleven major market sectors — consumer discretionary, consumer staples, energy, financials, healthcare, industrials, information technology, materials, real estate, telecommunication services, and utilities — as well as the smaller industry groups within those sectors.

REMEMBER

As you're building your portfolio, you should research the indexes each ETF family uses and be sure that the choice of index matches your trading goals. Generally we recommend picking one family of ETFs and sticking with that family to avoid unwanted duplication. Also, this practice will ensure that you're building a portfolio with the sectors you intend to use.

Two of the largest families managing market-weighted ETFs are iShares (managed by BlackRock) and State Street Global Advisors. For example, iShares Dow Jones sector ETFs use the Dow Jones U.S. index. This index is a market-capitalization index designed to represent 95 percent of the U.S. equity market. The managers of these ETFs use the Industrial Classification Benchmark (ICB) system to determine the compositions of each sector and subsector. The ICB classifications were jointly developed by Dow Jones and the British indexer FTSE. (FTSE also develops indexes for many country-based stock exchanges, such as the Stock Exchange of Thailand and the Cyprus Stock Exchange.) The ICB has 10 industries, 18 super sectors, 39 sectors, and 104 subsectors.

State Street Sector SPDRs, which stands for Standard & Poor's depository receipts, use the S&P 500 as the underlying index, which includes the 500 leading companies in the United States. They use a different classification system, the Global Industry Classification Standard (GICS), to determine the composition of each sector. This standard was developed jointly by Morgan Stanley Capital International (MSCI) and Standard & Poor's (S&P). The GICS has 11 sectors, 24 industry groups, 68 industries, and 157 subindustries.

The GICS takes a market-orientation approach. For example, it groups consumers into two sectors, consumer discretionary and consumer staples, which both contain goods and services. This differs from ICB, which groups consumer companies by consumer goods and consumer services.

When developing a sector strategy, the market orientation can be a significant difference. Consumer staples are considered noncyclical. Consumers have to buy these products regardless of what's happening in the economy. Consumer discretionary is more impacted by cycles. As the economy expands and the average consumer has more disposable income, they're more likely to buy discretionary items such as new clothes or a second car, for example. The consumer discretionary sector includes industries like automobile manufacturers, travel companies, and restaurants. In a grouping by consumer goods and consumer services, however, you get a mix of noncyclical and cyclical stocks.

REMEMBER

Understanding the sector composition is crucial for implementing a profitable sector strategy. Always be sure to research the underlying indexes as you choose ETFs for your portfolio.

Equal-weighted ETFs

Equal-weighted ETFs give all stocks a similar weighting no matter what size the stock. This weighting assumes that all stocks have the same impact on the index. This type of ETF outperforms a market-weighted ETF when small-cap stocks are outperforming large-cap stocks. Each of this type of sector ETF is rebalanced quarterly to maintain an approximately equal weighting among the stocks in the underlying index.

Because the number of small-cap companies far surpasses the number of large- or mega-cap companies, this type of ETF needs to do a lot more trading to remain in balance than one with just a few large companies. So be sure to compare your fees with the market-weighted sector ETF options. Ask yourself: Is paying more worth it to get the exposure to small-cap stocks? Obviously, when small caps are outperforming large caps, the answer is probably yes.

Two examples of this type of ETF are the Rydex S&P 500 Equal Weight Sector ETFs and the Guggenheim S&P 500 ETFs, which are both based on the S&P 500 index and GICS standard.

WARNING

If you choose to work with equal-weighted ETFs, your portfolio will be biased toward small stocks and may not be representative of the overall economy. Because large-cap stocks are more representative of the economy, this type of ETF may not be the best choice for a sector rotation strategy.

Fundamentally weighted ETFs

Fundamentally weighted ETFs are relatively new to the ETF scene. They're based on the underlying fundamentals, such as sales, cash flow, book value, and dividends. Companies that are the largest by whatever fundamentals chosen by the ETF manager have the largest weight in the index.

Some players in this market are nine PowerShares FTSE RAFI sector ETFs. The ICB is used to determine the composition of each sector. Information technology and telecommunications have been combined into one sector for these ETFs.

REMEMBER

A fundamentally weighted index may be more closely aligned with the overall economy than a market-weighted one because the weights of the individual companies are based on the size of the company, not just the market cap.

Sector Rotation Strategies

In Chapter 5, we introduce you to sector rotation strategies. ETFs make implementing these strategies easier by minimizing the time you need to spend on individual stock research. You can use that time instead to follow sectors. After you've researched and selected the family of ETFs you want to use, you can spend most of your time researching what analysts are saying about where the economy is going. You then can rebalance your portfolio to follow economic trends. In this section, we review those trends and see which sectors do best in which trends.

REMEMBER

When using a sector rotation strategy, you're looking for the sector that has reached a low and is now beginning to show signs of strength. You want to catch the sector that is most likely to recover and rotate in as it begins to strengthen. This is the classic buy low and sell high strategy.

Early recovery

When consumer expectations and industrial production begin to rise and interest rates are bottoming out, you know you're entering the early stages of recovery. In the early stages of recovery, materials sectors, such as XLB (Materials Select Sector SPDR Fund), and energy sectors, such as XLE (Energy Select Sector SPDR Fund) or IXC (iShares Global Energy ETF), tend to take the lead. Finding the right ETFs in these sectors is a good way to overweight your portfolio as the economy moves into recovery.

Full recovery

After the economy fully recovers, you'll start to see signs that consumer expectations are falling. Productivity levels and interest rates flatten out. During this economic period, companies in the consumer staples and services sectors tend to take the lead. But be ready to move when the economy heads into its next recession. You should always have some portion of your portfolio in the noncyclical industry ETFs that supply the staples of life, even in times of recession. One possible option may be XLP (Consumer Staples Select Sector SPDR Fund).

Early recession

You can recognize the earliest part of a recession by certain signs: Consumer expectations fall more sharply, and productivity levels start to drop. Interest rates also begin to drop. The utilities, such as XLU (Utilities Select Sector SPDR Fund), and finance, such as XLF (Financial Select Sector SPDR Fund), sector ETFs are ones to hold because the underlying stock prices tend to rise in the early part of a recession. Investors tend to seek stocks that provide some safety and pay higher dividends. Gold and other valuable mineral stocks also tend to look good when investors seek safety. Although the 2008 recession was an anomaly, generally you see banks, insurance companies, and investment firms perform well during the early parts of a recession.

Full recession

You may not think to look at consumer stocks when the economy is in a full recession, but during a full recession consumer expectations actually improve. Spending begins to increase. Yet industrial productivity likely remains flat, and businesses don't increase their production levels until they believe consumers actually are ready to spend again. Interest rates drop or stay low because neither businesses nor consumers are spending, so credit becomes more available. In the 2007–2009 recession, credit remained tight as banks worked out their problems with mortgage and credit card debt losses. In future recessions, this may not be as severe. During a full recession, ETFs that focus on cyclical, such as XLY (Consumer Discretionary Select Sector SPDR Fund), and technology stocks, such as XLK (Technology Select Sector SPDR Fund) or IXN (iShares Global Tech ETF), tend to lead the way to the next recovery.

Analyzing ETFs

REMEMBER

When analyzing ETFs, you need to consider two things: First you must research the underlying indexes and classification benchmarks so you know what types of stocks are likely to be part of the ETF. Then you need to research the fund's trading history to know how it performed in the various types of markets.

For example, if you believe that a full recession is underway, then you may want to consider weighting your portfolio more heavily with cyclical and technology stocks. Look at the charts for the ETFs you're considering and see how well they did during the last full recession. Fortunately, because ETFs trade just like stocks on the major exchanges, you can analyze their price charts in almost identical ways. The technical concepts that apply when looking at the chart of a stock are also applicable to the chart of an ETF.

Just like you would for a mutual fund, you want to look at the ETF's historic performance. Although history is no guarantee the ETF will perform in the same way in the future, it still gives you some reason to base your decision on the ETFs you want to use.

TIP

An excellent website for researching what the analysts are saying not only about individual ETFs but about sector choices as well is NASDAQ (www.nasdaq.com/investing/etfs). There you find a treasure trove of ETF stories about where the market has been and where it's going, along with ETF options to follow the trends. You may want to subscribe to both the latest ETF news and ETF commentary feeds available on this website. The subscriptions are free.

Another fantastic resource is ETF.com (www.etf.com). This site provides an extensive collection of helpful research tools to make sure that your ETF research is as complete and thorough as possible. The site also provides a number of free newsletter services to which you may want to subscribe.

Lastly, Morningstar (www.morningstar.com/Cover/ETFs.aspx) is a good source for ETF research. There you can find a lot of information about individual ETFs as well as ETF trends.

TIP

After you've done your research, you can pick entry and exit points by using the comparative performance charting tool, PerfCharts, at StockCharts.com (http://stockcharts.com). PerfCharts allow you to dynamically compare the performance of up to ten different stocks or funds on the same chart. Create your own with a unique group of symbols, or use the predefined PerfCharts to analyze popular groups, such as the major market indexes or U.S. commodity groups. To get started, click the tab for Free Charts at the top of any StockCharts.com web page, and then look for the PerfCharts box.

The S&P sector ETFs PerfChart is an excellent tool for visualizing relative strength. It allows you to quickly determine which sectors are moving up and which are moving down, helping you make sure you're focused only on the top-performing sectors. The S&P sector ETFs PerfChart on StockCharts.com can be accessed at the following link: https://stockcharts.com/freecharts/perf.php?[SECT].

Portfolio Construction

Constructing an ETF portfolio is not much different from constructing a stock-based portfolio. You follow the same basic techniques we discuss in Chapters 15 and 16. The only difference is that you use ETFs for building your trading system rather than stocks.

ETFs can be created from trading tools besides domestic stocks, such as commodities and currencies. If you're more adventurous and understand the risks involved in other types of trading vehicles and strategies, you may want to check out some of the following ETFs.

International trading with ETFs

If you want to add an international component to your trading strategy, ETFs make that much easier. You don't have to worry about the difficulties of researching international stocks individually. You can just research the ETFs for the countries you want to add to your strategy.

WARNING

Be careful, though, because now you're adding in the market risks of international trading, which include currency risks (the fluctuation of currency values among the countries represented in the ETF) and political risks (the politics of every country whose stocks are in the ETF).

Commodities and ETFs

You can also decide to add commodities to your trading mix. ETFs with commodities baskets or single commodities are available. But this type of trading is different, so be sure to study the basics of commodity trading before you start risking your money. If the topic interests you, pick up a copy of *Commodities For Dummies*, by Amine Bouchentouf (Wiley), before you get your feet wet.

Currency trading and ETFs

You can even trade currency using ETFs. Most major currencies have an ETF that you can trade with a basket of assets in that currency. You can find out more information about currency trading in *Currency Trading For Dummies*, by Kathleen Brooks and Brian Dolan (Wiley).

Leveraged ETFs

Leveraged ETFs amplify the returns of a particular index by using financial deriv-atives and debt. For example, a 2:1 leverage fund means that every dollar invested by a trader in the fund is matched with a dollar of debt. Theoretically, if all goes well, the leveraged ETF returns double. So if the index on which the leveraged ETF is based goes up 1 percent, the ETF's value goes up by 2 percent.

WARNING

That increase may sound great to you, but the opposite is also true. If the ETF makes the wrong bet on the trend and the index goes down 1 percent, the ETF value goes down by 2 percent. Leveraged ETFs definitely take a strategy for mini-mizing risks and make it instead a strategy that could compound the risks you take.

Inverse ETFs

If you want to hedge your bets and invest in an ETF that will move in the opposite direction of the index, then choose an inverse ETF. This can provide a simpler alternative to traditional short selling. For example, the ProSharesShort QQQ ETF (PSQ) is the one to choose if you expect a downturn in the NASDAQ 100 Index.

So if you're expecting the underlying index to go up but you want an insurance policy in case the index goes down, you may choose to balance your trading port-folio with an inverse ETF for the sector you're betting on.

Chapter **15**

Executing Your Trades

You've picked your stock, and you're ready to enter a position. As long as you place the trade while the market is open, you have some flexibility in the way your order is entered and executed. However, if you can't monitor the market during business hours or if you enter your order after the market is closed, you need to be much more precise when placing your order and indicating the type of fill (or terms of the order) you're willing to accept. Otherwise, you may run into a nasty surprise when you review your broker's fill report and discover how the trade was actually executed.

This chapter reviews available alternatives when you enter an order to buy, sell, or sell short and explains how the choices you make can affect the trade. We also review margin requirements, discuss how trading affects your tax return, and identify situations in which you must be aware of stock-trading regulations.

Entering and Exiting Your Trade

When you want to enter or exit a trade, you have to tell your broker what you want to do. To do that, you enter an *order* with your broker. This order tells the broker the number of shares and the symbol for the stock, fund, or other security you plan to trade. Your order also specifies the type of transaction you'd like to execute and how you'd like the broker to handle your transaction. (See Chapter 2 for more about the types of orders available.) We discuss your choices for instructing your broker how to handle your order in this section.

Before entering your trade order, you probably want to check for a stock quote. Ideally, your quote system for your broker provides information similar to that shown in Figure 15-1.

FIGURE 15-1:
A quote screen
for AT&T stock.

T (AT&T, Inc.) NYSE				©StockCharts.com
Monday 8-Dec-2008 1:35 pm				Last Trade:
Open: 28.90	Bid: 29.86	P/E: 13.21		▲ +6.07%
High: 30.22	Bid Size: 64	EPS: 2.26		Chg: +1.71
Low: 28.84	Ask: 29.87	Last Ticks: ↓		Last: 29.86
Prev Close: 28.15	Ask Size: 23	Last Size: 100		Volume: 26,267,612

Chart courtesy of StockCharts.com

REMEMBER

The fields depicted in Figure 15-1 are as follows:

>> **Description:** The name of the stock and its symbol (in this case **T**, AT&T, Inc.).

>> **Exchange:** The exchange on which the stock is traded (in this case, the NYSE).

>> **Net percentage change** (symbolized with ▲ or ▼): The change in price expressed (+ or –) as a percentage difference between the previous day's close and the current closing price.

>> **Net change** (Chg): The change in price (+ or –) from the previous day's close.

>> **Last:** The price recorded for the most recently executed trade when the markets are open. It will be the same as the close price when the markets are closed.

>> **Volume:** The daily trading volume.

>> **Open:** The price obtained for the first trade of the day.

>> **High:** The highest trade price of the day.

>> **Low:** The lowest trade price of the day.

>> **Previous Close:** The last trade price for the previous day.

>> **Bid:** The highest price someone is willing to pay to buy the stock.

>> **Bid Size:** The number of shares being bid at the bid price.

>> **Ask** (or offer): The lowest price someone has offered to accept to sell the stock.

>> **Ask Size:** The number of shares being offered at the ask price.

>> **P/E:** The price/earnings ratio (see Chapter 6).

>> **EPS:** Earnings per share (see Chapter 6).

>> **Last Ticks:** One or more symbols showing the direction of the last few trades in the stock during the day or at the end of the day for which the quote is effective. A plus sign or up arrow indicates a trade that was higher than the previous trade, or an *uptick*. A minus sign or down arrow indicates a trade that was for less than the previous trade, or a *downtick*. And an equal sign or a dash indicates a trade at the same price as the previous trade.

>> **Last Size:** The number of shares for the most recent trade.

Keeping straight the bid and the ask

Most of the information displayed on the quote system is straight fact, but a few items need additional explanation. For example, many new traders are confused by the *bid* and *ask* prices through which stocks are auctioned. Although it seems backward, if you look at it from the point of view of the *market maker* (the people who either manage trading activity or actually execute the trades; see Chapter 2 for more detail), it starts to make more sense. These professional traders make money in several ways. One of the most common is through trading with *retail investors* (that's what market makers call you and us, the individual investors participating in market trading activity). Market makers buy shares from a retail investor at one price and then turn around and sell those shares to another retail investor at a higher price. They buy at what is referred to as the *bid* price and then sell at what is referred to as the *ask* price. In addition to facilitating smooth market trading activity, the goal of market makers is to sell for a price higher than they buy, thus generating a profit.

A *market order* tells your broker to buy or sell at the current market price. This means that if you use a market order when buying, your order is likely to be filled at the ask price. When selling, your market order is likely to be filled at the bid price. Occasionally, your broker may be able to fill your order between the bid and ask prices, but you never should count on it, because it doesn't happen very often. Your order can, however, become the highest bid or the lowest ask if you use a *limit order.* A limit order allows you to set the price at which your trade is executed. You specify the highest price you're willing to pay when buying or the lowest price you're willing to accept when selling. If you place your limit order between the current bid and ask prices, your order becomes either the best bid price if you're buying or the best ask price if you're selling.

WARNING

You run the risk of having your order not execute at all when using a limit order if the security is trading heavily and the current market price moves away from your limit price. Also, the NYSE and NASDAQ each handle this order a little differently. Your broker can help you sort through the details if you encounter problems.

Understanding the spread

The *spread* is the difference between the bid and ask prices. It is sometimes referred to as the *inside spread*, which is the difference between the highest bid and the lowest ask. Back when stock prices were quoted in increments of eighths (12.5 cents) and quarters (25 cents), the minimum spread was either an eighth or a quarter. Today, with decimal pricing, the spreads tend to be tighter and can be as low as a penny per share on the most actively traded stocks. While the major exchanges don't support spreads less than one cent, some ECNs (electronic communications networks; see Chapter 2) permit tighter spreads for a small number of securities.

TIP

When you place a limit order within the spread so that your limit price is between the current bid and ask prices, your order will usually become either the best bid if you're buying or the best ask if you're selling. This approach makes sense whenever the spread is particularly wide and the price isn't moving very fast. When the spread is narrow, the way it is in Figure 15-1, using a market order is probably best — that is, as long as the market is open and the stock is widely traded. However, because you're letting the market dictate your order's fill price instead of specifying it yourself using a limit order, you run the risk of your trade executing at a price you didn't expect, either much higher or much lower than your target. Be aware of this concern and use market orders carefully, particularly outside of open market hours.

The biggest problem with trying to squeeze a profit out of the inside spread is that prices move. Keep in mind that stock quotes are only snapshots of current bid and ask prices. By the time your order reaches the market, these quotes can (and do) change. Even the fastest real-time quote systems lag a bit behind the real-time market prices trading on the exchanges, so it's possible that the limit order you just entered between the spread is now outside the spread and won't be filled — and believe us when we say that that can be disappointing.

Devising an effective order-entry strategy

During trading hours, you can be reasonably confident that a market order will be filled at or near current market prices. But if you're like most people, you don't spend all your time during the day diligently tracking the market's trading activity. As such, you need another strategy for entering and exiting positions. You can use one or more of several alternative approaches to better control the terms and prices that you're willing to accept when your orders are filled.

Using limit orders

If you're buying a stock, choose the maximum price that you're willing to pay, and then pay no more. That means you can't use market orders to enter your positions. Instead, you can use limit orders, which enable you to set the highest price that you're willing to pay for a stock, making that your *limit price.* If you're selling short, choose the lowest price at which you're willing to sell, and set that as your limit price.

Limit orders are effective for opening a position, but they can be problematic for exiting a position. For example, if you need to exit your position because the breakout has failed (see Chapter 9), you simply need to exit the position without trying to finesse the price. Failed trades recover infrequently, and they often get worse. You have no reason to be patient when things are going against you. In this situation, the quick fill of a market order can be helpful.

Similarly, whenever you have a profitable trade and you're trying to protect your profits, a limit order rarely is your best choice for exiting the position. You're better off exiting the position by using either a market order or a stop order after you've identified a reversal pattern.

Using stop orders and stop-limit orders to enter a trade

Traders normally talk about using stops for exiting or trading out of a position, but stops are also effective for opening a position. If you identify the stock that you want prior to an actual breakout, you can enter a buy stop at a price above the breakout point. You can enter these orders on a *GTC* (good-'til-canceled) basis, so that even if the trading range lasts a while, your order is poised to trigger a transaction whenever the breakout occurs.

TIP

Most brokers limit the length of time that orders can remain open, so make sure you know your broker's GTC policies and note that NASDAQ doesn't have any provisions for handling stop orders. If you're trying to use stops when trading NASDAQ stocks, your broker has to provide the mechanism for triggering these trades when your stop price is hit. Make sure that your broker can handle the stop orders that you want to use.

WARNING

The downside to this approach is obvious — you're unable to confirm the breakout when using an automatic buy order. If the breakout fails and you've triggered a buy order on the breakout, you now hold a position that's losing money.

Although we generally recommend waiting a few days to confirm the breakout, using this strategy at times may be more appropriate than others. For example, if you're convinced that the market is in a bull market phase (as described in Chapter 13), the stock's trading range is long and tight, and you can identify an obvious breakout, then entering a GTC buy stop order at a price that's a bit higher than the breakout price is probably okay. However, you need to be much more tentative when the market is only in a bullish transition or pullback phase, or when you're monitoring second and subsequent breakouts. When that's the case, make sure the breakout is confirmed — that means the stock remains above its breakout price for a bullish breakout — after a few trading days before entering your order. If you have any doubt, wait for confirmation.

WARNING

Another problem with this approach is that after the stop price is reached, your order is triggered and it becomes a market order to buy or sell. You're in the exact situation you'd be in if you'd entered a market order while the market was closed. You have no control over the fill price after your stop is triggered.

For example, say the stock price gaps higher (see Chapter 10) as it breaks out of its trading range and surpasses your stop price by two or three dollars. Your order is triggered and will likely be filled at a price that's much higher than your stop price and much higher than you had anticipated. If the stock price falls below your fill price, you're now holding a losing position. The only way to avoid this problem is by using a stop-limit order, which means when your stop price triggers the release of your order, the order becomes a limit order rather than a market order and is filled only if the stock price pulls back below your limit price (see Chapter 2 for more on limit and market orders). Again, be sure to confirm that your broker permits stop-limit orders on NASDAQ stocks.

You can also use a stop order or a stop-limit order to open a short position. You specify a sell stop or a sell stop-limit order while designating your trade as a short sale. Again, you must confirm that your broker supports these types of orders for NASDAQ stocks.

MANAGING AND MONITORING GTC ORDERS

WARNING

You, and you alone, are responsible for monitoring your open orders. It's not uncommon for many stocks to break out almost simultaneously, so you need to be careful not to overcommit. If, by some fluke, all your open orders trigger simultaneously or within a short period of time, you must maintain enough purchasing power to adequately fund all your trades. Otherwise, your broker will call and demand that you pay for all those trades that you inadvertently executed. Expect repercussions from your broker, including restrictions on your account, if you don't send the money immediately.

Using stop orders to exit positions

After your buy or sell order is filled, you need to enter your stop-loss instructions. You want to protect your open positions and simultaneously stay clear of short-term traders trying to *run the stops*. Running the stops is a little game played by short-term traders where they try to find and execute open stop orders before driving the stock price in the other direction. It can be very lucrative for them and infuriating, not to mention expensive, for you. You can try to avoid being run over when they're running the stops by keeping your stop prices away from the most obvious location. For example, if a breakout occurs at $35.75, don't put your stop-loss one cent below at $35.74. Move down a few cents, to $35.69, or even $35.63, to stay away from the obvious stop-loss spots. Stop-loss measures, and the reasons for them, are discussed more fully in Chapter 12.

Timing your trades: Entering orders after the market closes

In most cases, as long as you enter your trades during market hours, using a market order is an acceptable strategy. However, if you plan to check your charts each evening and then enter your trades before heading to work in the morning, you must use a different approach. Otherwise, you can suffer from opening price gaps and risk having your orders filled at prices that differ significantly from the previous closing prices. To make matters worse, you may discover that your position is losing money soon after being filled.

Don't be surprised to discover that many traders trade this way. Because of their daily schedules, they analyze stock charts in the evening and enter orders before the markets open. Unfortunately, common breakout and reversal patterns (see Chapter 9) cause many traders to react in a predictable fashion. After they enter buy orders for the same stock, a scarcity of that stock is likely to occur just after the market opens. Scarcity causes prices of individual stocks to rise, sometimes even dramatically, so that all those after-market orders are filled at prices significantly higher than the previous closing price. Making matters worse, after the buy orders are filled and buying pressure disappears, the stock price tumbles back toward the previous closing price.

Professional traders — including floor traders, market makers, day traders, and swing traders — exacerbate the problem even further. These short-term traders see the same technical signals on their charts that you notice on yours, and their goal is to profit from your enthusiasm (and perhaps your inexperience) as you try to open your position.

As a result, you need to think about the tactics these short-term traders employ before you enter any positions. When they see breakout or reversal patterns, short-term traders anticipate a flurry of buying activity in that stock, and they know that few people are going to be eager sellers when a stock breaks out of a trading range. Under those circumstances, the only way buyers can get an order filled is if they bid the price higher or accept whatever price is being asked for the stock. When that happens, the best asking price is going to be relatively high.

Someone will sell the stock to position traders but only at a relatively high asking price. Short-term swing traders and day traders, who may not even own the stock, offer those asking prices, agreeing to provide the stock to the position traders as long as the buying pressure pushes the stock's price upward. If the short-term traders don't own the stock, they must sell the shares short; in other words, they must borrow the stock before selling (see the later section "Selling Stocks Short"). After the short sellers absorb all that buying pressure, the rally fades, and the stock's price falls back toward the breakout price. That's when short-term traders buy the stock (at prices lower than they sold it) so they can cover their short positions, or in other words, return the shares that they borrowed to sell at higher prices to the position traders. How's that for taking a quick profit!

This scenario is at the heart of why being patient usually makes sense. By steering clear of these environments of high buying pressure, you're more likely to get a far better fill. Plus, you can determine whether enough buying interest is truly present to keep the stock price above the breakout price. Being patient doesn't always work, of course. Sometimes buying pressure drives the price higher, forcing short sellers to cover at a loss, which, in turn, drives the price even higher. This results in a *runaway stock.* When that does happen, you'll probably be left standing on the platform, watching the runaway stock as it leaves you behind. Fortunately, runaway stocks don't happen all that often. Thus, banking on runaway stocks is a poor tactic.

REMEMBER

Our advice remains the same: Don't chase these breakout and runaway stocks. When the cycle exhausts itself, as it ultimately must, the stock returns to a more rational price, and you can reevaluate whether your position continues to make sense. As a position trader, you can afford to be patient.

Reviewing a week in the life of a trader

To help you get a feel for entering and exiting positions, in this section we present a sample trade made by a hypothetical position trader. The idea is to help you understand the rationale and the timing. You can also use this example to practice picking entry and exit points based on historical pricing.

As a position trader, your week begins during the weekend. You have a few things to accomplish:

>> Evaluate the current state of the market.

>> Evaluate the current state of your existing positions.

>> Find potential replacement candidates for any failing positions.

>> Find candidates for new trading positions.

From an educational perspective, one of the most interesting periods to analyze in recent history is the financial crisis of 2007–2009. This was one of the most volatile periods the stock market has seen since the Great Depression. To illustrate exactly what it takes not only to survive but also to succeed as a trader in today's fast-paced market environment, let's take a closer look at the week of December 8, 2008.

Before we begin, let's recap the market's performance prior to that week. The broad market indexes peaked in October 2007. Stocks performed poorly over the next year, but they accelerated sharply to the downside in September 2008.

From its October 2007 intraday peak of 1,576 to its November 2008 low, the S&P 500, like most broad-market indexes at that time, lost over 50 percent of its value. In the months leading up to our sample week in December, the market saw several short, sharp rallies mixed into this distinct downtrend. Failed breaks to the upside printed in both the spring and summer months of 2008, for example. Downside pressure resumed, carrying stocks further into the ground. However, in November 2008, the S&P 500 shot up nearly 20 percent higher over the span of just five trading days.

Because the markets rallied 20 percent, the major media declared the bear market over. Rather than taking their word for it, we can use our analysis to see whether the persistent downtrend had ended.

The technical indicators on the charts and fundamental economic conditions showed a mixed picture for the first week of December 2008:

>> The economy was clearly still in recession, facing arguably some of the worst economic conditions in our lifetime.

>> The Fed lowered the Fed funds rate to its lowest point ever, near 0 percent, introducing relatively uncharted waters for the interest rate environment.

>> The consumer staples, utilities, and healthcare sectors were the best-performing sectors in the market. The sector rotation model (see Chapters 5 and 13) suggests that strength in these sectors often occurs during bear markets, before reaching the bear-market trough.

>> On the charts of both the S&P 500 Index and the NASDAQ Composite Index, the weekly MACD indicator (see Chapter 11) was far below its zero line. Although the indicator turned a little higher, it remained well below its signal line, suggesting that the market remained in a bear phase.

>> The bullish percent index (BPI; see Chapter 13) for all broad market indexes was signaling a bull confirmed condition.

Given the preceding factors, you can't conclude that a bull market had begun, despite what the mainstream media was saying. Instead, the market was most likely in a bearish pullback, but you couldn't rule out a bull market transition at that time.

Next, you would analyze your current positions in early December 2008, if you had any. Given the market's volatility, it would not be a surprise if you had already been stopped out of many of your short positions, as well as any long positions that you may have still had. And given your conclusion that the market was probably in a bearish pullback, you wouldn't initiate any new long positions.

Finally, you would try to look for new potential trading candidates. There was a lot of concern about major bankruptcies because high-profile bankruptcy announcements during that time period included Linens 'n Things, Circuit City, and Lehman Brothers, while GM was also teetering on the verge of collapse. Avoiding individual stocks at that time was still probably best, at least until you saw a clear indication of a new bull market. Instead, in December 2008, it made more sense to look at broad-market-index ETFs, as well as sector ETFs, to find trading candidates. (Chapter 14 takes a closer look at using ETFs as trading options.)

In December 2008 you couldn't be certain that the market was in a bearish pullback; it may have been in the beginning of a bull market transition. You would very carefully look for both long and short trading opportunities. For long positions, you would look only at the very strongest sectors, such as consumer staples, utilities, and healthcare. For short positions, you would look to the very weakest sectors, such as financial stocks and real estate. You could also look at broad-market ETFs for both long and short trading candidates, as well as inverse ETFs.

As you browse the daily ETF charts, it's not surprising that you find few exhibiting a long-lasting trading range (see Chapter 9). One that qualified at that time was the Utilities Select Sector SPDR Fund (XLU). You do find several patterns that may be attractive for short positions (see Chapters 10 and 11). For example, you find that the ProShares Short S&P500 Fund (SH) had recently made a new high and was in a pullback position. SH is an inverse ETF, so its price rises when the S&P 500 Index falls.

Your final step is to determine the breakout points and identify your entry prices (see Chapter 9) for each of the trading candidates you've found. You may enter buy stop orders for these trades now, or you may monitor the situation and enter the trades more actively as the trading signals occur.

TIP

As an academic exercise, look back at the charts of both XLU and SH, our two trading candidates, and explore how these two options performed in the months and years after December 2008. Determine good entry and exit points during this period to practice your trading on paper. You have the benefit of hindsight on your side, but it's a great way to learn how to recognize the trading signals and practice developing your own trading plans without putting your real investing capital at risk.

After you've entered your trades at the start of a trading week, your daily activities are comparatively easy. At the end of each trading day, you must

>> Evaluate the current condition of any new or existing positions.

>> Evaluate the current condition of any trading candidates you identified during your weekend analysis.

The markets gapped higher on Monday, December 8. XLU also rallied, but it didn't break out of its trading range. In fact, it remained in this trading range for the entire week. XLU stayed in a trading range until February 2009. After that it took a major drop to its low on March 2, 2009. After that drop in March 2009, it started a strong upward climb. See Figure 15-2.

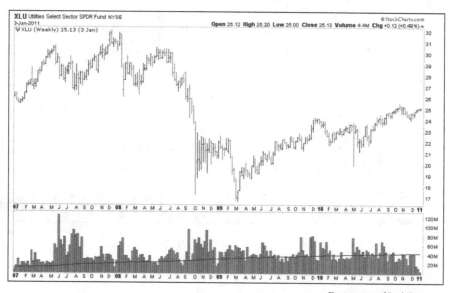

FIGURE 15-2:
A weekly chart of the Utilities Select Sector SPDR Fund (XLU), 2007–2011.

Chart courtesy of StockCharts.com

The price for SH, your short-side candidate, gapped lower at the open and traded in a narrow range throughout the day on Monday. Over the next several days, trading in SH was within a very narrow range. Although this isn't the classic breakout setup we discuss in Chapter 9, it's very similar. The 60-minute intraday chart for SH looked very much like a long-running trading range. The only difference is that this trading range was over a period of several days rather than several weeks or months. You decided that the SH trade was still viable, and you entered a buy-stop order just above the high of the intraday trading range. This trade was triggered during the day on Thursday, December 11.

Markets gapped lower the following morning, driving the price of SH higher. The opening price was the high price for the day. The ETF traded lower and ultimately touched the top of the prior intraday trading range, but it didn't fall back into the trading range, at least not during the week we're discussing.

Because we're omniscient (or maybe because we're writing this after the fact), we can tell you that this trade didn't work out. During the following week, SH fell back into the trading range and hit your stop price, giving you a 4.2 percent loss on this trade. SH continued to fall through December 2009 and then started an upward climb until March 2010. Since that time, it's been on a downward slide. See Figure 15-3.

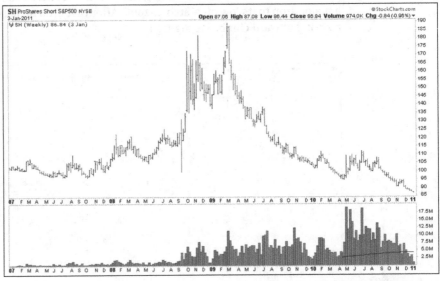

FIGURE 15-3:
A weekly chart of the ProShares Short S&P500 Fund (SH), 2007–2011.

Chart courtesy of StockCharts.com

Selling Stocks Short

When you sell a stock *short,* you sell something you don't have first and buy it later with the goal of profiting from a falling stock price. To sell a stock short, you borrow shares of a stock from your broker so you can sell them in the open market. Your broker gets those shares either from its own inventory or, more likely, from other clients. The proceeds of that sale go into your account. To close that position, you must buy the shares on the open market and return them to the broker. If the price you pay for the stock, or the *buy-to-cover price,* is less than your selling price, you earn a profit on the short sale. Conversely, if the buy-to-cover price is higher, you suffer a loss.

Let's say you borrow 100 shares of Company X and sell the shares short for $100 per share. When the price drops to $80 per share, you buy the shares back (you can also say you *covered the shorted shares*) and return them to your broker. You borrowed the shares, immediately sold them for $100 per share, and later bought them back for $80, netting a profit of $20 per share. It's exactly the same profit as if you had purchased the stock for $80 first and sold it for $100 later. Conversely, say you borrow 100 shares of Company Y and sell them for $100 per share. The stock price rises to $120 per share, and you decide to cover your loss. You buy back the shares and pay $120 per share, but you sold them for $100 per share. You have lost $20 per share on this trade.

Some of the quirks that are unique to selling stocks short include the following:

» **Paying dividends to the lender:** If the stocks pay a dividend during the time a short seller holds a position, short sellers pay the dividends on the ex-dividend date to the people who loaned them the stocks. Short sellers need to keep the ex-dividend date in mind whenever shorting stocks.

» **Being forced to close a position:** Whenever the original owner sells the stocks you borrowed, your broker can *call away* the shorted shares, which means your broker can force you to return the borrowed shares by buying them on the open market at the current price. This happens rarely and occurs only when no shares are available for shorting.

» **Mandating the execution of short sales from only a margin account:** Short sales must be executed in a margin account because your broker loans you the stock to sell short and charges you interest on any margin balance in the account.

» **Paying margin maintenance requirements:** Your broker can force you to close a short position if you're unable to satisfy maintenance margin requirements.

>> **Having minimal or even zero access to selling some stocks short:** Lightly traded stocks may be unavailable for selling short, and when they can be sold short, they may be more likely to be called away (which happens when the original owner sells the stock you borrowed and your broker is unable to borrow additional shares).

>> **Restricting short sales on certain stocks:** You can't short a stock that's less than $5 per share, and you can't short initial public offerings (IPOs), usually for 30 days following the IPO. Also, as we learned during the credit crisis, regulators can prohibit short selling on whole categories of stocks.

>> **Limiting short selling to only stocks on an uptick:** This *uptick rule* was eliminated in July 2007, but a modified version was implemented again in 2010. The essence of the old rule was that you couldn't sell a stock short in a falling market. Short sellers couldn't easily pile into a falling stock. The 2010 rule doesn't apply to all securities. Today it's triggered only when a security's price decreases by 10 percent or more from the previous day's closing price. The rule then stays in effect until the close of the next day. However, many people consider this new version of the rule to be ineffective.

TIP

One unusual aspect of shorting is that it creates future buying pressure. Every shorted sale must eventually be covered, and that means that every share of stock that's been shorted has to be repurchased at some point down the road. Future buying pressure can cause the price of a heavily shorted stock to jump dramatically if all the short sellers simultaneously clamor to get out of their positions as the price rises, a situation called a *short squeeze.* You can find out how many others are shorting the stock by looking at short-interest statistics, which are readily available online from a variety of sources, such as NASDAQ (www.nasdaq.com). From those statistics, you get some idea whether your short position is likely to be squeezed.

Avoiding Regulatory Pitfalls

Several regulatory pitfalls may cause you problems as you trade. You want to avoid running afoul of these regulations. Otherwise, you risk having severe restrictions placed on your account.

Understanding trade-settlement dates

In the United States, the Securities and Exchange Commission (SEC) regulates when traders must settle their securities transactions. Stock trades, for example, settle three business days after a trade is executed, meaning the buyer must pay for stock trades and the seller must deliver the stock within three business days after the trade is executed. For example, if your trade date is Monday, then the trade settles Thursday, three business days after the trade date. Short sellers are subject to the same settlement regulations as everybody else. That means the short seller must deliver the borrowed shares to the buyer three business days following the trade.

Most securities, including broker-traded mutual funds and bonds, settle in this three-day cycle. The shorthand for this settlement period is known as $T + 3$, which means *trade date plus three days.* Stock options and government securities, on the other hand, settle the day following the trade date, or $T + 1$.

Your broker may insist that the money for all trades be available in your account before allowing you to execute any trades. Brokers can exercise this restriction because they're permitted to set more stringent restrictions than regulations require. They can't, however, set more lenient terms. Regardless of your broker's restrictions, the trade settles during the period specified by SEC regulations. One consequence of this settlement cycle is that your broker is unlikely to allow you to withdraw funds that are part of the trade until the trade settles. However, brokers typically do allow you to trade with those funds as if they are available as long as other trading regulations aren't violated.

Avoiding free riding

WARNING

Whenever you choose to trade in a cash account, you must take care to avoid free riding. *Free riding* occurs whenever you buy and sell a stock without depositing sufficient funds before settlement to pay for the transaction. For example, if you have $5,000 in your cash account and you buy 1,000 shares of a $10 stock, for a total transaction cost of $10,000, you receive a money call to deposit $5,000 to settle the trade. Of course, for the sake of simplicity, we ignored commission costs in this example.

One way that a trader may mistakenly violate the free-riding rules is trying to use the same capital on two transactions in a single day. Here's the scenario: Say you have $10,000 of equity in your account and you buy 1,000 shares of a $10 stock. Later that same day, you're stopped out of the position. So far there is no problem. But if you try to reenter the position on the same day, then you receive a money call for the full price of the second trade. The bottom line: You can't use the same capital to open two positions on the same day in a cash account. That's *free riding.* Note, however, that these trades are permitted in a margin account. Trading in a margin account means you're not at risk of violating free-riding regulations.

WARNING

If you fail to satisfy the money call within the specified time, your broker either issues a warning or places your account on restricted status. When you're restricted, you must have enough funds in your account to cover your trade before the broker executes your order. Restrictions usually are imposed for 90 days.

Avoiding margin calls and forced sales

Although trading on margin is very powerful, it's also potentially very risky. You may recall from our discussion about differing types of accounts in Chapter 2 that a margin account enables you to borrow money from your broker, which, in turn, permits you to leverage your trading capital. This leverage can improve your total return when things go well, but it can also amplify any losses when a trade goes against you. A margin account is required if you plan to sell stock short.

Before putting your margin to work, you must become familiar with the rules governing its use. The Federal Reserve determines the maximum amount that your broker can loan you. Currently, the Fed permits your broker to loan you up to 50 percent of the value of each trade. The Fed hasn't changed the margin requirement values since 1974. Prior to 1974, however, the Fed had adjusted margin requirements 22 times to limit stock market speculation and inflationary pressures.

Understanding margin fees

Your broker charges interest on the average daily margin balance, regardless of whether it's held as cash or stocks. The margin balance is an adjustable rate loan for which the interest rate is based on the current *broker call rate*, which sometimes is known as the *money call rate*. Brokers usually quote their respective margin rates as the broker call rate plus a percentage, where the added amount depends on the size of your loan. You can find the current broker call rate online with a quick Google search.

Understanding margin collateral

Your trading positions represent the collateral used to secure your margin loan. Brokers require the value of your collateral to be sufficient to cover any outstanding loan. The amount required by your broker, called the *minimum maintenance margin,* can range from 25 percent upward. In other words, your broker requires the equity in your account to be at least 25 percent of the market value of your margined stocks.

If the equity value of your account falls below the minimum maintenance margin, you receive a *margin call,* a demand from your broker to deposit more money in your account. If you fail to satisfy your broker's demand for additional funds, your broker liquidates some or all of your trading positions. In fact, your broker may even liquidate your positions before you satisfy the margin call if the value of the equity in your account continues to fall. Falling stock prices mean falling equity values.

As an example, say that you have $10,000 in your account and you buy 1,000 shares of a $20 stock, which is $20,000 worth of stock. Current margin regulations require that you maintain a deposit of at least 50 percent of the value of that trade in your account to open that trade and 25 percent of the total value of the position to maintain it. After purchasing the stock, your account has $10,000 of equity and $10,000 in a margin loan. A margin call occurs in our example when the price of the stock falls dramatically the next day from $20 to $12, representing a loss of 40 percent. At this point, you still owe the $10,000 margin loan to your broker, but the total equity in your account now is only $2,000. The 25 percent minimum maintenance requirement is $3,000 (that's 25 percent of $12,000, or 1,000 shares at $12 each), so you'd receive a maintenance margin call to deposit $1,000 to bring your account up to the $3,000 minimum equity amount.

Notice in the example that you're also dangerously close to owing more to your broker than the stock is worth. If the stock's price falls much further, the broker likely will liquidate your position to satisfy your outstanding loan. Brokers are allowed to liquidate your position at any time without your explicit approval. In fact, they're allowed to liquidate any position in your account to satisfy your loan.

This example illustrates the risks of using margin. The value of the stock fell 40 percent in the example, but you lost 80 percent of your equity. Another small drop down to a 50 percent loss in the stock will result in a complete 100 percent loss for you. Always remember that leverage cuts both ways. Earning double the profits may be nice, but doubling your losses is immensely painful. Our recommendation is to never satisfy a margin call — close the offending position instead. In our example, you should have set stops so you'd be able to get out of the losing position long before you got the margin call. But after that margin call is generated, you need to liquidate the losing position(s) immediately to pay off the margin loan.

When you open a margin account, you must sign a *hypothecation agreement,* a binding agreement that explicitly entitles your broker to liquidate positions to satisfy outstanding margin loans. The hypothecation agreement also permits your broker to loan any stock in your margin account to another client to provide shares for that client to short the stock. When you short a stock, the shares of the stock that you sell must come from somewhere, and that somewhere is most often from other clients who own the stock. If you're the one shorting stock, one "gotcha" can accompany this scenario. If the stock you borrowed is sold to someone else, then your broker can call away your short position in a forced sale. Although forced sales like this don't happen very often, they are nevertheless a risk that you must fully understand and be ready to assume if you short stock.

Avoiding pattern-day-trader restrictions

Another risk you run when using a margin account is being classified as a *pattern day trader*. A *day trade* is defined as entering and exiting a single position in the same day. You can buy a stock and sell it or you can short a stock and cover the position. Either way, if both transactions occur on the same day, it's considered a day trade. If you day trade four or more times within a five-business-day period, you're classified as a *pattern day trader* unless your day trades represent fewer than 6 percent of the total number of trades executed during the same period, which is a huge threshold. After you're classified as a pattern day trader, your account must have at least $25,000 of equity before you're permitted to execute additional day trades. Day trading margin rules are discussed in Chapter 18.

The Tax Man Cometh

Trading profits are taxable and are usually taxed as income at the trader's marginal income tax rate. Traders rarely hold positions long enough to qualify for the special (typically much lower) capital gains treatment that is available to long-term investors. Still, paying taxes is better than losing profits or principal.

One tax trap that snares traders is the *wash sale rule*. Normally, you can deduct trading losses from trading gains before calculating your income tax burden. However, if you sell a stock for a loss and then repurchase the stock within 30 days, you can't deduct the trading loss. Fortunately, the loss isn't lost forever. You can use it to adjust the cost basis on the trade by the amount of the loss, which ultimately reduces the amount of tax owed when the position is finally closed. This adjustment effectively raises the cost of a stock purchase, for tax purposes, so you owe less tax. A similar adjustment is available when selling short.

Day traders receive special tax treatment, but you must be a bona fide day trader to qualify. The details are reviewed in Chapter 18.

Chapter **16**

Developing Your Own Powerful Trading System

A *trading system* is a collection of technical and fundamental analyses tools woven together to generate buy and sell signals. Trading systems often are built using common indicators, oscillators, and moving averages (see Chapter 11). You can combine these various technical analysis tools to create a virtually unlimited number of trading systems. For the novice trader, the advantage to this approach is that you don't need to invent something new to create and personalize an effective system.

The downside, however, is equally obvious. Many traders use these common tools and end up with a system that offers little competitive advantage and only modest (if any) profits. In addition, these systems can be difficult to use because the signals of one trading system mirror the signals of many others, which makes entering and exiting positions troublesome.

Ultimately, you want to develop or adapt a trading system that closely fits your personality, trading time frame, schedule, and trading objectives. This chapter helps you methodically develop and add to a trading approach that uses your own personalized repertoire of trading systems. It also helps you recognize and avoid destructive and costly habits that can sabotage your trading efforts. In addition, we discuss ways for you to evaluate some of the claims made about trading systems that are for sale and whether buying someone else's trading system makes sense.

Understanding Trading Systems

Although individual trading systems differ in many ways, you can think about them on the basis of a couple of broad characteristics to get a good overview. The first characteristic has to do with the two ways a trader interacts with the system. In this case, trading systems are either

>> **Discretionary trading systems:** A system that presents trading candidates for your consideration but leaves the final trade execution decision to you.

>> **Mechanical trading systems:** A computer-based system that automatically generates buy and sell signals that will always be traded.

The other way to categorize a trading system is by how it treats trends in the markets. In this case, trading systems are either

>> **Trend-following trading systems:** A system that tries to identify trade entry and exit points for new or existing trends.

>> **Countertrend trading systems:** A system that tries to identify trade entry and exit points by finding tops and bottoms.

Although these categorizations are not mutually exclusive of each other (mechanical and discretionary systems, for example, can both be trend-following systems), each approach has its fair share of both champions and detractors, so we discuss the strengths and weaknesses of each type of system in the sections that follow.

REMEMBER

As you read through our descriptions of the trading systems, understand that *no* system generates profits without any losing trades. Put another way, no system works in every situation. Keep that fact firmly in mind when you're developing and designing your own personal trading system. Your goal is to design a trading system that is useful to you across a large number of stocks and a large number of situations. Believe us when we say that you will run into trouble whenever you try to tailor a trading system to a specific stock. Additionally, try to ensure that your system works across long periods of time and throughout many different market conditions.

Discretionary systems

A *discretionary trading system* makes you an active participant in all phases of the trades you make and provides you with a great deal of leeway when making trading decisions. With this approach, evaluating the economic data, analyzing the broad-market indexes, determining which sectors are showing strength, and identifying high-relative-strength stocks that are breaking out of long trading ranges and hoping to catch a new trend all are up to you. You make decisions based on what you see in the charts and in the fundamental economic data, and you enter and exit (buy and sell) positions based on that information. When you're relying on a discretionary trading system, your judgment is a key factor.

TIP

A discretionary system requires a great deal of discipline, which can cause problems for some traders. This type of system works well for traders who are capable of making good decisions quickly under pressure. But discretionary systems may prove troublesome if you allow your emotions to wreak havoc with your ability to think clearly, act rationally, and make thoughtful trading decisions.

When emotions cloud your trading decisions, you may end up

>> Overtrading

>> Prematurely liquidating your positions

>> Holding positions too long

>> Anticipating trading signals in attempts to get better entry and exit prices

WARNING

Another problem with discretionary systems is that they're difficult to test. This is possibly their greatest drawback. System testing is useful because it helps you understand situations in which an indicator works well and those in which it fails. With a discretionary system, you can test the indicators, but you can't reliably test your discretion. We talk about testing trading systems in more detail later in this chapter.

Mechanical systems

A *mechanical system* addresses some of the problems that arise when using discretionary systems. Mechanical systems usually are computer-based programs that automatically generate buy and sell signals based on technical and/or fundamental data. You're expected to blindly follow the resulting trading signals. Put another way, mechanical trading systems take your judgment out of the equation. In fact, some mechanical systems even enter buy and sell orders directly with your broker without your intervention.

TIP

If your greedy impulses or your fear of losing routinely cause you to make poor trading decisions, a mechanical system may be a better choice for you. An automated approach tends to reduce the stress and anxiety that arise when you have to make difficult decisions quickly. As such, you can make and execute trading decisions in a consistent, methodical way. A mechanical trading system also enables you to automatically include rigorous money management protocols in your trading methodology.

Another benefit of the mechanical approach is having the ability to thoroughly test the system. Through testing you can confirm whether your trading system performs the way you expect it to and explore ways to improve your system before actually committing your trading capital. You can adjust and fine-tune your system after seeing the test results. Unfortunately, fine-tuning your system may lead to other problems. We discuss ways to avoid them in the later section "Identifying system-optimization pitfalls."

Trend-following systems

Trend following is favored by many technicians for one simple reason: Trends offer excellent opportunities for profit. Unfortunately, the popularity of the trend-following approach is one of its greatest weaknesses. Too many of these systems generate very similar buy and sell signals, which, in turn, makes outperforming the average trader difficult for any individual trend-following trader.

Even the best trend-following systems have a relatively large percentage of failed trades, primarily because they depend on several extremely profitable trades to make up for the large percentage of losing trades. If your trend-following system is also a discretionary system, your discretion (or lack of it) can cause you to miss a few of these profitable trades. In this case, your overall results will suffer.

REMEMBER

Trend-following systems are typically based on either moving averages or break-out patterns (see Chapters 9 and 11). Moving average–based trading systems are the most popular and can be quite profitable; however, they work only when a stock is trending. These trading systems depend on long-lasting trends to generate enough profit to outweigh a relatively large number of losing trades. In fact, the number of losing trades can easily outnumber the winning trades with this type of trading system. When a stock is *range bound* (stuck moving sideways within a specific price range), a moving average–based system generates a large number of losing trades. Because of the high overall number of trades, this system is often accompanied by relatively high transaction and slippage costs (see the later section "Accounting for slippage"). Smart money management protocols are critical when using a trend-following trading system.

TIP

You can make some adjustments to a trend-following system that may improve its performance. For example, you can insist that its trading signals be confirmed by another condition before actually entering any positions. If your system triggers a buy signal, for example, you may want to see whether the signal remains in effect for at least a day or two before entering a position. We show some examples of moving-average and breakout systems, along with some ideas to improve the performance of these systems, in the section "Developing and Testing Trading Systems," later in this chapter.

Countertrend systems

For many traders, the quest to find a profitable countertrend trading system is all consuming. *Countertrend systems* appear desirable because their goal is to buy low and sell high. These systems try to identify *inflection points,* or the moments when stocks change direction, so traders can take positions close to when they occur. This approach may work in a few narrowly defined situations, such as in a trading range (Chapter 9) or a trend channel (Chapter 10), but it's likely to fail in a spectacular and expensive way if attempted on a broader scale.

The vast majority of trading systems follow market trends. This is simply a higher-probability practice. Trend-following systems tend to outperform countertrend systems, especially for position traders. Swing traders and some day traders sometimes use a countertrend approach, but even then, they usually do so in conjunction with a trend-following component. (Flip to Chapters 17 and 18 for more about swing trading and day trading.)

Countertrend systems usually depend on oscillating indicators, reversal patterns, and channeling strategies to find turning points. Some countertrend systems also are based on cycle theory, and others are based on volatility, expansion, and contraction.

WARNING

We discourage you from spending too much time evaluating countertrend systems, at least until you're confident in your ability to use trend-following systems to successfully make your trades. Countertrend systems generate a large volume of trades, and the more you trade, the more you spend on transaction and slippage costs. These costs alone often swamp potentially profitable systems. Although a countertrend strategy can sometimes work profitably in a trading range or trend channel (see Chapters 9 and 10), it's still risky, especially for a new trader. Until you can confidently (and honestly) consider yourself a thoroughly experienced trader, stick with the proven techniques that are more likely to lead to profitable results over the long term.

Selecting System-Development Tools

As a trader, it's natural to want some way of confirming that your newly designed system can perform profitably before you commit real trading capital. That means you need a way to test your system, which, in turn, means using computer software to precisely define the system and evaluate its performance. Typically, this requires simulating trades by using historical data.

TIP

Regardless of whether you decide on a mechanical or a discretionary approach to trading, testing your system brings with it a long list of benefits. Although thoroughly testing a discretionary system is difficult, you can still test the component indicators to learn when they do and don't provide effective trading signals. To begin, you need a computer, development and testing software, and historical data.

Choosing system-development hardware

Doing the math that's required when testing your system can really slow down your computer, and it can generate a lot of data. Almost any computer will do the job when you're getting started, but if you end up testing many system ideas, you definitely need a large amount of disk storage and a fast computer. The computer equipment required to run a proprietary trading platform, including products such as TradeStation, is usually enough for system development and testing. (See Chapter 4 for more information about the hardware requirements for a typical proprietary trading platform.)

Deciding on system-development software

You'll come across a wide array of trading system–development and testing products on the market. Some proprietary trading platforms, such as TradeStation, include system-testing capabilities. Spreadsheet software, like Microsoft Excel, also is useful for analyzing simple trading systems and the results generated by specialized development and testing software.

TIP

Some system-development programs provide a great deal of statistical analysis, so choosing between spreadsheet tools and system-development tools is a trade-off between thoroughness and expediency. After you've been through the testing exercises a few times, you get a feel for the strength of each approach. So it's likely that you'll decide to use both a system-development program and a spreadsheet program when creating and testing your new trading systems.

Trading system–development and testing software

You need to consider several of the following criteria when evaluating your trading system–development and testing software:

>> All trading system–development and testing programs use some type of computer language to describe and test your system. Some are terse and difficult to use; others are more intuitive. Traders with strong computer or programming skills have little problem mastering any of these languages, but others may struggle. Pay careful attention to this development language before selecting a system. Be certain that you're actually able to use the system you choose.

>> You need to integrate your trading system with your stock charts. Some system-development software requires you to actually write computer code that enables you to display your trading system and stock charts simultaneously. Avoid these systems if you're uncomfortable writing computer code.

>> The manner and effectiveness by which your system-development and testing software reports on how your trading system is performing is critical. Some systems provide extremely detailed statistics about the performance of your trading systems. Others, however, list little more than the buy or sell signals. In general, more information is better.

>> Make sure your system-development and testing programs are capable of exporting the data they generate, historical price data included, into a spreadsheet program for further analysis.

TIP

TradeStation (www.tradestation.com) is the gold-plated system-development platform. It has many built-in tools that make your development and testing job relatively easy. For those of you on tight budgets, one of the less-expensive alternatives you may want to consider is the charting and system-development program AmiBroker (www.amibroker.com). Although flexible and powerful, AmiBroker isn't as feature-rich or polished as TradeStation, and it requires significantly more effort on your part. For example, AmiBroker includes well-known technical-analysis indicators like moving averages and MACD (see Chapter 11), but the number of indicators included is a tiny subset compared with what TradeStation offers. Similarly, you have to use AmiBroker's formula language to create and enter any other indicators that you may be using.

Spreadsheet software

A spreadsheet program is another invaluable testing and analysis tool. Although a spreadsheet program can't do everything that a specialized system-development and testing program can do, it can add quite a bit of analysis horsepower to your system-development tool kit. You can actually code and test simple trading systems directly into the spreadsheet. You can also evaluate the results of your system tests more thoroughly using the spreadsheet's built-in statistical and analysis functions.

You can, for example, copy the price data for a stock into your spreadsheet, calculate moving averages and other indicators, and then configure buy, sell, or sell-short signals. You can also export trading signals from your system-development program and import the results into your spreadsheet for further analysis.

TIP

One of our favorite spreadsheet projects is calculating the maximum favorable and unfavorable moves after our system has triggered a buy or sell signal. Simple to do, it helps you understand the strengths and weaknesses of your trading system in great detail. You can see whether problems with your trading system may be solved by using different exit procedures or tighter (or looser) stop-loss points.

For example, although your entry signals may show promise, your exit signals may be causing you to leave a lot of money on the table. These situations are hard to see when you're working only with charts; however, they sometimes jump out when you're working with raw data during your spreadsheet analysis. You can find an example using this testing technique in the later section "Using breakout trading systems."

Finding historical data for system testing

When you need to test your system, you can, of course, test it in real time, with real money, out in the real markets. But getting some idea of how your system will perform before risking your hard-earned capital is usually a smarter choice. Typically, that means testing your system by evaluating how it performs when simulating trading using historical price data. Ten to twenty years of historical end-of-day data for the indexes and stocks you plan to trade is usually more than enough to properly simulate trades for testing your system.

Many sources can provide the data you need to do this. You can download historical data from the Internet, and some online data is available free of charge. Some proprietary trading platforms likewise include access to historical data. You may want to get data from more than one source to confirm its accuracy.

TIP

Yahoo Finance provides free historical data and permits you to download the data into a spreadsheet. To access the Yahoo data feed, get a quote for the stock and select "Historical Data." Then click "Download Data."

Many online services offer data in a more convenient format but for a price. Some sell historical data recorded on CDs. Sources for intraday price data also are available. Here are the URLs for a few of the many sites offering various forms of historical data:

- >> **Historical data:**
  - • **Yahoo Finance:** `http://finance.yahoo.com`
  - • **Google Finance:** `www.google.com/finance`
  - • **StockCharts.com:** `https://stockcharts.com/h-hd`
- >> **Intraday data:**
  - • **eSignal:** `www.esignal.com`
  - • **IQ Feed:** `www.iqfeed.net`
  - • **QuoteTracker:** `www.quotetracker.com`
- >> **Historical data on CD:**
  - • **Commodity Systems Inc. (CSI):** `www.csidata.com`

Developing and Testing Trading Systems

The ideas that you may want to include in your system development and testing are virtually limitless. Many new traders begin system testing by combining a few off-the-shelf indicators in an effort to obtain better trading results. Doing so is as good a place as any to begin.

However, we want to caution you to keep your systems simple enough that you can understand not only the system but also the result. Simplicity usually is better when trading, especially when you're first becoming familiar with the processes of system development and testing. We describe the process by looking at a couple of examples in the sections that follow.

Working with trend-following systems

Many trend-following systems use a moving average for their starting points. In this trend-following example, the system is designed for position trading, which means we use a relatively long moving average. Short selling isn't permitted with this simple system.

The first step is to define buy and sell rules for your initial testing. The actual code for defining these rules depends on your specific system-development package.

Therefore, trading rules are described as generally as possible. The rules for an initial test may look like this:

>> Buy at tomorrow's opening price when today's price crosses and closes above the 50-day exponential moving average (EMA).

>> Sell at tomorrow's opening price when today's price crosses and closes below the 50-day EMA.

To test whether using a moving average as a starting point is a good idea in a trend-following system, apply these two rules to ten years of historical data for the stocks of your choice. After testing this idea, you find that this simple system works fairly well when stock prices are trending, but it's likely to trigger many losing trades when the prices of stocks are range bound. You can try to avoid these losing trades, and possibly improve your overall trading results, by filtering out trading-range situations. One way to accomplish that goal is by changing the buy rule to read as follows: Buy at tomorrow's open when the following conditions are true:

>> Today's closing price is above the 50-day EMA.

>> The stock crossed above the 50-day EMA sometime during the last 5 days.

>> Today's 50-day EMA is greater than the 50-day EMA from 5 days ago.

These added conditions serve as signal confirmation. When you test these rules, you find they reduce the number of whipsaw trades for most stocks, but they're also likely to delay buy and sell signals on profitable trades and thus usually result in smaller profits on those trades. However, this adjustment makes the overall system more profitable because the number of losses is reduced.

You can find out whether other changes that you can make in your simple system can actually improve profitability. You may, for example, test different types of moving averages. Try, for example, a simple moving average (SMA) instead of an exponential moving average (EMA). Or you may want to try using different time frames for your moving average, such as 9-day, 25-day, or 100-day moving averages. See Chapter 11 for more details about the multiple types of moving averages.

Identifying system-optimization pitfalls

Most system-development and testing software comes equipped with a provision for system optimization, which allows you to fine-tune the technical analysis tools used in your trading system. You can, for example, tell the system to find the time frame of the moving average that produces the highest profit for one stock and then ask it to do the same thing for a different stock. Some systems enable you to test this factor simultaneously for many stocks.

WARNING

Although this approach is alluring, using it is likely to cause you trouble. If you find, for example, that a 22-day moving average works best for one stock, a 37-day moving average works best for the next stock, and another stock performs best using a 74-day moving average, you're going to run into problems. The set of circumstances leading to these optimized results won't likely repeat in precisely the same way again in the future. We can almost guarantee that whatever optimized parameters you may find for these moving averages won't be the optimal choices when trading real capital.

This is a simple example of a problem that's well known to scientists and economists who build mathematic models to forecast future events. It's called *curve fitting* because you're molding your model to fit the historical data. You can expend quite a bit of effort fine-tuning a system to identify all the major trends and turning points in historical data for a particular stock, but that effort isn't likely to result in future trading profits. In that case, your optimized system is more likely to cause a long string of losses rather than profits.

REMEMBER

Testing a long moving average and comparing the results to a short moving average is fine, and so is testing a few points in between a long moving average and a short moving average. As long as you use this exercise to understand why short moving averages work best for short-term trades and why longer moving averages work better for traders with longer trading horizons, you'll be fine. Otherwise, you're probably moving into the realm of curve fitting and becoming frustrated with your actual trading results.

Testing with blind simulation

TIP

Blind simulation is a method for setting aside enough historical data so you can test your system-optimization results and avoid the problem of curve fitting. For example, you may test data from 1990 through 1999 and thus exclude data from 2000 through the present. After you've developed a system that looks good enough for you to base your trades on, you can then test your system against the data that was excluded. If the system performs as well with the excluded data as it did with the original test data, you may have a system worth trading. If it fails, you obviously need to rethink your system.

Another approach is choosing your historical data with extreme care. You can expect trend-following systems like a moving-average system to perform well during long, powerful trends. If your stock had a strong run up during the long-lasting 1990s bull market, that kind of price data can skew your results, magically making any trend-following system appear profitable. Whether that success actually can be duplicated during a subsequent bull market, however, must first be thoroughly tested.

TIP

If the majority of your profits come from a single trade or only a small number of trades, the system probably won't perform well when you begin trading real money. You may want to address this problem by excluding periods from your test data when your stock was doing exceptionally well or when the results of any trades were significantly more profitable than the average trade. This technique is a valid approach to eliminating the extraordinary results arising from extraordinary situations in your historical data. Using it should give you a better idea of your system's potential for generating real profits in the future.

Using breakout trading systems

Similar to moving average–based systems, a *breakout system* can take many forms. You may already be familiar with the trading-range breakout system we describe in Chapter 9. To test a different approach, you can define a breakout system as follows:

>> Buying at tomorrow's opening price when today's closing price is above the highest high price that occurred during the last 20 days

>> Selling at tomorrow's opening price when today's closing price is below the lowest low that occurred over the last 20 days

These trading rules are loosely based on the rules for *Donchian channels* (sometimes called *price channels*), which comprise a breakout system developed by Richard Donchian in the 1950s. Donchian was one of the early developers of trend-following trading systems.

A spreadsheet may be helpful for evaluating this system. You can, in fact, configure this system into a spreadsheet, include buy and sell signals, and perform analyses to determine how well the system performs. You also can use the spreadsheet to dig into the system's results to find out what works and what doesn't. Figure 16-1 shows an example.

Re-creating the spreadsheet in Figure 16-1 is straightforward. After downloading the historical price data into a spreadsheet format, all you have to do is encode the formulas into the correct columns. The formulas are described in the nearby sidebar "Creating the Donchian channel spreadsheet."

	A	B	C	D	E	F	G	H	I	J	K	L	M
						Donchian	Donchian	Change					
	Date	Open	High	Low	Close	High	Low	Flag	Buy / Sell	Buy Price	Gain (Loss)	MFE	MAE
	9/4/07	48.93	50.00	48.91	49.68	49.06	44.39	FALSE	-				
	9/5/07	49.56	49.65	48.87	49.18	50.00	44.39	TRUE	Buy	49.56	0.00%	0.18%	-1.39%
	9/6/07	49.23	49.36	48.81	49.14	50.00	44.39	TRUE	-	49.56	-0.67%		-1.51%
	9/7/07	48.53	48.60	47.95	48.23	50.00	44.39	TRUE	-	49.56	-2.08%		-3.25%
	9/10/07	48.62	48.75	47.81	48.20	50.00	44.39	TRUE	-	49.56	-1.90%		-3.53%
	9/11/07	48.51	48.99	48.43	48.93	50.00	44.39	TRUE	-	49.56	-2.12%		-2.28%
	9/12/07	48.84	49.37	48.78	48.94	50.00	44.39	TRUE	-	49.56	-1.45%		-1.57%
	9/13/07	49.29	49.35	48.94	49.18	50.00	44.39	TRUE	-	49.56	-0.54%		-1.25%
	9/14/07	48.80	49.31	48.73	49.22	50.00	44.39	TRUE	-	49.56	-1.53%		-1.67%
	9/17/07	49.00	49.10	48.59	48.81	50.00	45.59	TRUE	-	49.56	-1.13%		-1.96%
	9/18/07	49.09	50.08	48.83	50.04	50.00	46.08	TRUE	-	49.56	-0.95%	1.05%	-1.47%
	9/19/07	50.29	50.59	49.98	50.17	50.08	46.39	TRUE	-	49.56	1.47%	2.08%	
	9/20/07	50.06	50.26	49.92	50.03	50.59	46.71	TRUE	-	49.56	1.01%	1.41%	
	9/21/07	50.28	50.52	50.01	50.36	50.59	46.71	TRUE	-	49.56	1.45%	1.94%	
	9/24/07	50.49	50.96	50.33	50.59	50.59	46.71	TRUE	-	49.56	1.88%	2.82%	
	9/25/07	50.42	51.07	50.36	51.07	50.96	46.71	TRUE	-	49.56	1.74%	3.05%	
	9/26/07	51.36	51.51	51.12	51.32	51.07	46.71	TRUE	-	49.56	3.63%	3.93%	
	9/27/07	51.62	51.65	51.36	51.58	51.51	47.05	TRUE	-	49.56	4.16%	4.22%	
	9/28/07	51.54	51.68	51.18	51.41	51.65	47.75	TRUE	-	49.56	4.00%	4.28%	
	10/1/07	51.45	52.16	51.38	52.00	51.68	47.81	TRUE	-	49.56	3.81%	5.25%	
	10/2/07	52.04	52.06	51.72	52.01	52.16	47.81	TRUE	-	49.56	5.00%	5.04%	
	10/3/07	51.84	52.07	51.50	51.65	52.16	47.81	TRUE	-	49.56	4.60%	5.06%	
	10/4/07	51.75	51.83	51.34	51.77	52.16	47.81	TRUE	-	49.56	4.42%	4.58%	
	10/5/07	52.17	52.90	52.06	52.82	52.16	47.81	TRUE	-	49.56	5.27%	6.74%	
	10/8/07	52.80	53.16	52.71	53.15	52.90	47.81	TRUE	-	49.56	6.54%	7.26%	
	10/9/07	53.27	53.45	53.03	53.38	53.16	48.43	TRUE	-	49.56	7.49%	7.85%	
	10/10/07	53.39	53.57	53.21	53.51	53.45	48.59	TRUE	-	49.56	7.73%	8.09%	
	10/11/07	53.79	53.94	52.28	52.66	53.57	48.59	TRUE	-	49.56	8.54%	8.84%	
	10/12/07	52.90	53.54	52.80	53.53	53.94	48.59	TRUE	-	49.56	6.74%	8.03%	
	10/15/07	53.61	53.71	52.70	53.12	53.94	48.59	TRUE	-	49.56	8.17%	8.37%	
	10/16/07	52.79	53.28	52.68	52.87	53.94	48.83	TRUE	-	49.56	6.52%	7.51%	
	10/17/07	53.62	53.66	52.68	53.55	53.94	49.92	TRUE	-	49.56	8.19%	8.27%	
	10/18/07	53.33	53.89	53.12	53.78	53.94	49.92	TRUE	-	49.56	7.61%	8.74%	
	10/19/07	53.77	53.77	52.39	52.44	53.94	50.01	TRUE	-	49.56	8.49%	8.49%	
	10/22/07	52.16	53.12	52.02	53.07	53.94	50.33	TRUE	-	49.56	5.25%	7.18%	
	10/23/07	53.61	54.21	53.34	54.18	53.94	50.36	TRUE	-	49.56	8.17%	9.38%	
	10/24/07	53.74	53.94	52.60	53.77	54.21	51.12	TRUE	-	49.56	8.43%	8.84%	
	10/25/07	53.89	53.98	52.75	53.05	54.21	51.18	TRUE	-	49.56	8.74%	8.92%	
	10/26/07	54.08	54.20	53.44	53.93	54.21	51.18	TRUE	-	49.56	9.12%	9.36%	
	10/29/07	54.19	54.33	53.84	54.15	54.21	51.34	TRUE	-	49.56	9.34%	9.62%	
	10/30/07	53.94	54.56	53.90	54.26	54.33	51.34	TRUE	-	49.56	8.84%	10.09%	
	10/31/07	54.47	55.07	54.04	55.03	54.56	51.34	TRUE	-	49.56	9.91%	11.12%	
	11/1/07	54.68	54.77	53.97	54.00	55.07	51.34	TRUE	-	49.56	10.33%	10.51%	
	11/2/07	54.42	54.55	53.60	54.42	55.07	52.02	TRUE	-	49.56	9.81%	10.07%	
	11/5/07	53.86	54.40	53.59	54.07	55.07	52.02	TRUE	-	49.56	8.68%	9.77%	
	11/6/07	54.33	54.69	53.78	54.68	55.07	52.02	TRUE	-	49.56	9.62%	10.35%	
	11/7/07	54.22	54.58	53.31	53.35	55.07	52.02	TRUE	-	49.56	9.40%	10.13%	
	11/8/07	53.14	53.33	50.80	51.73	55.07	52.02	TRUE	-	49.56	7.22%	7.61%	
	11/9/07	50.73	51.12	50.00	50.00	55.07	50.80	FALSE	Sell	49.56	2.36%		

Spreadsheet courtesy of Michael Griffis

FIGURE 16-1: Spreadsheet analysis for Donchian channels.

If you're like most traders, the first thing you'll do is calculate some statistics about the system. For example, you can use spreadsheet functions to calculate the following:

» Total gain or loss for the system

» Average gain (the numerical average)

>> Median gain (the middle result)

>> Maximum gain for any single trade

>> Maximum loss for any single trade

>> Standard deviation

You can then look at aggregate results to find out whether the system actually made money. In the case of the Donchian channel breakout system, initial results don't look promising. The system lost money during the entire test period.

If you're like most traders, your impulse is to discard the idea and move on to another. But with the Donchian channel breakout system, you need to dig a little further before you do. During the time frame of this test, the system triggered 30 trades, 18 of which were losing trades. However, 13 of those losing trades were profitable at some point during the process, and all the winning trades gave back a large part of the profits before the sell signal was triggered. In fact, many of the profitable trades gave back significantly more than half of the profits before the sell signal.

Figure 16-1 shows how a single position from the spreadsheet progressed. The entry trade was triggered when the price of QQQQ closed above the September 4 Donchian high. In this simulated trade, the stock was purchased at the September 5 opening price of $49.56 and then sold on November 9, the day after the price of QQQQ closed below the November 8 Donchian low.

If you look through the last three columns, you'll notice that this simulated trade was profitable but closed well below its most profitable price. If that happens once during simulated trading, you may not need to worry much about it, but if it occurs frequently, you need to think of ways to remedy the problem.

TIP

In the Donchian channels system, buy signals apparently work better than sell signals. Therefore, you need to consider different types of stops and sell signals. One simple idea that's worth testing is stopping out (selling at a predetermined price) of a position if the stock's low (instead of its close) falls below the Donchian low. Another is to shorten the time frame for the exit signal by using a five- or ten-day Donchian channel. Or you can, for example, use a trailing stop or some completely different criteria to exit these positions.

In any case, this example gives you ideas about how you can use a spreadsheet to test and analyze any trading system. It also provides you with some suggestions about how you can use this kind of analysis to improve your system's results.

CREATING THE DONCHIAN CHANNEL SPREADSHEET

The opening, high, low, and closing prices for the QQQQ exchange-traded fund were copied into Columns B through E of the spreadsheet found in Figure 16-1.

You need at least 20 rows worth of data before you can calculate the first Donchian price channels. (These first 20 rows are not shown in Figure 16-1.) The following calculations assume that column headers are in the first row, and the price data begins in the second row. So the row containing data for 9/4/07 is Row 21. After entering a formula in the following columns, copy the formula for that column to every row that has price data.

The remaining columns are configured as follows:

- **Column F** is the *upper Donchian channel*. Use the spreadsheet MAX function to find the highest price value for the previous 20 trading days. Start this calculation in Row 22, giving 20 rows of data. The calculation for Row 22, Column F, is =MAX(C2:C21).

  Notice that the formula doesn't include the current row. If it did, the current close would never cross above the Donchian channel line.

- **Column G** is the *lower Donchian channel*. Use the MIN function to find the lowest low for the previous trading day. Start this calculation in Row 22, using 20 rows of data. The calculation for Row 22, column F, is =MIN(D2:D21).

  As for the upper Donchian channel, the formula doesn't include the current row.

- **Column H** is the *change flag* indicator. This flag is a simple way to avoid triggering more than one sequential buy or sell signal. It's also useful for calculating the remaining cells. Simply stated, the cell displays either TRUE for a buy signal or FALSE for a sell signal. If yesterday's close is greater than the Donchian high, turn on the TRUE condition. If yesterday's close is less than the Donchian low, turn on the FALSE condition. Otherwise, copy the TRUE or FALSE condition from the previous day into this column.

  In Row 22, Column H, type the formula =FALSE(). Then in Row 23, Column H, the formula is =IF(E22>F22,TRUE(),IF(E22<G22,FALSE(),H22)).

- **Column I** is the *buy/sell* indicator. This column shows when a buy or sell signal first is triggered. It compares the current change-flag value with the previous value. If they're equal, a dash goes in the cell. Otherwise, the word *Buy* is shown when the change flag is TRUE and *Sell* is shown when it's FALSE. The formula for Row 23, Column I, is =IF(H23=H22,"-",IF(H23,"Buy","Sell")).

(continued)

(continued)

- **Column J** is the *buy price.* This column shows the trade entry price. If the buy/sell flag indicates a buy, then put today's opening price in the cell. Remember the trading rule is to buy at the opening price on the day following the trade entry signal and sell at the opening price on the day following the trade exit signal. Therefore, the sell signal requires a special case. If the change flag indicator is TRUE for either today or the previous day (the special sell signal case), copy the trade price from the previous day to today. Otherwise, the change flag is FALSE, so leave the cell blank. The formula for Row 23, Column J, is =IF(I23="Buy",B23,IF(OR(H23,H22),J22,"")).

- **Column K** is the *gain/loss* indicator. This column shows a running total of the gain or loss in the trade, assuming the trade closes at the current opening price. The first row after a buy signal always shows 0 percent. The last row following a sell signal is the actual gain or loss from the simulated trade. The formula for Row 23, Column K, is =IF(OR(H22,H23),(B23-J23)/J23,"").

- **Column L** is the *MFE,* which is short for *most favorable excursion.* This column shows a running total of the best possible outcome for the trade as though it were closed at the high price of the day. This column is useful for what-if analyses but not for estimating your actual gains or losses. You rarely, if ever, sell at the high price for the day or the MFE for a trade. The calculation is simple. If the change-flag indicator is TRUE and if today's high is greater than the purchase price, calculate the percentage gain. Otherwise, leave the cell blank. The formula for Row 23, Column L, is =IF(H23,IF(C23>J23,(C23-J23)/J23,""),"").

- **Column M** is the *MAE,* or *most adverse excursion.* This column shows a running total of the worst possible outcomes for the trade as though it were closed at the low for the day. This column is useful for what-if analyses but not for estimating actual gains or losses from the trade. You rarely, if ever, sell at the low price for the day or at the MAE for a trade. The calculation is simple: If the change-flag indicator is TRUE, and if today's low is less than the purchase price, calculate the percentage loss. Otherwise, leave the cell blank. The formula for Row 23, Column M, is =IF(H23,IF(D23<J23,(D23-J23)/J23,""),"").

Make sure you have copied the formulas in each column to every row that includes price data.

To evaluate the results, you can copy the trading signals, gain and loss values, and MFE and MAE values from your system to a new spreadsheet. Paste the values using the spreadsheet's Paste Special function. You then can sort and analyze the data in any way you choose.

Accounting for slippage

Slippage is the term traders use to describe the costs of trading, which is made up of two components. The first is the actual transaction or commission cost for executing your trade. The second is more difficult to measure because it's the sum of the costs of unfavorable fills. If, for example, you're planning to buy at tomorrow's opening price based on today's closing price, those two prices can be much different. An unfavorable fill is a cost of trading and accounted for as slippage.

TIP

Most trading system–development packages have a provision for estimating slippage costs when testing your trading ideas using historical data. If you know your transaction costs, enter the exact amounts. Otherwise, estimate the transaction cost. You probably need to overestimate the cost of unfavorable fills because it always seems to end up being worse in actual trading than most traders ever imagine. You may want to start with an estimate of 25 cents per share and adjust it as you gather data on your actual slippage costs.

Keeping a Trading Journal

One of the most impactful, high-leveraged activities you can adopt is to keep track of all your trading activities in a trading journal. Doing so tracks your experiences in the market, helps you process and carefully analyze them while also keeping them in a permanent place, and then allows you to return to those journal entries at a later time to learn from your past experiences. When kept right, your trading journal becomes an invaluable reference manual that can help you recall both what you've done right and what you've done wrong in the past, thus keeping you on the right track moving forward and preventing the same mistakes again in the future. A trading journal can help you analyze your trades and trading systems to determine which aspects of trading you do well and which ones you need to work on.

When you develop a trading system, save ideas and test results in your journal. When you enter a position, record everything about the trade. Include your thoughts as you contemplate making the trade. When you have a what-was-I-thinking moment later on, you can find the answer in your journal.

TIP

Using a loose-leaf binder to hold your trading journal is probably best. Print before and after charts for each trade and include them in the journal. Keep detailed notes about each trade and about the system you used to trigger the trade. At a minimum, your notes need to include the following:

>> Trade date

>> Stock symbol

- >> Number of shares and why you chose that number

- >> Whether you bought long or sold short

- >> Which system triggered the entry signal

- >> Which system triggered the exit signal

- >> Where you placed your initial stops

- >> If and why you moved your stops

- >> What caused you to exit the position and why

- >> The percentage gain or loss from the trade

- >> Whether any economic reports or announcements were made around or during the time of the trade

- >> Your thoughts, hopes, and fears that you had before opening the position and while the position was open

You can also use your journal to keep track of more than just your trading history. Save Internet articles or blogs that influenced your thinking. Cut out and archive the new high and new low lists from the newspaper. Keep a record showing leading and lagging industries. Save sector charts along with your trade records. Whatever information you use to make trading decisions needs to be in your trading journal.

REMEMBER

You can improve only the things that you measure. Record statistics about your trades. Include the duration of each trade, the MFE, and the MAE. After you close a trade, write down what you could have done differently. Find out whether you can identify signals that can help you recognize similar situations in future trades.

REMEMBER

Although keeping the journal is important, it's useful only when you review it regularly. Spend a little time every week or month reviewing all your trades so you can pinpoint consistent mistakes or missed opportunities. Be brutally honest with yourself and use your journal as an opportunity to step back, take a cold, hard look at your trading decisions, and evaluate how you can improve moving forward. Every trader, no matter how experienced, always has room to grow. Your trading journal should become the soil that nurtures that growth.

Evaluating Trading Systems for Hire

You'll see advertisements on the Internet, in trade magazines, and in newspapers for foolproof systems that promise amazing returns. Sometimes you'll even see claims for systems that regularly return hundreds of percent with little or no risk.

Although some stocks do actually achieve astronomical returns of hundreds and sometimes thousands of percent, those cases are rare. Consider this: A system that offers profits of 100 percent per year supposedly grows $10,000 into $10 million dollars in only ten years. *Be skeptical.* Experienced traders know that no system consistently returns 100 percent per year.

Consider this: If you created such a system, would you sell it?

When evaluating these systems, the devil is in the details. Advertisements often are unclear about how a system actually works in real-world trading, and some vendors make claims based on nothing more than the results of system testing based only on simulated trades and historical data. In fact, the system's author may never have traded the system using real capital.

Constructing a system that shows great profits when simulating trades with historical data is easy. If you designed a trend-following system and tested it against data during the period 1997–2000, or 2003–2007, you can be fairly certain that the system is going to perform well in simulated testing. But that doesn't mean you should use it to trade real money.

REMEMBER

If a system sounds too good to be true, it probably is. So do your own homework. Find out what works and what doesn't, and save your hard-earned trading capital for trading.

5

Risk-Taker's Paradise

IN THIS PART . . .

Swing trading doesn't involve a visit to the park. Find out the strategies of these short-term holdings.

Day trading can sometimes seem like a computer game, but lots of money is at stake. Find out how it works.

Options and futures offer another way to trade. Discover how they work.

Trading currency can add a new dimension to your portfolio, but it can be a wild ride. Find out why.

Chapter **17**

The Basics of Swing Trading

Swing trading is a trading strategy that tries to take advantage of short-term opportunities in the market. It occupies the middle ground between position trading and day trading. Swing traders use trend-following and counter-trend strategies to participate in trading-range and trending stocks. This turbo-charged trading style requires an exceptional understanding of the inner workings of the markets and excellent analysis capabilities.

In this chapter, we discuss a few of the basic techniques used by swing traders along with the risks that are unique to the discipline. We also talk about tax issues and account restrictions unique to swing trading.

Selecting Stocks Carefully

REMEMBER

Swing trading is a technical discipline. Although no hard-and-fast rule defines it, swing traders often trade in 100-share increments and usually limit the number of simultaneous positions to ten or fewer. A swing trade can last as little as a few hours to as long as a few weeks, but typical swing trades span no more than a few days. On this kind of timescale, fundamental analysis has little impact on a stock's price movement; therefore, swing traders make stock selections using technical-analysis tools. Careful trade management is crucial to swing-trading success.

Stock selection is even more important for swing trading than it is for position trading. When you're looking for a stock to move right away, you base your decisions on selection criteria that are different from when you're positioning for a move that may last several weeks to several months. Following are a few of the important selection criteria that swing traders use:

>> **Volume and liquidity:** Swing traders typically focus on actively traded and relatively large stocks. The goal is finding stocks that are easy to buy, sell, and sell short. When trading time frames are short, you need to be able to execute your orders quickly. Unfortunately, stocks with the greatest liquidity and trading volumes are closely followed by the largest number of professional traders, which usually constrains the number of profitable swing-trading opportunities, so swing traders often scout opportunities outside of the 25 or so stocks that have the highest trading volume and greatest liquidity.

>> **Trending:** Trending stocks provide the best opportunity for swing-trading profits. You may use either the methods described in Chapter 9 for identifying trending stocks or the *average directional index* (ADX) indicator. This indicator has three components: the ADX reading and two *directional movement indicators* — the +DMI and the –DMI. An ADX reading of more than 30 or so indicates a trending stock. A comparison of the two DMIs shows you whether the ADX is trending up or down. If the value of +DMI is larger than the value of –DMI, then the stock is trending higher. If the value of –DMI is larger than the value of +DMI, the stock is trending lower. The ADX indicator is included in most charting applications.

>> **Volatility:** Swing traders depend on larger, or more volatile, short-term moves for profits. As a result, they want to trade stocks that have histories of making large moves in short periods of time. One popular approach to finding them is keeping an eye on the *average daily ranges* (ADRs), which are simple moving averages that track the day-to-day differences between an individual stock's daily high and low prices. If you're swing trading, you want stocks that show high ADRs. Volatility also can be measured using historic volatility, which we discuss in the later "Trading volatility" section.

>> **Sector selection:** Just like position trading, swing traders try to trade stocks in the strongest sectors, and the weakest sectors are candidates for short sales. Use the techniques described in Chapter 13 to identify strong and weak sectors.

>> **Tight spreads:** As a means of controlling slippage (see Chapter 16), you need to pay close attention to the difference between the bid and ask prices of the stocks you're considering as swing-trading prospects. Stocks with wide

spreads make profitable swing trading difficult. Low-priced stocks rarely are good candidates for swing trading because the spread, as a percentage of the stock price, is usually too wide.

Looking at Swing-Trading Strategies

Swing trading fluctuates between the use of trend-following and countertrend strategies:

» When a stock is trending strongly, swing traders primarily employ trend-following techniques but may use countertrend techniques to fine-tune exit points.

» When a stock is range bound, swing traders use countertrend methods to identify entry and exit points.

Trading trending stocks

TIP

Technical-analysis patterns that we cover in Chapters 9 through 13 are all applicable to swing trading. Patterns repeat in all time frames; the difference is in how swing traders use and interpret these common patterns. Trend-following strategies are more aggressive for swing trading than they are for position trading. Although swing traders use some of the same indicators and patterns used by position traders, they often use them in different ways. We explain a few examples in the sections that follow.

Trading pullbacks

A *pullback* is another name for a consolidation within a trend. Consolidation patterns include the flags and pennants discussed in Chapter 10. Swing traders use daily charts and intraday charts — ranging from 1-minute bars to 60-minute bar charts — to identify the dominant short-term trend and any pullback patterns within the trend. They try to enter a position when the price of a targeted stock stops declining or pulling back so they can capture the next move higher in the trend. Conceptually, pullback trading is simple, but in practice, it's trickier than it sounds.

After you identify a trending stock and find a flag or pennant pullback pattern by visually examining the daily charts, you must try to enter a position just as the pullback is ending. The classic setup is finding an orderly pullback in which the high of each bar on a chart of the pullback is lower than the previous one. Figure 17-1 shows an idealized example of the type of pattern you're trying to find.

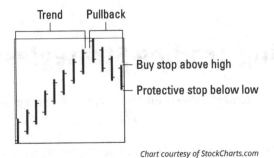

FIGURE 17-1:
An example of an orderly pullback.

Chart courtesy of StockCharts.com

Entering a position is done by placing a buy stop order with your broker. A buy stop is like any stop order; when the price is hit, the order is executed. (See Chapter 12 for details.) Entering a position to trade pullbacks is an iterative process, so we recommend using a day order instead of a good-'til-canceled order (see Chapter 15). Here are the steps:

1. Select your buy stop price so it's just above the intraday high price shown in the last bar of the chart.

2. If the stock price trades above your buy stop price, your order is executed.

   Otherwise, the order is canceled at the end of the day.

3. As long as you're still interested in this trade, adjust your buy stop price to just above the intraday high of the most recent bar on the chart and reenter your order.

4. After your order is filled, place a stop-loss order (see Chapter 12) using a stop price just below the intraday low of the lowest bar in the pullback on the chart.

5. As long as the trade is active, continue adjusting the stop price to be just below the intraday low of the most recent bar on the chart.

Figure 17-2 is a price chart of the stock of National Oilwell Varco, Inc. (NOV), that's showing a strong uptrend. Several opportunities for trading pullbacks are also shown on this chart.

The first pullback occurred after NOV traded to a new high of $30.44 on January 23, 2007. That new high is labeled Bar #1 on the chart. After identifying the pullback, you begin the iterative process of setting the buy stop price just above the high of the last bar on the chart. At the end of each day, you reset the buy stop price, again setting it just above the high of the last bar, and reenter the order.

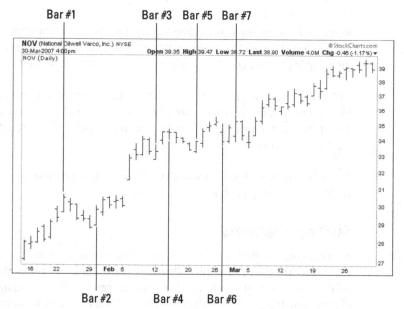

Bar #1   **Bar #3**   **Bar #5**   **Bar #7**

Bar #2   **Bar #4**   **Bar #6**

FIGURE 17-2:
A chart of National Oilwell Varco (NOV) showing pullback trading examples.

Chart courtesy of StockCharts.com

In this example, the trade is triggered on Bar #2, which occurred January 30. You had set the buy price just above the January 29 high, which was $29.44. NOV opened January 30 at $28.90. The trade was triggered when the stock climbed above $29.45, rising as high as $30.01 before backing off to close at $29.80. You could expect your order to fill very near your $29.45 buy stop price. For the sake of our example, we assume a fill price of $29.50.

Immediately following the trade execution, you set a stop-loss order below the low of the previous bar, $28.74 in this case. Or you may set the low at $28.90, the trade day's low. Either approach makes sense, so it's your call. Each day that the trade remains active, reset the stop order just below the low of the previous bar on the chart.

The thrust of this trend lasted through February 12, 2007, a duration of ten trading days. This position hit the stop price on February 12, labeled Bar #3 on the chart in Figure 17-2, when the stock traded below the February 9 low of $33.03.

The next opportunity to trade a pullback occurred during the pullback that began after NOV traded at a new high on February 13, labeled Bar #4. The trade was triggered on February 21, shown as Bar #5, when NOV traded above the February 20 high of $33.85. The position hit its stop price on February 27, shown as Bar #6, when the stock traded below the February 26 low of $34.91. Given slippage and transaction costs, this trade was no better than a break-even trade.

The next opportunity came following the poorly formed pullback that began with Bar #6. You entered the trade on Bar #7 when NOV traded above the February 28 intraday high of $35.00. The trade would stop out two bars later for a loss.

NOV traded at $66.32 on April 26, 2012. There were many trading opportunities for a swing trader using this stock between 2009 and 2013. Practice finding good swing trades by working with historical charts and look for trends similar to the ones noted earlier.

Swing trades don't always work out, of course. Complications and frequent losing trades always are possible.

Surfing channels

Another trend-following approach to swing trading uses a channeling strategy to identify entry and exit points. Chapter 10 explains the channeling strategy and how to construct the channel lines. After you identify a channel on the daily charts, you treat channel lines as lines of support and resistance. Figure 17-3 shows an example.

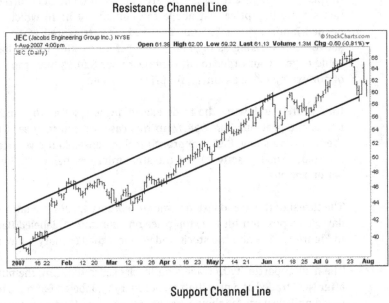

FIGURE 17-3:
A chart of Jacobs Engineering Group, Inc. (JEC), in a trend channel.

Chart courtesy of StockCharts.com

After identifying support and resistance levels for a channeling stock, you can monitor its chart for reversals near the channel lines. As the stock price approaches the lower or *support channel line*, you have an opportunity to take a position in the direction of the trend. After entering a position, your stop-loss order is entered just below the support channel line. As the stock price approaches the upper or *resistance channel line*, it signals when to exit your position.

TIP

You can use intraday charts to fine-tune this strategy. As a stock price falls toward its lower channel or support level, begin watching intraday charts for indications that the stock is changing direction and heading higher. If you see an intraday low near the location of the support channel line, followed by a higher high and a higher low, you can use that situation as an entry signal. After entering a long position, you place a stop-loss order just below the support channel line.

You hold this long position until either it stops out or the stock approaches its upper channel-resistance level. Again, you need to monitor the intraday charts for hints of a change in direction and exit the trade whenever you see the reversal. After that, you wait for the stock to head back toward the lower channel line to initiate a new long trade.

Trading range-bound stocks

Unlike the typical position trader, a swing trader is more likely to use counter-trend strategies (see Chapter 16) and actively participate when a stock is range bound. The swing trader tries to make trades based on price movements from the bottom to the top of the range and back down again. You can use either daily or weekly charts to identify the trading range. An example using a daily chart is shown in Figure 17-4.

Your trading approach to range-bound stocks is similar to the one for trading a channeling stock that we describe in the previous section, "Surfing channels." As the stock price approaches the support level, which is just above $59.00 in Figure 17-4, you have an opportunity to take a position. You can use a few approaches to enter a position.

You can, for example, simply choose to place a buy order using a limit price just above the support line. Another approach that may give you a little more control and provide better entry and exit points is to monitor the stock to find pivot points as it trades near the support line. A *pivot point* is a three-bar pattern in which the low price of the middle bar is lower than the lows of the bars on either side of it. The entry and exit points for this kind of trading are similar to the ones used for trading based on a pullback pattern. After identifying a pivot point, you enter an order on the next bar. You place the protective stop either immediately below the low of the pivot bar or just below the support channel line.

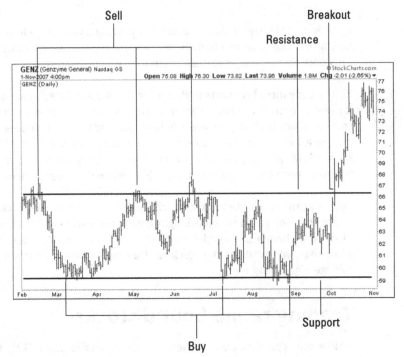

Sell   Breakout

Resistance

GENZ (Genzyme General) Nasdaq GS   © StockCharts.com
1-Nov-2007 4:00pm   Open 75.08 High 76.30 Low 73.82 Last 73.96 Volume 1.8M Chg -2.01 (-2.65%) ▼
GENZ (Daily)

Support

Buy

FIGURE 17-4:
A chart of
Genzyme General
(GENZ) stock
prices bound
within a trading
range.

Chart courtesy of StockCharts.com

TIP

Using intraday charts is another way to fine-tune your entry point. As the stock approaches the support line, you enter a position as soon as you see a reversal pattern on the intraday charts — for example, a higher high and a higher low, or a gap higher (see Chapter 10).

You exit these kinds of positions when the stock reverses near its resistance line. You can then take a short position in the stock — using any of the entry techniques described earlier — or wait for the stock to return to the support line to initiate another long position.

If the stock breaks through its upper resistance level, you interpret that condition exactly the way a position trader does — a very bullish indication that the stock is likely beginning a new trend, immediately closing any open short positions and converting to a trend-following strategy (see the earlier section "Trading trending stocks").

SWINGING WITH GANN AND TAYLOR

Swing trading has been around in one form or another since the earliest days of markets. The term itself probably originated with W. D. Gann when he invented the swing chart during the 1920s. George Douglass Taylor popularized the phrase, and a short-term trading technique, when he introduced a now classic three-bar trading pattern in his 1950 book, *The Taylor Trading Technique.*

Taylor's ideas serve as the basis for much of today's swing-trading methodology. According to Taylor, trending stocks tend to rally, rest, and then continue to trend. Swing traders watch for these rest periods and attempt to enter the market just in advance of the thrust of the new trend.

Taylor's method, sometimes called *the book trader's method,* was originally developed to trade futures contracts in the grain markets. Taylor theorized that the market cycles through three distinct phases or days. The first phase is the buy day, the second is a sell day, and the third is a sell-short day. Although these three days don't necessarily fall on consecutive days, for the sake of following the discussion, we assume they do.

Taylor first determines the short-term trend, finds the position of the short-term cycle within the trend, and then uses this information to determine when to buy, sell, or sell short. The buy day begins the cycle. A typical buy day begins with weakness, and the trader takes a long position near a previously identified support level based on the weakness. This position is held overnight into the next day, the sell day. The sell day typically opens strong, but the strength fades before the close. The trader sells at the early signs of weakness. The final day of the cycle is the sell-short day. The trader watches for any strength near resistance levels on the third day and sells short into this strength. The short position is held overnight and then covered during early weakness the following buy day. The cycle begins in earnest again with the trader initiating a long position after covering the short position.

Taylor's approach is difficult to execute. Like all swing trading, it requires constant monitoring of the market and an excellent understanding of support and resistance levels. It is a discretionary approach that is difficult to test. Few stocks actually follow a three-day script on consecutive days. Many stocks trend for several days before pulling back or rising, so the three-bar method must be adjusted to account for these differences. Nevertheless, Taylor's thinking is evident in much of today's swing-trading methodology.

Trading volatility

Swing traders try to trade stocks that move up and down more than average. To find these stocks, swing traders spend a great deal of effort measuring and analyzing volatility, usually in the form of historic volatility. Although the math required to calculate historic volatility is complex, the concept is simple. *Historic volatility* measures a stock's price movement. The faster it moves, the higher the historic volatility. Fortunately, many charting and analysis programs include a method for calculating historic volatility, so you don't have to program in the formula.

REMEMBER

Historic volatility isn't concerned with the direction of a stock's price movement. A high historic volatility value doesn't reveal whether a stock's price is rising or falling. Although swing traders want to know that a stock trends in one direction or the other, they don't really care which direction. Downside movement is just as attractive as upside movement to the swing trader.

TIP

You can use historic volatility for swing trading in several different ways. One popular approach uses historic volatility for finding stocks that have been very volatile but currently are experiencing quiet periods. These temporarily quiet stocks often return to previous levels of historic volatility, and that presents a swing-trading opportunity. Swing traders identify these stocks by comparing measurements of historic volatility across longer and much shorter periods of time and expressing that comparison as a ratio. The ratio looks like this:

Historic volatility ratio = Short-term historic volatility
÷ Long-term historic volatility

One common ratio compares a 6-day historic volatility with a 100-day historic volatility. Whenever the value of that ratio is less than 50 percent, the stock is a candidate for a swing-trading position.

After this stock takes a short low-volatility rest, it is likely to return to its historic level of volatility with a fast move. Remember that volatility tells you nothing about the direction of price movements, so to get around this limitation, be sure to place buy and sell-short stop orders, respectively, above the high and below the low of the current bar. When the stock decides which way it will go, one of your stop orders will be filled, and that should get you pointed in the right direction. Using more traditional technical-analysis tools is another approach to evaluating a stock's current trend so you can then trade in the direction of that trend.

WARNING

Risks accompany both approaches. Using the first approach, the stock may take off in one direction and quickly reverse course, and you may end up holding a position with a highly volatile stock heading the wrong way. This same scenario also can happen with the second approach. Another potential problem occurs when the stock price gaps through your entry order because your order may end up getting filled at a price that's significantly different from what you expected.

Money management issues

Because of the short duration of each trade, swing trading generates a large volume of trades. Execution and slippage costs (see Chapter 12) can be very high. Profits are relatively small when measured on each trade, so losses must be carefully controlled.

TIP

You need to adhere closely to the money management rules we discuss in Chapter 12. In addition, each swing trade must represent only a small percentage of your trading capital. Ten percent of your capital per trade is too much. Risking less than 5 percent — and perhaps as little as 2 percent — of your trading capital on any one swing trade is a more conservative approach. This approach is similar to the one used by professional traders. When profit potential is small, don't take big risks, or you won't be a swing trader for long.

Using Options for Swing Trading

Stock options can be used as substitutes for the underlying stocks when swing trading. A *stock option* is a limited-duration contract that grants the *option buyer* the right to either buy or sell a stock for a fixed price. The *option seller,* usually called the *option writer* or the *option grantor,* is granting the right to the option buyer to either buy or sell a specific stock for a fixed price.

Each option represents 100 shares of stock. A *call* is an option to buy 100 shares of a specified stock. The call buyer is acquiring a limited-duration right to buy 100 shares of a stock from the option grantor at a fixed price, called the *strike price.* A *put* is an option to sell 100 shares of a specified stock. The put buyer is acquiring a limited-duration right to sell 100 shares of a stock to the option grantor at the specified strike price. (Options are discussed in more detail in Chapter 19.)

You can, for example, substitute a call option for a long stock position or a put option for a short stock position. You realize any profits by selling the options outright, or you can exercise an option and take possession of the shares of stock. Swing traders, however, are more likely to sell the option than exercise it.

Although using options as stock substitutes has several advantages, doing so also has risks of its own. The primary advantage: An option costs far less than the underlying stock, which enables you to limit your risk to the price of the option.

Each option is a substitute for 100 shares of stock or 100 shares of an exchange-traded fund (ETF). One call option, for example, gives you the ability to buy 100 shares of a stock at a fixed price for a certain length of time. As an example, assume that the QQQQ exchange-traded fund is trading at $27.10 per share. At the time of the example, you can buy one call option with a $27 strike price for $2.26 per share, or a total of $226, before transaction costs. That one option enables you to buy 100 shares of QQQQ for $27 before the option expires.

Say that the option in this example has approximately six weeks before expiration. Your option position is therefore profitable as long as the QQQQ exchange-traded fund trades above $29.26 (excluding transaction costs) before the expiration date. (We determined the break-even price by adding the $27 strike price to the $2.26 cost of the option, which totals $29.26.) Your risk is the price of the option. In other words, you can't lose any more than $2.26 per share, or $226, on this trade.

Unfortunately, option pricing isn't as straightforward as stock pricing. The preceding pricing example is merely a snapshot that varies with changes in the price of the QQQQ exchange-traded fund. The following factors affect option prices:

>> Options expire and their prices decay as the expiration date draws closer. This price decay is caused by the option's falling time value.

>> The prices of current-month options decay at faster rates than longer-dated options.

>> In percentage terms, *out-of-the-money* options often move at a faster rate than *in-the-money* options. (An option is said to be in the money if it has intrinsic value, and it's out of the money if it has no intrinsic value. For a call option, that means the price for the underlying stock is greater than the specified strike price. For a put, that means the price for the underlying stock is less than the strike price. See Chapter 19 for additional details.)

WARNING

Trading options that are far out of the money is rarely a good strategy.

>> Volatility is a component of option pricing. Option prices rise and fall as the volatility of the stock rises and falls.

>> Except in a few unusual circumstances, an option's price doesn't move in lockstep with the underlying stock's price. If a stock moves $1, the option, in general, moves some amount less than $1. The more an option is in the money, the closer the change in an option's price will be to the change in the underlying stock's price.

Another factor to consider when substituting options for stocks is that the option's *spread*, or the difference between the bid price and the ask price, is extremely wide when considered as a percentage of the option price.

Before you decide to substitute options for your stock trades, make sure that you understand the option-pricing model; we discuss it in Chapter 19. And be careful that you don't overtrade with options. If you normally buy 100 shares of a stock, then you need to buy only one option contract. Although the price of ten option contracts may be attractive when compared with the price of the stock, ten option contracts nevertheless represent 1,000 shares of stock. When buying options for ten times the number of shares that you normally trade, you're increasing your exposure to risk by a factor of ten.

WARNING

When trading options, you can't make money in as many ways as you can lose it. Being right on the stock's direction but still losing money on an option trade is possible because of pricing issues. That's why gaining an understanding of the option-pricing model is so important before you try to substitute an option for a stock. We discuss options more fully in Chapter 19.

Getting a Grip on Swing-Trading Risks

Swing trading is risky and demands a great deal of time. As a swing trader, you must monitor the market during every trading hour. You also must be able to control your emotions so you stay focused and trade within your plan.

Ask any swing trader; you're likely to hear that strict adherence to money management reduces risk. The counterargument is that swing trading exposes a great deal of capital to risk but makes only small profits. Some traders are able to swing trade profitably, but you need to realize that the odds are stacked against you. Only you can decide whether it's worth the effort.

Some argue that swing trading combines the worst aspects of position trading with the worst aspects of day trading. Like in day trading, swing-trading profits are small, and slippage costs are high. Swing-trading positions are held overnight, so swing traders can't take advantage of the special margin provisions that are available to day traders, who close all positions by the end of the trading day. And swing traders are subject to the same account restrictions as day traders are, but they may not qualify for the special tax advantages afforded to full-time day traders.

Taxes (of course)

Special tax treatment is available from the IRS for full-time traders. The benefits enable full-time traders to be taxed as a business rather than as an investor, and that means you can deduct the cost of the computer hardware and software used for trading, and you can treat your home-office expenses, including the costs for data acquisition, as ordinary business expenses. Furthermore, you can convert capital gains and losses to ordinary gains and losses under the Mark-to-Market accounting rules in the IRS Code Section 475. Mark-to-Market rules enable you to avoid wash-sale regulations and deduct all losses against other income without hitting the $3,000 cap imposed on other investors.

Unfortunately, swing traders do not necessarily trade every day, so some swing traders have a difficult time qualifying for these special tax provisions. If you are unable to qualify as a full-time trader, then your swing trades will be taxed in the same way as every other investor. You must report gains and losses on IRS Schedule D, and you must adhere to wash-sale regulations. You may also run into difficulty if you try to report your trading expenses as a business deduction.

The rules are complex. You need to consult with your tax advisor to determine your eligibility. Information about the rules is in IRS Publication 550, in the last section of Chapter 4, "Special Rules for Traders in Securities." We provide more information in Chapter 18.

Pattern-day-trading rules apply

Swing traders are subject to the same rules as day traders. If a swing trader opens and closes a position in a single stock during one day and does this more than four times in a five-day period, the swing trader is categorized as a pattern day trader. If this occurs, the swing trader must maintain an equity balance of $25,000 in his account or his broker will prohibit him from making any day trades. Additional information about the pattern-day-trading rules is provided in Chapter 18.

This scenario actually is quite likely for the swing trader because of the number of stops that are hit. As a swing trader, you may as well plan to maintain a minimum equity balance in your trading account in excess of $25,000.

Chapter **18**

The Basics of Day Trading

D ay traders sometimes enter and exit trading positions more than 100 times in a single day. They may even get into and out of a position within the span of only a minute or two.

Some players compare watching the charts and jumping quickly in and out of positions to the rapid-fire action and excitement of a video game. However, much more is at risk. Instead of merely losing a game, a bad move can mean the loss of your entire portfolio, or maybe even more. Yes, day traders sometimes end up in negative positions, owing money to the firms with which they're trading. We explain how that can happen later in this chapter.

For now, you need to know that day traders rarely hold a stock overnight and that watching a computer screen for hours at a time is a critical part of the day for this high-stress type of trading. Although neither of us is or ever has been a day trader, in this chapter we nevertheless explain how this type of trading works, give you some common strategies used by these types of traders, explore restrictions the United States Securities and Exchange Commission (SEC) places on day traders, and show you the high levels of risk day traders face.

What Day Trading Is All About

Day traders try to fashion a career out of buying and selling stocks quickly throughout the day. A certain amount of day trading is critical to maintaining the liquidity of the stock market because the techniques they use keep the market moving. They're known as *institutional day traders* — market makers.

Retail day traders, on the other hand, are a different bunch. They may make dozens or even hundreds of trades a day, but they also close out all their positions at the end of each day. Retail day traders use technological developments that first became available in the late 1990s to get in on the action that used to be the sole province of the institutional day traders.

Institutional day traders (market makers)

Market makers are a critical part of the New York Stock Exchange (NYSE). All are members of an exchange either as an individual, a partnership, or part of a corporation. They're responsible for making markets in certain exchange-traded securities, maintaining inventories of the securities for which they're responsible, and making sure the market for those securities is orderly.

Market makers play a critical role in maintaining the liquidity and efficiency of NASDAQ-listed stocks and stocks that are sold over the counter and not listed in a particular exchange. They're usually part of a brokerage firm or bank that facilitates the buying and selling of stocks in these markets. A market maker must be ready to buy and sell stock on a regular and continual basis. More than 500 firms operate as NASDAQ market makers.

Market makers trade into and out of positions throughout the day, often executing orders in a matter of seconds. We discuss these types of traders in greater detail in Chapter 2.

Retail day traders

Retail day traders try to make money in a totally different way. The playing field of day trading opened for retail day traders in the late 1990s, when computer software was developed that enabled individual investors to have direct access to securities markets in ways that previously were technologically available only to licensed and registered professionals. Today, regulators believe retail day traders are responsible for about a third of NASDAQ's trading volume. Although stocks listed on the NASDAQ are a common choice for day traders, the preferred trading platform for most day traders is the *electronic communications network,* or ECN, because being connected to the markets in this manner makes becoming the highest bid or lowest ask price easier than doing so via directly trading on the NASDAQ (see Chapter 2). Since the NYSE bought ARCA (an ECN), the difference between NASDAQ and listed stock has shrunk, and we're now seeing significant day-trading volume on both NASDAQ and NYSE stocks.

It's all about access

Brokerage firms that promote day trading provide their customers with real-time links to the major stock markets and the NASDAQ system, which, in turn, gives them information not readily available to average retail investors. Brokerages also provide customers direct entry into their order-processing systems. This direct access enables day traders to send their orders to a particular market or market maker and to determine the order route — a task that only licensed professionals previously were able to accomplish. Although other online and traditional brokerage houses may provide real-time quotation information, they don't offer their customers linkages to markets and market makers. Instead, some have preset algorithms that determine where a customer's order is routed for execution, which may or may not be the cheapest way to go. Many times the algorithms are set based on trading agreements among firms without regard to cost effectiveness.

Why does direct access matter so much? Speed and, again we say, speed! Systems that provide more and more direct access give day traders the opportunity to execute their trades within seconds. In addition, by using a more direct route, traders can choose market makers whose bid or ask prices look the best and fill their orders instantly.

Traders also can post bid or ask prices directly on an ECN, or they can cancel orders with the click of a button, all because they have direct access. When establishing a position using a limit order through a traditional online broker, traders must go to the website and cancel their orders, and under those circumstances, they can't know whether their orders have been filled until they receive notice of cancellation.

REMEMBER

Day traders aren't looking to make a large profit on one huge sale every day, but instead they seek smaller profits on much more frequent changes in the positions they establish during the day. Mere seconds are critical when you're trying to get in and out of a position, trying to make money on small stock price differences that may be much less than a single point, which, in trading lingo, translates to a dollar in the nontrading world. Although swing traders and position traders seek profits of several points (dollars) with each position they enter, day traders may exit their position after earning a profit of only a few cents. Traders usually buy or sell at least 1,000 shares at a time, so 25 cents translates into a $250 profit for every 1,000 shares traded. In only a matter of seconds, what looked like a good price to a day trader can be lost.

By controlling where their orders are sent, day traders also gain better control over the costs of their trades. One of the ways that some traditional brokers make money on trades they execute for customers is charging a fee called a *payment for order flow*. These fees can be a penny or more per share of stock, providing something of a kickback to the brokerage house and enabling deep discount brokerages to charge smaller upfront commissions that barely cover the cost of their trades. Although online discount brokers send trades to particular markets or market makers through which they've established trading deals, day traders have the inside information to select the routes that give them the best prices.

Brokers must inform clients in writing upon opening an account whether they accept payments for order flow. If they do, the brokers must provide a detailed description of the type of payments. They must also disclose on trade confirmations whether they receive payment for order flow. Customers have the right to request the source and type of the payment for any particular transaction. So look for the details about payment for order flow when you choose your broker and look for details on your trade confirmations. For more information, read this primer on trade execution (https://www.sec.gov/investor/pubs/tradexec. htm) from the SEC.

Day-trading firms

In addition to direct access, day-trading firms provide (for a fee, of course) their customers with training in how to participate in this rapid-fire, price-sensitive buying and selling and then encourage their trainees to use their strategies and their software. These firms developed proprietary software and systems that day traders use to analyze and chart activity and execute orders. This software usually is available only at on-site trading facilities or downloadable to your computer rather than being used through websites.

REMEMBER

Day trading through a website isn't usually done because the added seconds it takes to download price information and then send back an order is likely to result in the loss of your order to some other trader. Even when a trader has high-speed Internet access, the trader can spend too much time waiting for pages to load and sending orders. So to be successful, day traders need the instant access they get through proprietary software.

Day-trading firms are organized in one of two ways — as *traditional broker-dealers* (day traders open accounts with the firm and trade using their own accounts) or as *proprietary trading firms* (or a prop firm for short) that either sell interest in the firms to traders who want to day trade or hire traders as independent contractors. Typically, a proprietary trading firm is organized as a limited liability company (LLC), which is a corporate structure used to minimize the legal exposure of the firm. LLCs are not a separate entity for tax purposes, but they still enjoy many of the legal protections offered to C corporations.

TIP

You can find a directory of proprietary trading firms at Traders Log (www.traderslog.com/proprietarytradingfirms). Some of these firms offer stock trading, and others focus on futures and options trading.

As part owners or contractors rather than customers, day traders are associated with the firm, and as such, they can trade using a portion of the firm's capital. Most of these arrangements require traders to put up at least $25,000 to buy in. More often, however, the buy-in required is closer to $100,000. This arrangement enables day traders to use much more leverage than traditional broker-dealer arrangements do, where borrowing on margin is limited to amounts held in individual traders' accounts under Regulation T margin requirements. (We explain how margin accounts work in Chapter 15.) In addition to buying into the LLC, traders for these firms also are required to get a Series 7 license, and some firms require Series 55 and Series 63 licenses.

Understanding Account Restrictions

The Federal Reserve's Regulation T is one of the key restrictions in the SEC arsenal of tools for controlling day trading. Rules related to the settlement of stock transactions and borrowing from others to meet margin requirements also limit what day traders can do.

The Fed's Regulation T: Margin requirements

The world of day trading became much more restricted in August 2001 when amendments to Regulation T were approved that focus on pattern day traders. Your broker and the Financial Industry Regulatory Authority (FINRA) consider you a *pattern day trader* whenever you buy and sell (or short and cover) any security on the same day within a margin account four or more times during any rolling five-day period. Days when the markets are closed — Saturday, Sunday, and market holidays — are not included when calculating the rolling five-day period.

WARNING

After you're designated a pattern day trader, you're required to maintain a minimum of $25,000 of equity in your margin account before you're ever permitted to do any more day trading. For most day traders, that means having at least $25,000 in cash at the end of every trading day. This limitation can impact other investing activities in your account, so if you're considering day trading, be sure to talk with your broker to gain an understanding of the impact that margin account minimums have on other stock transactions you may want to make within your account.

After you've been designated as a pattern day trader and maintain the $25,000 minimum in your margin account, you're entitled to borrow up to four times any amount you maintain in your margin account. For example, if you maintain $50,000 in your account, this gives you up to $200,000 of *day-trading buying power*. But remember, this extra buying power is limited only to intraday trades. If you hold positions overnight, you can't take advantage of the day-trading margin when opening a position. You must adhere to the traditional 50 percent initial margin requirements.

Typically, day traders are *flat*, or back into a cash position by the end of the trading day for all day trades; otherwise, you risk a margin call (see Chapter 15). Whenever your day-trading activities result in a margin call, you have at most five days — but some brokers require payment in fewer days — to deposit cash or securities in your account to meet the call. If you fail to meet the margin call, your account will be restricted to traditional margin requirements.

Although brokerage firms aren't required to monitor whether day-trading accounts fall below the $25,000 minimum throughout a given trading day, customers must cover any losses incurred in their accounts from the previous day's trades before they're allowed to continue day trading. If a day trader exceeds the four times leverage rule during the day, a brokerage firm can impose additional restrictions on the account to protect itself from additional risk and prevent any recurrences of such activities.

Members of FINRA are required to issue day-trading margin calls to pattern day traders who exceed their day-trading buying power. Traders then have five days unless their broker has stricter rules to meet these calls. Until a margin call is met, the day-trading account's buying power is restricted to traditional margin requirements, which allows the day trader to leverage equity only two times. For example, if a day trader has $50,000 of equity but the account is restricted due to exceeding buying-power constraints, the day-trading buying power is only $100,000. These stricter requirements begin on the trading day after buying power is exceeded and stay in place until the trader either meets the call by depositing the necessary cash or securities or until five business days have passed. After five business days have passed and the day trader still has not met the call, the day trader is limited to trading only on a cash-available basis for 90 days or until the call is met.

Traders can't meet the call and then just take the money right out again. Funds deposited to meet the call must be left in the account for at least two business days. Traders also can't use *cross-guarantees* (guarantees from third parties) for the margin call. The cash or securities must be deposited directly in the account.

Settlement: No free rides

An official stock transaction is settled three days after the date of the trade, meaning that day traders frequently are buying and selling stocks before their transactions are officially settled. Day traders can't *free ride,* meaning they can't buy a security and sell it an hour later without first having enough funds to cover the settlement of the initial trade. If a trader buys a stock or other security, he or she must have the funds to cover the initial trade even if the security is sold for a profit within the same day.

A margin account with leverage of four times excess equity is what enables day traders to get around this rule. To play within these rules, all the trader needs to have is sufficient cash to pay for the shares or sufficient reserve in his or her margin account. Brokers can restrict the use of margin funds for three days until a stock transaction is settled, but they're not required to do so.

REMEMBER

Before trading, be sure that you understand the restrictions your broker imposes on margin accounts related to stock transaction settlements. The settlement time for options is the next day, as opposed to the three-day waiting period for stocks. To trade using options, funds must be in the account before you place the trade or you'll be stuck wiring funds around, which can add plenty to the costs of your trading.

Strategies for Successful Day Trading

As mentioned throughout this chapter, day traders often trade stocks in lots of 1,000 shares or more, putting large portions of cash at risk with every trade. Although the profit potential is great, so is the risk of losing all your money and maybe even owing money if you use borrowed cash in your margin account.

WARNING

Before you ever consider day trading, you need to understand the risks you're taking and how to control them. Otherwise, money can flow out of your account very quickly. Studies show that it generally takes six months to learn how to be a successful day trader, and during that learning curve, you can count on losing money. Success rates of day traders range from 10 percent to 30 percent of those who try it. In other words, 70 percent to 90 percent of the people who attempt day trading don't succeed and frequently end their day-trading careers in debt. We explain more about risks in the later section "Recognizing That Risks Are High," but first we need to review some of the basic strategies that day traders use.

Technical needs

Number one on the list of things you need to become a day trader is a very good computer and Internet setup. They're necessary for successful day trading. Most traders have two or more monitors with a PC built to handle a large number of data feeds at one time. Windows 7 or 8 is the preferred platform of day traders because most of the trading platforms are written for these environments and because they're able to handle multiple monitors. Windows 10 has gotten mixed reviews because of its automatic updates that sometimes are not compatible with a trading platform. If you do have Windows 10, check with the provider to find out if there have been problems using Windows 10.

Daily computer maintenance is critical for day traders. Computer problems are the last thing you want to experience in the middle of your trading day, especially when buy positions are left open. You can lose a lot of money if you're waiting for your computer to reboot and a trade goes sour. Traders recommend that you clear the *cookies* (files that websites send to your computer when you're using them) from your Internet cache on a daily basis and that you *defragment* (reorganize your files so the computer runs more efficiently) your computer at least once a week.

Another key step is finding an Internet service provider (ISP) that is reliable and offers high-speed access to the Internet. Many traders have more than one ISP lined up, so they have a backup in case the first one goes down. Again, you don't want to lose even mere seconds when you're in the middle of your trading day, especially when you have open positions.

Trading patterns

Day traders make use of patterns seen in technical analysis that are similar to the ones we discuss in Part 3 of this book. One common pattern that day traders look for is a price gap in a stock at the opening of the market. They find that prices usually move in the same direction as the opening price gap during the first few minutes that the market is open, and then the market tends to reverse and fill the gap (see Chapter 10). Trading that doesn't fill the gap during the first five to ten minutes can signal a dominant trend for the day for that particular stock. Some traders watch this action to find their targets for the day and the directions they plan to play them. There is no consensus on this, of course. Others believe that early market moves give false signals and that using those moves for planning your trading day can be dangerous.

Traders watch for many of the same patterns they find when looking for breakout signals and signs of reversals (see Chapter 10). The key difference is that a day trader looks for intraday signals, while longer-term traders format their charts for longer periods of time.

Scalping

Scalping basically means you move into and out of a position for a very limited profit in an extremely short time frame, usually just a few minutes or possibly only a few seconds. The scalper's objective is to make profits of only fractions of a point on any given trade, rather than the several points' profit that most traders seek. Day traders execute their trades in a much narrower time frame, so scalpers look for only 10 to 25 cents per share, hoping to make small gains as often as possible. When scalping with higher-priced ($100 or more per share) or faster-moving stocks, one point can be considered a scalp.

WARNING

For most stocks, scalping doesn't pay if you trade fewer than 1,000 shares. Here's why: A 10-cent scalping profit on 1,000 shares is only $100 before paying transaction fees or commissions. There will be little profit after fees and commissions if you're trading lots with fewer than 1,000 shares.

Trend traders

Not all day traders use the scalping technique. Some are trend traders. Instead of jumping into and out of a trade for a fraction of a point, they look for profits of at least one or two points and may stay in a position for minutes or even as long as an hour. *Trend traders* make fewer trades than scalpers do but seek higher profits per trade and may trade in blocks of fewer than 1,000 shares because they can make a nice profit as trend traders with considerably less share volume. In fact, traders who look for more than a one-point profit sometimes hold a stock for several hours unless the stock is high-priced or its price is moving fast.

Recognizing That Risks Are High

Reading about trading patterns and the high volume of stock trading, you've probably already figured out for yourself that the risks are high. Within a matter of minutes, trading in and out of stocks in 1,000-share blocks can be costly whenever a stock quickly moves in a direction you weren't anticipating.

In fact, the U.S. Senate investigated the risks of day trading after a shooting spree at an on-site day-trading facility in Atlanta, Georgia, left nine people dead in July 1999. The shooter, Mark Barton, was a chemist before getting involved in day trading and losing $105,000 in just one month. He killed himself after the shooting spree.

Senate investigators found that the revenue of the 15 largest firms that specialize in day trading for 1999 was $541.5 million, or 276 percent higher than their revenue in 1997. Profits went up by more than $66 million, and by 1999, the 15 firms had opened 12,000 new accounts. Investigators also found that the 4,000 to 5,000 most active traders were borrowing huge sums of money and losing it. In that year traders paid an average of $16 per trade and made an average of 29 trades per day. Using these statistics, investigators concluded that a trader needed to make more than $111,000 a year in stock market gains just to break even with that level of costs.

A study by Ronald L. Johnson done for the North American Securities Administrators Association released in 1999 found that 70 percent of a sampling of accounts at one trading firm lost money. He concluded that 70 percent of people who attempt day trading will not only lose but will also likely lose everything they initially deposited in their day-trading account. He found that only 11.5 percent of day traders made short-term trading profitable.

Another study, released in May 2004 by university professors who looked at day traders on the Taiwan Stock Exchange, found that 82 percent of traders lost money. Some may profit most days, but they end up in a losing position after calculating costs of operations.

Liquidity

To be considered liquid, a trader must have the ability to change holdings quickly into cash. Although you can see that a day trader must trade a large number of shares to make a profit, he or she must also have significant cash and securities in his or her account to be able to continue trading activities.

Slippage

Slippage can cost day traders significantly if they're not careful how they execute their trades. *Slippage* relates to the difference between what you expect your exit or entry stock prices to be and what you actually end up paying for and getting out of that stock when your order is finally executed. Depending on the volatility of the market, a stock price sometimes can vary by as much as one or two points from the time you see the stock quotation until the time your order is actually executed.

Traders can control slippage with the right type of order. The three basic ways to enter a position are at market, with a stop order, or with a limit order. Day traders rarely use market orders, which means buying or selling a stock at the market price. Instead they use stop or limit orders to better control when their orders are filled and how much they pay for the stock. We discuss types of orders in Chapter 2.

TIP

Most traders recommend that you never enter a position without immediately placing a stop-loss order at an exit price that you decide is the most you're willing to lose on a particular position. Although a stop order means that once a stock hits the exit price, the order changes to a market order and may result in your selling the stock at less than that price, it nevertheless is safer than placing a limit order, which can mean that you miss the exit point altogether and possibly lose even more. Stop-loss orders can cause some slippage, but you usually lose less with these types of orders than with limit orders. A limit order can be completely missed when your stock breaks into a downward trend because the fall in price was too abrupt or rapid for it to be executed.

When buying stock, traders use limit orders because they place limits on the entry prices traders are willing to pay. Traders certainly don't want to end up paying higher prices than they intend, which, in turn, raises the bar for making a profit higher than is reasonably possible to attain.

Trading costs

Many of the day-trading firms set a per-share cost for stock trades or a per-trade cost. Per-trade costs vary from $4.95 to $9.99 per trade depending on how much trading you do in a month. In addition, you may be charged a fee for routing as well as for the trading platform provided.

Cost of trading is the same whether you have Level I or Level II access (see Chapter 3 for information on Level I and Level II quoting alternatives). The number of trades you do impacts whether you have to pay for Level II access. To get Level II access for free, your broker will set a minimum number of trades you must make per month; otherwise, the monthly fee for Level II access can be $150 or higher. Options-trading fees vary by broker as well.

In addition to these fees, per-share charges can range from $0.005 per share to $0.01 per share, depending on the exchange on which you choose to trade. If your computer crashes or your Internet access goes down, phone orders can cost you $15 or more per trade.

So if you trade 30 times a day for 20 days a month, the number of your trades totals 600. At $4.95 per trade, your commission costs are $2,970 per month, and if you trade 1,000 shares with each trade, that adds up to a total of 600,000 shares per month. Even at the lowest per-share exchange cost of $0.005, that means an additional $3,000 in per-share charges. Thus, your monthly cost for this volume of trading would be $5,970. Some brokers offer a higher per-trade price without fees for per share, so shop carefully for a trading cost that will best meet your trading style.

TIP

NerdWallet reviewed the best platforms for day traders: `https://www.nerd wallet.com/blog/investing/best-online-brokers-platforms-for-day-trading/`.

In addition to these costs, many traders also pay for newsletters or join trading chat rooms that give them alerts for the best opportunities each day. These services can add another $200 to $250 to your monthly costs. So before you see even one penny of profit, your monthly outlay can be $6,000 or more (that's $72,000 annually or more). You can easily understand why so many day traders never see a profit for at least six months and why such a high percentage of day traders actually give up before their businesses turn profitable.

Taxes (of course)

On top of all these costs, you must consider taxes that you'll have to pay on any short-term profits at your current individual tax rate and not the preferred tax rates given to long-term investments that are held more than a year. However, full-time day traders have tax advantages that other traders and investors don't have, provided that they meet the following qualifications:

>> **Buy and sell a high volume of stocks every day.** If you're day trading full time, proving that you're meeting the requirements to qualify for the special day-trading tax breaks is easier. If you work full-time and trade part-time, qualifying for the tax break may be more difficult.

>> **Establish (in their accounts) that they regularly and continually make numerous trades just about every day the market is open.** A broker designating you as a pattern day trader and requiring you to maintain a margin account minimum of $25,000 may help prove you're a day trader in the eyes of the Internal Revenue Service (IRS).

>> **Make a profit buying and selling stocks with short-term horizons rather than profit by holding stocks for long-term gains or dividend income.**

REMEMBER

If you successfully prove to the IRS that you're a day trader, you can consider your day-trading activities as a business and thereby write off your trading costs as a sole proprietor on Schedule C of your tax return. The reason doing so gives you such a great tax advantage is that other investors are able to write off only the costs that exceed 2 percent of their adjusted gross incomes. Any losses reported on your Schedule C business return can be written off against your adjusted gross income and thus reduce your tax bill, which, in turn, can help you qualify for other tax breaks.

In addition to the costs of making your trades, you can write off many more items against your business on Schedule C. You also can write off any interest you pay on your margin account and possibly depreciate up to 100 percent of any equipment that you bought to start and continue to run your trading business as a Section 179 business deduction. This deduction could be as much as $500,000 in 2017. If you use a space in your home exclusively for your trading activities, you also can take a home-office deduction.

TIP

Any gains that you make on your trading activities are considered capital gains and, as such, are exempt from any self-employment taxes that other sole proprietors must pay on their business profits. You still have to report your gains and losses on Schedule D, and to avoid additional scrutiny, you may want to attach a note to your Schedule C explaining why you have losses and no income. The IRS red flags returns from people who report losses on Schedule C for several years in a row, a factor that also can trigger an audit.

Avoiding the Most Common Mistakes

If the risks and costs don't scare you away from day trading, you need to become familiar with some common mistakes that lead to failure for many day traders. Some traders talk about their more common mistakes, especially the ones that cost a lot of money while they were building their businesses. Here are some of the more serious mistakes new day traders make:

>> **Breaking stop-loss rules:** When a stock starts dropping, newer, not-yet-disciplined traders tend to panic as their picks begin losing money, so they decide to hold the stock rather than exit when their initial stop-loss is reached. However, traders go broke using that strategy because they don't stop their losses as planned. You must set your exit prices based on your technical analysis for both losses and profits when you first buy the stock. Follow those rules mechanically when the target price is hit, and don't let your emotions get in the way.

>> **Chasing trends:** New traders who aren't yet confident in the way they read patterns often wait to see confirmation that they're right before they enter a position. That hesitation causes them to miss planned entry points and, if they're right, can end up forcing them into buying at a stock price that's higher than they intended when an upward trend is expected or selling at a lower price than they intended when a downward trend is expected. By missing intended entry prices, traders end up chasing the trends and finding that their original entry and exit points no longer are valid because many others already acted on the trend, and the stock is no longer available at the planned prices.

Experienced traders just walk away from that particular trade instead of getting caught up in trading points that don't match technical analysis and thereby chasing a trend.

>> **Not waiting for the right trade:** A new day trader must exhibit the patience required in waiting for the right trade to match what the technical analysis indicates. Experienced traders know to wait for the right timing instead of forcing a trade, entering at the wrong price, and overtrading their account.

REMEMBER

>> **Not establishing set rules before the trading day begins:** To avoid getting caught up in the emotions of a big win or loss, you need to decide your entry and exit points before the trading day begins and never deviate from them after the day begins. Experienced day traders know that you either focus on your trades or think about your rules. You don't have time to do both, and trying to do so can be a recipe for disaster. Staying objective and following your rules is crucial to maintaining the control a day trader needs.

>> **Forgetting that fundamentals don't matter:** New day traders get caught up in the idea that the company whose stock they've purchased is a good company and that when its stock loses ground, it's therefore bound to head back up. Experienced traders know that how good the fundamentals look doesn't matter and that when the market is selling down, even the price of a good stock goes down. Day traders must follow market signs and not worry about how good or bad the fundamentals of the company they're trading may appear.

>> **Averaging down:** Although investors may *average down,* meaning they buy a stock and if the price goes down they buy even more shares, believing that it's a good stock that will recover, this technique doesn't work at all for day traders, and most experienced traders of every variety will tell you that using it is a fatal mistake. Day traders instead believe that you need to set a stop price and get out (called *stopping out*) of a losing stock and possibly reenter again at a lower price. Doing so gives you time to look objectively at what is happening with the stock and determine whether getting back in is worthwhile. Stopping out also is likely to cost you less than averaging down, and you won't risk getting caught with a margin problem. Averaging down can tie up too much money that you can otherwise use for a more profitable trade with a different stock. The worst feeling, even for an experienced trader, occurs when a stock plunges far below the stop position because deciding whether to take the large loss is difficult. In most cases, if you're uncertain of your next move, experienced traders recommend that you get out of the position before the situation grows worse or out of control.

>> **Not knowing when to take profits:** New traders sometimes make the mistake of either taking profits too early or not taking profits at all. Both can result in unnecessary losses. Most of the time, indecision strikes when traders

are afraid they'll lose a profit if they hold it too long or miss a profit if they exit too soon. Just as with losses, you need to determine exit points before entering a position, and you must follow rules. Remember that as a day trader, you must focus either on your trade or on your rules. Day traders who move into and out of positions within seconds or minutes don't have time to do both.

>> **Walking away from the computer with open positions:** Experienced day traders never walk away from their computers when they still have an open position. Although we touch briefly on holding open positions overnight in the introduction to this chapter, this rule is even stricter. Because experienced day traders respond to price changes that occur in mere seconds or minutes, they definitely don't want to be away from the screen while a position is still open.

WARNING

Day trading is a high-risk career choice that you should consider only after doing a considerable amount of initial research, hunting down good resources for educating yourself about the risks and rewards, and finding all the techniques you need to use to day trade successfully. Even before you get started, be sure to check out the firms you're planning to use as resources by calling up their disciplinary records and complaint histories through the SEC or state regulators. You're putting a good deal of money at risk, so take the time to find out all you can before spending even that first dime.

You also may want to consider taking your Series 7 exam, the exam all stockbrokers are required to pass. Although you must be sponsored to take the exam, many training centers near your home or online can help you find a sponsoring broker. Even though you may never want to work as a broker, the information you're required to know for the exam gives you a much stronger awareness of the securities markets and the laws by which they're governed. Studying for the test, you'll also discover more about the various investment products on the market and the risks you take when buying and selling each type. For more about the Series 7 exam, read *Series 7 Exam For Dummies*, by Steven M. Rice (Wiley). For a closer look at day trading, read *Day Trading For Dummies*, by Ann C. Logue (Wiley).

Chapter **19**

Doing It by Derivatives

Traders can raise the bar on the leverage they're allowed by opening the door to the derivatives markets. *Derivatives* are any financial instruments that get or derive their value from another financial security, which is called an *underlier*. This underlier is usually stocks, bonds, foreign currency, or commodities. The derivative buyer or seller doesn't have to own the underlying security to trade these instruments.

You may unwittingly encounter derivatives if you trade those exchange-traded funds (ETFs) that offer to return two or even three times the value of an underlying stock index. Those ETFs use derivatives to amplify the reward — and the risk. And you may recall that derivative trading, especially those derivatives tied to the value of underlying mortgage assets, exacerbated the mortgage mess that started the financial collapse of 2008.

WARNING

Derivatives traders use futures and options, which are the two most common types of derivatives, to make money in a highly risky venture. In this chapter, we introduce you to a variety of derivatives, how they're traded, and the risks involved in trading futures and options. However, you need to seek additional training before jumping into this kind of trading.

Types of Derivatives: Futures and Options

Derivatives are marketable instruments, which over time acquire and relinquish value based on an underlying asset (see the later section "Options lingo"), including such commodities as coffee or soybeans, bonds, and even stocks. They are commonly used by commercial and institutional organizations to *hedge* against the risks of financial losses suffered by the underlying assets that they hold. Trading a derivative, for example, can minimize your financial loss whenever a major change occurs in the price of an asset that you own. Hedging is a popular tactic used by growers, producers, portfolio managers, and users of the commodities.

The two basic and most common types of derivatives are contracts for options and for futures. Traders buy and sell them as a way to speculate on the direction that the volatile prices of underlying assets will take further down the road. If their hunches are right and the prices move in the directions they expect, traders can make a significant profit. If, on the other hand, they're wrong, they can lose the amount they paid for an option or future and possibly even quite a bit more. Before we explain all the risks, we devote the next few sections to accurately defining futures and options.

Buy now, pay later: Futures

Futures are legally binding contracts between two parties, one of whom agrees to buy and the other who agrees to sell an asset for a specific price at a specified time in the future. The specific price is known as the *futures price*. The specified date in the future is known as the *delivery date*. Futures were first used in the 18th century in Japan as a means of trading rice and silk, but they didn't appear in U.S. markets until the 1850s, when futures markets were developed for buying and selling commodities such as wheat, cotton, and corn.

Futures contracts are one of the most volatile trading instruments. Prices can change rapidly, causing traders to face sudden and sometimes huge losses or gains. Futures contracts are traded based on the prices of underlying commodities, indexes, bonds, and stocks. Most people who enter futures markets do so not to actually buy and sell the actual goods or underlying financial asset but rather to speculate on or to hedge the risks of the changing prices of the assets that they do hold.

WARNING

Futures contracts are riskier than options because you actually have to come up with the underlying commodity, bond, stock, or currency to satisfy the contract, sell the future at a loss before the settlement date, or pay the difference in cash to settle the contract. Futures are binding contracts that require you to fulfill the obligations specified in the contracts. Options are less risky because they're not an obligation to perform. Rather, they give the buyer of the option the right to exercise the option, but the buyer isn't obligated to do so. We explain options in the later section "Wait and see: Options."

What's your position?

When people talk about futures, they're bound to say something about their positions. Here's what they mean:

>> **Short positions:** The party in the contract who agrees to deliver the commodity, stock, or bond holds a short position. Traders who take short positions are expecting the price of the underlying commodities to go down.

>> **Long positions:** The party in the contract who agrees to buy the commodity, stock, or bond in a futures contract holds a long position on the security. Traders who take long positions are expecting the price of the underlying commodities to go up.

Making money using futures

Traders can make money from trading futures on the basis of the daily movements of the markets for the various types of underlying commodities, stocks, bonds, or currencies involved in the contracts they buy and/or sell.

For example, typical futures contracts for wheat are signed between wheat farmers and bread producers. On one side of this contract, farmers agree to sell a specific amount of the wheat they grow at a specific price and a specified time, and on the other side, producers agree to pay that price for the contracted amount of wheat to be delivered to them by the specified time. Farmers benefit by ensuring that they can get a specific price or income from their wheat, and bread producers benefit by knowing how much they have to pay for the wheat they need to make the bread that they, in turn, sell to earn a living.

The value of that futures contract is adjusted daily. Assuming the farmer agreed in February to sell 10,000 bushels of wheat to the bread maker at $4 per bushel in July, and assuming that before the July settlement date the price of wheat rises to $5 per bushel, the farmer holding the futures contract has lost $1 per bushel of wheat, or $10,000. These types of price adjustments actually are calculated daily throughout the time that the futures contract is in force, and that means the farmer's or bread maker's account is credited or debited as wheat prices fluctuate.

The farmer and the bread maker will probably never actually exchange their goods. Instead, the obligations of the futures contract eventually are settled with cash.

In this scenario, the bread maker will probably buy his wheat at the current price of $5 per bushel when he needs it, but because he speculated correctly on the price, it's only really costing him $40,000 (instead of $50,000 at the current market price) to buy the wheat. Although the bread maker pays $50,000 for 10,000 bushels of wheat, he has saved $10,000 because of the money he made on the wheat futures contract. The farmer, on the other hand, sells his wheat at $5 per bushel and gets $50,000 cash but actually keeps only $40,000 because he has to cover his loss from the futures contract.

You can see from this example that futures contracts are actually financial positions. This financial position, or the buying and selling of futures contracts, is what traders are speculating about. If futures traders believe the price of wheat is rising, they buy futures contracts so they can benefit from the gain made by the price. But when the situation is reversed and the price of wheat drops to $3 per bushel, then the trader who buys can be on the losing side of that futures contract and be liable for a $10,000 loss. The buyer puts up a margin, which is only a small percentage of the price of the actual commodity, stock, bond, or currency underlying the contract.

Commodities futures

People who buy commodities futures basically are agreeing to buy a certain amount of a commodity at a set price at some point in the future. Conversely, people who sell those same futures are agreeing to provide a certain amount of a commodity at the agreed-upon price by the agreed-upon time. The example of the farmer/bread maker in the preceding section illustrates this type of future. Buyers or sellers can enter into futures contracts on many commodities, including farm products (pork bellies, wheat, corn, and soybeans), precious metals (gold, copper, and silver), and many others.

Traders usually don't get directly involved as buyers and sellers of the actual commodities because they usually get out of their futures contracts before the underlying commodities on which their trades are based ever change hands. Instead, they're speculators, buying and/or selling futures contracts based on which way they think the commodity price is going to move. Speculation, as you know, is wrought with risk, and the reason the risk is so great is that a commodity contract controls a large amount of the commodity (or commodity value) compared with the relatively small margin that it takes to enter into a contract. The result is extensive *leverage*, which means controlling a large position with only a small cash deposit. If the price moves in a direction that's the opposite of what the trader anticipates, he or she may have to take a huge loss to get out of the contract.

Index futures

Index futures are based on the expected direction of the value of indexes like the S&P 500 and the New York Stock Exchange Composite indexes. They can be the riskiest types of futures. No underlying commodities, stocks, or bonds ever change hands with these futures contracts. Any differences in these contracts must be settled with good old cold, hard cash. Margin also is high on these types of futures. For example, a Dow Jones Industrial Average contract has a value that's 25 times the value of the underlying DJIA Index.

Smaller index futures contracts, known collectively as *e-minis,* are targeted at individual traders. These mini contracts are available for indexes such as the S&P 500, the NASDAQ 100, the S&P mid-cap, and the Russell 2000. Their respective individual values range from 20 times to 100 times those of the underlying indexes.

The S&P 500 e-mini contract, for example, is 50 times the value of the S&P 500 index. In other words, if a trader takes a position in the S&P 500 e-mini contract, every time the underlying S&P 500 index moves one point, the value of the S&P 500 e-mini contract changes by $50. Another way to think about this is for every 0.25 point, the value of the S&P 500 e-mini contract changes by $12.50. If you take a long position in the S&P 500 e-mini contract when the underlying index is at 1,500, and the index moves to 1,510, you have a $500 profit. The trader who took the other side of this trade, the short position, is in exactly the opposite position, losing $500.

Bond futures

Bond futures are based on the price of future delivery of a specific type of bond in a specific denomination at a specific interest rate on a specified date. Speculators basically are betting on whether the price of that bond goes up or down. Changes in interest rates have a big impact on bond values. In general, when interest rates fall, bond prices go up, and when interest rates rise, bond prices go down. Speculators in bond futures basically enter positions based on whether interest rates will go up or down. For example, a speculator who thinks interest rates will go up sells contracts for the future delivery of bonds. If interest rates indeed go up as expected, the price for the underlying bonds goes down, and speculators can do one of two things:

>> Buy the lower-priced bonds and, in turn, earn a profit by selling them to the buyer to settle at the higher price named in the original futures contract.

>> Close the contract to realize a profit.

Stock futures

Stock futures are contracts in which you agree to either deliver or purchase upon delivery 100 shares of a particular stock on or before a designated date in the future (known as the *expiration date*). For example, a trader who enters into a contract to buy 100 shares at $30 a share for a total of $3,000, and who expects the price of that stock to go up, can lock in the lower price and then buy the actual stock at that lower price on the expiration date or close the contract and realize a profit. Traders who enter into this type of contract generally must have about 20 percent of the cash value of 100 shares of the underlying stock in their brokerage accounts, so a trader in this example would have to have $600 in a brokerage account.

Foreign currency futures

Future currency contracts are contracts that involve the future delivery of certain foreign currencies. We discuss these types of futures in Chapter 20.

Wait and see: Options

Options are financial instruments that give the buyer the right, but not the obligation, to buy or sell a particular asset at a predetermined date in the future at a specified price.

Although futures have been available in the United States since the 1850s, options did not become available until 1968, when they were part of a government pilot program. The Chicago Board of Options Exchange opened in 1973. The big advantage that options have over futures is that you buy the right to exercise the option contract, and yet you still can decide to allow the option to expire without ever exercising that right. When you let an option expire, you lose only the amount you paid for the option and not the full amount that otherwise can be lost in trading the underlying asset. Option sellers take the riskier stance because they can lose the value of whatever asset they promised to sell or buy if the option buyer decides to exercise the option.

Options lingo

REMEMBER

Trading in options has a language all its own, and you need to understand it before we get into the mechanics, so here are some key terms:

>> **Puts:** A *put option* is a contract that gives the buyer the right to sell a particular asset at a specified price at any time during the life of the option.

- » **Calls:** A *call option* is a contract that gives the buyer the right to buy a particular asset at a specified price at any time during the life of the option.

- » **Option grantor:** The person who writes or sells any option is called the *option grantor*. This person or financial entity must come up with the underlying asset promised in the option, even if doing so means a loss, whenever an option buyer decides to exercise an option. For example, if an option grantor agrees to sell you 100 shares of ABC stock for $50 per share on or before May 1, and the stock price rises to $60 on April 20, then the grantor must sell you that stock for $50 and take the $10-per-share loss. You get to sell ABC at the current price and reap the benefits.

- » **Covered calls:** If an option seller holds an *equivalent position,* or owns the same number of shares of the underlying asset that is offered in the call, then the contract is considered a *covered call.* Options traders selling covered calls are trying to take advantage of a neutral or declining stock. If the option expires unexercised, the writer (seller) of the option keeps the premium. If, on the other hand, the holder (buyer) of the option exercises it, the stock must be delivered. However, because the option writer already owns the stock, the risk is limited. The opposite scenario is an *uncovered call,* which is when the writer sells a call for a stock that he or she doesn't own. The seller of an uncovered call is taking virtually unlimited risk.

- » **Covered puts:** When the seller of a put option also has sold short an equivalent amount in the underlying security, then this option is considered a *covered put.* If the writer has neither established a short position in the underlying security nor deposited a corresponding amount of cash equal to the value of the put, then the put is called a *naked put.* The seller of a naked put also is taking virtually unlimited risk.

- » **Option holder:** The person who buys the option is called the *option holder.* If the option buyer buys the right to sell an asset at some time in the future, then he or she buys a put option. If the option buyer buys the right to purchase an asset at some time in the future, then he or she buys a call option. The most an option holder can lose is the amount paid for the option contract.

- » **Underlying asset:** An option contract is based on an underlying asset — usually either a futures contract or specific number of shares of stock — that can be bought or sold.

- » **Premium:** The actual price paid for the option is called the *premium,* which is what the option holder pays to the option grantor to gain the right to either buy or sell the underlying asset. Premiums for options are set by the open market. Option buyers must pay the premium plus whatever fees their brokers charge for such transactions.

>> **Expiration date:** The *expiration date* is the last day that an option buyer can exercise the rights specified in the contract. Options based on futures contracts usually expire one month before the settlement date of the underlying futures contract. After an option expires, the option holder no longer has any rights, and the option has no value. So option buyers lose whatever premium they paid plus any commissions or transaction costs that had to be paid when the option was purchased. In that case, the option is said to expire worthless.

>> **Exercise:** Option buyers can exercise the rights they purchase with the option any time before the expiration date — if, that is, the option they purchased is an *American-style option. European-style options,* on the other hand, can be exercised only on their expiration dates. Exercising a call option means the option buyer buys the underlying asset at the price set in the option, regardless of the current market price for the asset. Exercising a put option means the option buyer sells the underlying asset at the price set in the option. An option buyer can always decide not to exercise the rights set forth in his or her option and simply let it expire. The option holder also can sell the option contract at its current market value.

>> **Strike price:** The *strike price* is the price of the underlying asset at which the option can be exercised.

>> **Offset:** If option buyers or sellers want to realize their profits or limit their losses, they can *offset* their option through a sale or purchase that is called *liquidating an option* or *closing an option.* When an option is liquidated, no position is actually taken in the underlying asset. Offsetting is usually done on the same exchange where the buyer first bought or sold the option. If she can sell the option for more than she bought it, then she will realize a profit. If she sells the option for less than she paid, then she will take a loss.

>> **In the money:** An option is said to be *in the money* when it is worthwhile to exercise the option and buy or sell the underlying asset. A call option is in the money when the market price for the underlying asset is above the strike price set in the option contract. A put option is in the money when the price for the underlying asset is lower than the strike price set in the option contract.

>> **At the money:** An option is deemed to be *at the money* when the strike price for the option is the same as the market price for the underlying asset.

>> **Out of the money:** An option is said to be *out of the money* when exercising the option isn't worthwhile. A call option is out of the money when the strike price is higher than the market price for the underlying asset. A put option is out of the money when the strike price is less than the market price for the underlying asset.

Option pricing

The three factors affecting the price of an option premium are as follows:

>> **Date of expiration:** As the option moves closer to its date of expiration, the value of the option declines, and that's why an option is considered a *wasting asset.* The more time that you have until an option expires, the greater possibility you have for the option to reach the point of being in the money. Longer options therefore have higher premiums.

>> **Strike price:** For out-of-the-money options, when the current market price moves more and more out of the money and away from the strike price, the premium price gets lower and lower for put options and higher for call options. The premium for an in-the-money call option, on the other hand, rises in value if the underlying asset moves further into the money in relationship to the strike price.

>> **Volatility:** The more volatility that's expected by the market for the underlying asset, or stock, the greater the chance that the option will become worthwhile to exercise. When the market for an asset is volatile, premiums for options on that asset are higher.

Option-pricing techniques are considered to be among the most mathematically complex of all applied areas of finance. One common example, the Black–Scholes option-pricing model (named for its developers Fischer Black and Myron Scholes), takes into consideration the stock's price, the option's strike price and expiration date, the risk-free return, and the standard deviation of the stock's return, which are all measures of volatility.

When you get a quote for an option, you may have to choose from numerous strike prices and expiration dates that are available. When you're thinking about buying a call option, and its strike price is low and yet close to becoming worthwhile to exercise, the premium price (the price you pay for the option) will be much higher than for an option with a higher strike price. If you're thinking about buying a put option, then you'll pay more of a premium for an option with a high strike price than you will for one with a lower strike price.

Just to give you an idea of how the pricing of options is affected by strike price and time, Table 19-1 is an options quote for an imaginary stock we call ABC. *Settle* is the time of expiration for the option.

TABLE 19-1 **ABC Stock Sample Option Quotation (In Dollars)**

Strike Price	Calls/Settle			Puts/Settle		
	Apr	May	June	Apr	May	June
$50	4.50	4.60	5.40	0.25	0.50	1.50
$52	3.50	3.60	4.40	0.50	1.00	3.50
$54	2.50	2.60	3.40	0.75	2.00	5.50
$56	1.50	1.60	2.40	2.00	3.00	7.50
$58	0.50	0.60	1.40	4.00	5.00	9.50

You can see from the options quotes for ABC stock that a May call with a strike price of $54 commands a premium of $2.60 per share. To buy an option for 100 shares, the premium would be $260 plus whatever fees your exchange or broker charges. Buying a call is much less of a cash outlay than if you were to buy 100 shares of ABC stock at $54. That would cost you $5,400. The premium of $260 is paid to the option seller, minus any fees charged by the broker or exchange.

Fees include commission charges plus any costs involved in executing the order on the trading floor of the exchange. Commissions vary greatly from broker to broker, so be certain you understand all the possible fees before initiating a trade. Some brokers charge commissions per trade, but others charge on the basis of a *round trip*, including both the purchase and the sale of the option. Some brokerage firms charge per-option transaction fees, while others charge on the basis of a percentage of the option premium that's usually subject to a minimum charge.

WARNING

Commission charges can have a major impact on whether you're able to earn a profit or have to suffer a loss on an option. A high commission charge reduces your potential for making a profit and can even drive what little profit you make into a loss. So be careful. Know what charges you have to pay and compare them with other brokers before you trade.

Options and futures are quoted with bid and ask prices just like stocks, and the spreads with options can grow pretty wide as a percentage of the option's premium, which, in turn, can have a significant impact on the profitability of your option position. The wider the spread, the harder it is for you to make a profit. As an option trader, you typically buy at the ask, the higher price, and sell at the bid, the lower price. That means that any trade must recover the difference between the bid and the ask before you can earn a profit. As with stock trading, you can use a limit order to put your order between the bid and the ask, but there is no guarantee that your order will be filled. See Chapter 15 for more about bid-ask spreads.

Buying Options and Futures Contracts

All types of options and futures are traded on a commodities exchange. In addition, some types of options can be traded on stock exchanges. More than 20 different exchanges are available for trading either options or futures contracts or both in North America. The chart at https://www.interactivebrokers.com/en/index.php?f=1562 from Interactive Brokers lists all the exchanges and the types of contracts in which they trade. The chart also provides trading hours.

At the top of this chart, you'll find links to exchanges in Europe, Asia/Pacific, and Global Exchanges.

You can trade stock options and some index options in a traditional stock account. You must sign special risk-release forms, but otherwise, the account remains the same. (For more about establishing an account, see Chapter 3.) Naked short positions require a margin account.

Opening an account

If you want to trade futures or options on futures, you must do so through an individual account that you open with a registered *futures commission merchant* (FCM) or through your stock broker. Your broker transmits any transactions through an FCM as an introducing broker. Your broker won't collect the funds from you for your options trades. You have to deposit them directly with the FCM.

CONSIDERING THE NEW MINI OPTIONS

Beginning March 2013, mini-options contracts became available that allow you to trade options based on 10 shares rather than 100 shares on some higher-priced stocks, such as Amazon, Apple, and Google. Therefore, instead of having to own 100 shares of these higher-priced stocks, you can buy options when you hold just 10 shares.

The basics of trading these mini-options contracts are similar to the 100-share contracts, but they enable smaller investors to trade options on these higher-priced shares without as large of an initial investment. Because mini-options hit the market in March 2013, we can't yet say how effective this trading option will be; this trading opportunity is still relatively new, and there isn't yet much data regarding how effective they can be. Based on initial pricing, the spread for mini-options is higher, so that does make them riskier with less chance of making money on the trade. If you do decide to trade mini options, protect yourself by using limit orders based on the bid-ask spread for the full-sized contract.

You have the choice of opening either a discretionary account or a nondiscretionary account. A *discretionary account* is an account in which you sign a power of attorney over to your FCM, your broker, or a *commodity trading advisor* (CTA) so he or she can make trading decisions on your behalf. A *nondiscretionary account* is an account in which you make all the trading decisions.

You also may want to consider trading through a commodity pool. When trading through a *commodity pool,* you purchase a share or interest in a pool of other investors, and trades are executed by an FCM or CTA. Any profits or losses are shared proportionately by the members of the pool.

When you open an individual account, you need to make a deposit that amounts to a *margin payment* or *performance bond* for the futures you trade. This payment is relatively small compared to the size of your potential market position, and it gives you the opportunity to greatly leverage your money. Small changes in options and futures prices can result in large gains or large losses in relatively short periods of time.

WARNING

Your broker calculates the values of the futures and option contracts in your account on a daily basis, and you need to maintain a margin level that's approximately 50 percent of the amount required when you originally enter your positions. If your holdings fall below that level, you'll be asked to come up with the cash to restore your margin account to the initial level, a situation that's known as a *margin call.* If you can't meet the margin call in a reasonable period of time, which can be as little as an hour, your brokerage firm closes out enough of your positions to reduce your margin deficiency. If your positions are liquidated at a loss, you can be held liable for that loss, which sometimes can be substantially more than your original margin deposit.

Calculating the price and making a buy

Before buying an option, you first must calculate the break-even price, but you must know the option's strike price, the premium cost, and the commission or other transaction costs to be able to do it. With those three details in hand, you can determine a break-even price for a call option using this formula:

Option strike price + Option premium costs + Commission and transaction fees = Break-even price

Using the example in Table 19-1, here is the per-share break-even price for buying a May call option with a strike price of $54 and a commission of $25, or 25 cents per share:

$54 + $2.60 + $0.25 = $56.85

To make a profit on this call option, the stock price of ABC has to rise above $56.85. If the stock price doesn't rise above $56.85, you won't make a profit on this option purchase (unless you're somehow able to sell the option for more than $2.85 before the expiration date — see the next section). These calculations are correct only when your broker has one fee for a round-trip option exchange. If you have to pay fees in both directions, which is common, then you need to double the fee in the calculation.

When calculating the break-even price for a put option, you subtract the premium, commission, and transaction costs. Here is the break-even calculation for a May put option for ABC stock at a strike price of $54 with a commission of $25, or 25 cents per share:

$$\$54 - \$2.00 - \$0.25 = \$51.75$$

In this scenario, ABC stock has to drop below $51.75 for this put option to be worthwhile.

REMEMBER

If you're expecting a stock price increase, you want to consider purchasing a call option, but if you expect a price decline, you want to consider purchasing a put option. In both scenarios, you need to check the fundamental and technical analyses information you gathered on the underlying stock or asset so you can be certain that any break-even prices you've calculated reasonably match what your analysis indicates.

Options for Getting Out of Options

After you buy an option, you have to decide how you want to opt out of that position. You can choose one of the following three alternatives:

>> Offset the option.

>> Continue holding the option.

>> Exercise the option.

Offsetting the option

You offset an option by liquidating your option position, usually in the same marketplace that you bought the option. If you want to get out of an option before its expiration date, you can try to sell it for whatever price you can get. Doing so either enables you to take your profits or reduces your potential loss by the amount you receive for the option. As long as you bought your option in an active market, other investors usually are willing to pay for the rights your option conveys. The key, of course, is how much they're willing to pay.

Your net profit or loss for this option is determined by the difference between what you originally pay in premiums, commissions, and other transaction costs minus the premium you receive when you liquidate the option after deducting commissions and other transaction costs.

Holding the option

If your option is not yet in the money but you still believe it may get there, you can continue to hold the option until the exercise date. If you're right, you can exercise the option before the expiration date or liquidate at a later date, which means to buy or sell the option before the expiration date at some time in the future. If you're wrong, you risk the possibility that you won't find a buyer or that you'll have to let the option expire and take a loss that is equal to the amount of the premium, commission, and transaction costs you paid. Some traders take an even riskier position by buying options that are deeply out of the money for just pennies a share. Even if these options never grow any nearer to being in the money, as long as they move in the right direction, the premiums will rise. Although we don't recommend using this strategy, you can make profits as long as you're able to sell the option before its expiration date.

REMEMBER

Options decline in value as they get closer to their expiration dates, so if you think you've made a mistake and the market moves against your position, bite the bullet as soon as possible and try to liquidate your option to minimize your losses.

Exercising the option

You can exercise an option any time prior to its expiration date, as long as you're trading in American-style options. You don't have to wait until the exercise date to exercise an American-style option. (Some option contracts sold in the United States are European-style, which can be exercised only on the expiration date.) Exercising an option means

>> Buying the underlying asset when you own a call

>> Selling the underlying asset when you own a put

In general, call options are exercised only when the trader plans to hold the underlying asset, and put options are exercised only when the trader owns the underlying asset and wants to sell it. Option traders are more likely to realize any gains or losses by closing their option positions rather than exercising them.

The Risks of Trading Options and Futures

Trading in options and futures is risky business, and regulations governing those trades are stringent, even with regard to allowing you to open an account. Before opening an account for you, a broker must provide you with a disclosure document that describes the risks involved in trading futures and options contracts. The document gives you the opportunity to determine whether you have the experience and financial resources necessary to engage in option trading and whether option trading is appropriate for meeting your goals and objectives.

Topics that must be covered in the disclosure statement include the risks inherent in trading futures contracts or options and the effect that leveraging your account can have on potential losses or gains. The statement also must include warnings about trading futures in foreign markets because those types of trades carry additional risks from fluctuations in currency exchange rates and differences in regulatory protection.

WARNING

Commodities options and futures also can be risky because many of the factors that affect their prices are totally unpredictable, such as the weather, labor strikes, inflation, foreign exchange rates, and governmental policies. Because positions in futures and options are so highly leveraged, even a small price movement against your position can result in at least the loss of your entire premium payment and possibly even much greater liability for additional losses.

TIP

After you begin trading options and futures, you can't close your account until all open positions are closed — if, that is, you're trading through an account with a commodities exchange. This restriction doesn't apply to options traded in a stock brokerage account. Any accruals on futures contracts are paid out daily. Any funds in your margin account that are beyond your required margin or account-opening requirements can be withdrawn, but other such funds have to remain in the account until all your positions are closed. Any restrictions on the withdrawal of your funds are stated in the original disclosure document. Be sure that you understand those restrictions before committing your funds.

After opening your account, your broker usually mails or emails confirmation of all purchases and sales, a month-end summary of transactions that shows any gains or losses, and an evaluation of your open positions and current account values. You need to be able to get information from your broker on a daily basis after you begin to trade.

Brokers are required to segregate any money you deposit in your account from the brokerages' own funds. The amount that is segregated either increases or decreases depending on the success of your trades. Even if the brokerage firm segregates your funds, you still may not be able to get all your money back if the brokerage firm becomes insolvent and is unable to cover all the obligations to its customers. In other words, the money you put into your brokerage account is not insured.

Whenever problems with your broker arise and you can't resolve them without help, you have several dispute-resolution options. You can contact the reparations program of the Commodity Futures Trading Commission (CFTC) and ask for an industry-sponsored arbitration, or you can take your broker to court. Before deciding how you want to proceed, you must consider the costs involved with each option, the length of time it may take to resolve the problem, and whether you want to contact an attorney. You can get more information about dispute-resolution alternatives by contacting the CFTC at www.cftc.gov/ConsumerProtection/ReparationsProgram/index.htm or by calling 202-418-5250.

Minimizing Risks

In a nutshell, the best way to minimize the risks of derivatives trading is to take the time to find out as much as you can about the inherent risks of the derivatives you're trading and how others have dealt with them. The first step you can take is to check out the firms or individuals with whom you plan to trade. All firms and individuals that offer to trade options or futures must be registered with the CFTC (www.cftc.gov) and be members of the National Futures Association (NFA; www.nfa.futures.org). You can check out firms and individuals online at the NFA site by using its Background Affiliation Status Information Center (BASIC). On BASIC, you'll find the status of the firm or individual and any disciplinary actions taken by the NFA, the CFTC, or any U.S. exchanges. You can start a search on BASIC from the Investor Information page at www.nfa.futures.org/NFA-investor-information/index.HTML.

Next, be sure that you're familiar with the firm's commission charges and how they're calculated. Compare one firm's quotes with those of other firms you're considering. Whenever a firm has unusually high commission charges, ask for a detailed explanation for the higher charges and what additional services justify the higher cost.

Always make sure that you calculate the break-even price for any option you're thinking about purchasing, because you have to know at what point the option you're planning to buy will be profitable and whether the data you've collected justifies the option's premium costs.

You also need to understand the market for the underlying asset of the option or future you plan to buy and what can impact the market price of that asset. Be sure that your expectations for the potential profits from the option or futures contract you choose are reasonable.

You don't ever want to buy an option without first coming to a full realization that you can lose the entire value of your trade. If you want to take the riskier position as an option writer, be sure you can accept the possibility that your losses may exceed the premium you initially received for the option. Option writing comes with the potential of unlimited losses, as does futures trading.

Just as with stock trading, you can limit your losses by carefully setting your risk limits before you start to trade. Don't let yourself get caught up in the emotions of futures and options trading. Develop a plan before you buy that first option or future and stick with that plan, and be sure to diversify your holdings not only by asset types but also by time of expiration.

TIP

After you determine how much capital you want to put into trading derivatives, make sure that you know how much you can afford to lose on just one trade to be able to stay in business. You don't want to overexpose your cash position on one trade and risk the possibility that you won't have the money you need when the next opportunity comes along. By exposing your capital to a variety of markets, you also have a better chance that some of your trades will end up succeeding — how bad can that be?

WARNING

Be wary of firms that lead you to believe you can make lots of money trading options or futures with very little risk. That's never true. If a firm is using high-pressure tactics to get you to trade, that's a sure sign of a problem, so don't allow yourself to be rushed into a trading decision. If you aren't being given enough time to construct your own fundamental and technical analyses before you make a purchase, walk away from the deal.

REMEMBER

The risks associated with trading futures and options can be more than you initially paid for the trade, so be careful out there! We've given you an overview of the options and futures trading arena, but before you jump in, be sure you get significantly more training.

Chapter **20**

Going Foreign (Forex)

Trading money in the global markets can be a great way to make more of it, but beware that it also can be a lesson in how to lose money quickly. More than $5 trillion is traded every day on the *foreign exchange market* (Forex), and yet no centralized headquarters or formal regulatory body exists for this form of trade. London is the largest trading center, but New York, Tokyo, Hong Kong, and Singapore are important trading centers as well.

Forex is regulated through a patchwork of international agreements among countries, most of which have some type of regulatory agency that controls what goes on within their respective borders. Thus, Forex actually is a worldwide network of traders who are connected by telephone and computer screens.

REMEMBER

Because more international policing of money trading has occurred in recent years, authorities have had some successes exposing scams and frauds that victimize traders, especially newer ones, but a lot of fraud is still out there. So if you want to jump into this wild world of trading, you still need to be wary. Don't depend entirely on what we discuss here in this chapter to make your decision to start trading currency. Sure, we explain the workings of foreign exchange markets and how the language of the Forex market and its risks are unique, but you need to do a lot more training before you ever consider entering this extremely risky trading arena.

Exploring the World of Forex

If you've ever traveled outside the United States, you've probably traded in a foreign currency. Every time you travel outside your home country, you have to exchange your country's currency for the currency used in the country you're visiting. If you're a U.S. citizen shopping in England, and you see a sweater that you want for £100 (100 pounds — the *pound* is the name of the basic unit of currency in Great Britain), you'd need to know the exchange rate. In early 2017, for example, the rate was $1.24268 U.S. for £1 (one pound). So a £100 sweater would cost you $124.27 in U.S. dollars.

We include this example here to show you how Forex is used by the average shopper, but foreign currency traders trade much larger sums of money thousands of times a day. The majority of trades take place in five countries: the United Kingdom, the United States, Singapore, Hong Kong, and Japan. These five centers of currency trading handle 77 percent of Forex trading. As the United Kingdom moves out of the European Union as part of Brexit, these trading centers could change.

TIP

Currency trading is ongoing, 24 hours a day, with some countries just getting started as others are finishing up their business day. For example, when the trading day opens at 8 a.m. in London, the trading day is ending for Singapore and Hong Kong. When New York opens its trading doors, it's already 1 p.m. in London. Thus, traders must be alert around the clock, because a major event at an off hour anywhere in the world can shake the markets at any time.

Individual trades in the range of $200 million to $500 million are not uncommon. The Triennial Central Ban Survey of 2016 estimates that approximately $5.1 trillion are traded every day. In fact, its estimates indicate that quoted price changes occur as frequently as 20 times per minute, and the most active currency rates can change as many as 18,000 times in a single day.

Types of currency traders

Traders can be grouped into one of four basic types: bankers, brokers, customers, and central banks. Each plays a different role in the Forex market:

>> **Bankers, banks, and other financial institutions** do the lion's share of trading. They make profits buying and selling currency to each other and their customers. Approximately two-thirds of all Forex transactions involve banks dealing directly with each other.

>> **Brokers or dealers** sometimes act as intermediaries between the banks, helping them — or other traders looking for a good deal — find out where they can get the best currency trade. Buyers and sellers like working through brokers or dealers because they can trade anonymously through intermediaries. Brokers make profits on currency exchanges by charging a commission for the transactions they arrange.

>> **Customers,** which primarily are major companies, trade currency so they can operate globally or invest internationally. For example, if a U.S. car manufacturer buys parts from a manufacturer in Japan, then the U.S. car manufacturer needs to buy and pay for the parts in Japanese yen. Companies that trade currencies regularly have their own trading desks, whereas others conduct their currency trading through brokers or banks.

>> **Central banks,** like the U.S. Federal Reserve, that act on behalf of their governments, sometimes participate in the Forex market to influence the value of the currencies of their respective countries. For example, if the Federal Reserve believes the dollar is weak, it may buy dollars and even encourage central banks of other countries to do the same in the Forex market in order to boost the value of the dollar.

Why currency changes in value

Among the many factors that impact the value of a nation's currency are

>> Business cycles

>> Changes in tax laws

>> Inflationary expectations

>> Interest rates

>> International investment patterns

>> Policies adopted by governments and central banks

>> Political developments

>> Stock market news

Traders must monitor all these potential factors so they can stay on top of political or economic changes that impact the value of the currencies they hold. Currency trading, like other forms of trading, is affected by the basic economic principle of supply and demand. When a whole bunch of one type of currency is available for sale, the market can be flooded with it, and the price of that currency drops. When the supply of currency is low and the demand for it is high, then the value of that currency rises. Governments or through their central banks influence the value of their respective currencies by flooding the market whenever they want the value to fall or by making the supply scarce (by buying their own currency) whenever they want the value to rise.

What traders do

Currency traders look for a currency that offers the highest return with the lowest risk. For example, if a nation's financial instruments, such as stocks and bonds, offer high rates of return with relatively low risk, then traders who are foreign to that nation want to buy that currency, thus increasing the demand. Currency is also in demand when its country is going through a growth segment in its business cycle highlighted by stable prices and a wide range of goods and services available for sale. Forex traders who speculate on the values of currencies to earn their keep look for specific signs to indicate when exchange rates may change, including the following:

>> **Political instability:** Unrest in a country drives up demand for currency in safer markets, such as U.S. dollars, as speculators race to find safe havens.

>> **Rising interest rates:** Higher interest rates encourage foreign investments in countries where native investors are seeking better rates of return than they can get at home.

>> **Economic reforms:** Economic reforms in developing countries may help improve their currencies. As a result, investors see new opportunities for investing in the currencies of those successfully developing countries.

Traders try to predict these moves in advance so they can get in or out of a currency before others. Correctly guessing where a currency is going and taking a position in that currency at the beginning of the trend can mean huge profits for a trader. Traders make money either by buying the currency at a lower price and then selling it later at a higher price or by selling their holdings in currencies of other countries at higher prices before they have time to react negatively to improvements in the first currency. After the markets for their original holdings fall, they simply reestablish positions in them at bargain prices.

REMEMBER

When a trader purchases a large amount of a particular currency, then he or she is *long on the currency.* Conversely, when a trader sells a large amount of a currency, then he or she is *short on the currency.*

The Forex market is dominated by four currencies, which account for 80 percent of the market — the U.S. dollar, the euro, the Japanese yen, and the British pound.

These currencies always are liquid, which makes finding someone willing to buy or sell any of them easy for traders. Other currencies are not as liquid, and as is true with the stocks of small companies, you're sometimes unable to find any buyers or sellers when you're ready to trade for the currency of a smaller country. Currencies of developing countries are softest, usually facing lower demand than the currencies of developed countries. Soft currencies at times can be difficult to convert.

Understanding Money Jargon

The world of Forex has a language of its own. Prices are quoted two ways, meaning that when traders talk price with each other, they state their respective prices in terms of what *exchange rate* they'll pay to buy the currency and what they'll take when selling it. Bid and ask price differences, or *spreads*, usually are stated in *pips*, or a small fraction of a currency unit.

Pips are the most common incremental price movement quoted in the currency market. Some brokers quote in an even smaller measurement called *pipettes*. Although most transactions deal in thousands (individuals) or millions (interbank) of dollars, yen, euro, or other currencies, and a pip spread can equal thousands of dollars, most currency price quotes nevertheless are extended out four decimals (1.5432, for example). There are exceptions, such as the yen and nonmajor currency pairs that may be quoted to two decimal places. Many times traders quote only the last two digits, or the small numbers (such as 32 *exchange for* 22), because the incremental changes are so small that only the last two digits matter.

REMEMBER

As a trader, you need to think in terms of the host currency when receiving a quote for *direct exchange,* which is an exchange based on the value of the host country's currency. For example, quotes given to traders on the CME Group (formerly three separate exchanges: Chicago Mercantile Exchange, Chicago Board of Trade, and NYMEX) are based on the U.S. dollar because it's the host currency for the CME Group. You can see how that exchange works at www.cmegroup.com. Quotes for *indirect exchange* are just the opposite. They're based on the foreign currency for which you're seeking a trade rather than on the host currency. For example, if you're in the United States and receive an indirect price quote, you'd be getting a price based on buying a set amount of foreign currency in exchange for U.S. dollars. Most exchanges take place on the *interbank market* — currency exchanges among the world's banks — and are based on the U.S. dollar.

Traders use three different types of trades to exchange currency. They're known as spot, forward, and option transactions.

Spot transactions

Spot transactions account for about a third of all Forex transactions and involve trades in which two traders agree on an exchange rate and then trade currencies based on that rate. These transactions usually start with one trader contacting another and asking for a price on a particular type of currency without specifying whether he or she wants to buy or sell. The trader on the receiving end of the call gives the caller a two-way price — one if he or she wants to buy and the other one if he or she wants to sell. If they agree to do business, the two exchange their respective currencies.

Forward transactions

Traders use *forward transactions* when they want to buy or sell currency at some agreed-upon date in the future. A buyer and a seller set an exchange rate for the transaction, and the transaction occurs at the set price at the appointed time, regardless of what the current market price is for the currencies. Forward transactions can be a few days or even years in the future, although most futures contracts have standardized expiration dates depending on when you enter the position. The two types of forward transactions are futures and swaps:

>> **Futures:** These are forward transactions that have standard contract sizes and maturity dates. These types of transactions are traded on an exchange set up for this purpose.

>> **Swaps:** These are private contracts through which two parties exchange currencies for a specific length of time and then agree to reverse the transaction at a later date, which is set at the time of the initial contract.

WARNING

The risk that traders take in using forward transactions is that market rates can change, turning the contract to which they've just agreed into a losing trade. They still have to fulfill the contract at the fixed price because the price can't be revised after the contract is signed.

Companies that place orders for products from foreign firms usually use forward transactions so they can lock in an exchange rate at some time in the future when their orders are ready. Companies placing these orders don't want to lay out the cash upfront to exchange currencies, but they nevertheless want to be able to budget set amounts for their purchases. As such, they'd rather risk missing a better rate for the currency exchange in the future than a major shift in the product's price (perhaps brought on by a currency shock) that ends up costing them much more than they intended to pay.

Options

Option contracts were added to the Forex world to give traders a bit more flexibility than a forward transaction affords them. Like forward transactions, the owner of an option contract has the right to either buy or sell a specified amount of foreign currency at a specified rate up to a specified date. The big difference with option contracts is that traders who hold a contract aren't obligated to fulfill the transaction. They can, instead, simply decide to let it expire.

Option buyers have to pay for the right to buy or sell these transactions on or before a specified date. The set price at which the currencies are exchanged is called the *strike price*. When the date for the exchange arrives, the option holder determines whether the strike price is favorable. If it is, the option owner completes the transaction and earns a profit, but if it isn't favorable, the option owner allows the option to expire and absorbs the cost of purchasing the original option, which is less of a loss than actually exchanging the currencies. The two types of options currency traders deal with are

>> **Call options:** Options to buy currency at some set price in the future

>> **Put options:** Options to sell currency at some set price in the future

For example, suppose a trader purchases a six-month call option on 1 million euros at an exchange rate of 1.39 U.S. dollars to the euro. During that six-month period, the trader can (has the option to) purchase the euros at the $1.39 rate, buy them at market rate, or do nothing at all. As market rates for currencies fluctuate, options in those currencies can be sold and resold many times before the expiration date. Companies operating overseas use options as insurance against major unfavorable market shifts in the exchange rate and thus avoid locking their companies into guaranteed exchanges.

Trades are made using various currency symbols that are similar to the ones you need to know for stocks when seeking price quotes. Some of the more common currency symbols are listed in Table 20-1.

TABLE 20-1 ## Common Currency Symbols

Currency Symbol	Country & Currency Name
AUD	Australian dollar
CAD	Canadian dollar
CNY	Chinese yuan renminbi
EUR	Euro
GBP	British pound
JPY	Japanese yen
MXN	Mexican peso
MYR	Malaysian ringgit
NZD	New Zealand dollar
RUB	Russian ruble
SGD	Singapore dollar
USD	U.S. dollar

TIP

You can find current exchange rates for most major currencies online at the Universal Currency Converter (www.xe.com/ucc). You merely set an amount, the type of currency you want to convert, and the type of currency to which you want to convert to find out the exchange rate and how much the set amount of your currency is worth when converted or exchanged. Although this site won't give you a rate at which you're guaranteed to find a trade, it certainly gives you a decent estimate of what you can expect to find to within six decimal points.

Looking at How Money Markets Work

The currency exchange market is made up of about 2,000 dealer institutions that are particularly active in Forex. Most of the players are commercial or investment banks that are geographically dispersed in the key financial centers around the world. Among these 2,000 dealers, about 100 to 200 members carry on the core trading and market-making activities. Major players are fewer still.

When a dealer buys a U.S. dollar, regardless of where in the world the transaction takes place, the actual deposit is located either directly in a U.S. bank or in a claim of a foreign bank on a dollar deposit located in the United States. The same is true of the currency of any other country.

Different countries, different rules

The actual infrastructures of the various currency markets and how they operate are determined by each separate nation. Each country enforces its own laws, banking regulations, accounting rules, and tax codes, and each country determines its method of payment and the settlement system. Yikes! Doesn't that mean you have to know a lot about international monetary laws to be able to trade? Yup — especially if you want to be successful.

Luckily, considerable global cooperation exists among exchange regulators, which minimizes differences and helps protect Forex traders from fraud and abuse. In the United States, the U.S. Commodity Futures Trading Commission (CFTC) sets rules and investigates any problems involving U.S. currency trades. The CFTC reaches agreements, or *memoranda of understanding* (MOUs), with most major nations that have active currency exchanges. These MOUs form a method of cooperation between regulatory and enforcement authorities across international borders that combats fraud and other illegal practices that can harm customers or threaten market integrity.

WARNING

If you plan to become involved in Forex, be sure to visit the CFTC's website at www. cftc.gov to bone up on your knowledge of international laws and find information about recently exposed scams and other illegal activities. You certainly don't want to get caught up in a fraudulent deal and lose all your money.

The almighty (U.S.) dollar

The U.S. dollar is the most widely traded currency by far. Based on a Federal Reserve survey, the dollar is one of two currencies that are involved in more than 88 percent of all global foreign exchange transactions. The U.S. dollar wears many hats, serving as an investment currency in many capital markets, a reserve currency for many central banks, a transaction currency for many commodity trades, an invoice currency for many contracts, and a currency of intervention used by countries that want to influence the values of their own currencies.

Organized exchanges

The money market is largely unregulated as a *defined market*. By that, we mean that a commercial bank in the United States doesn't need any special authorization to trade or deal in foreign currencies. Securities and brokerage firms don't need special permission from the Securities and Exchange Commission (SEC) or any other regulatory body to carry out foreign exchange activities.

WARNING

Transactions can be carried out based on whatever terms the law permits and using whatever provisions are acceptable to the two parties, subject to the commercial law governing business transactions. Of course, that means the money market is the closest thing to the Wild West you'll find in the trading world. Almost anything goes. Institutions that participate aren't inspected specifically for their exchange practices, but regulatory authorities nevertheless look into trading systems as part of their regular examinations of financial institutions, just to be sure they're operating under the country's commercial banking or securities laws.

TIP

Although no official rules or restrictions govern the hours or conditions of trading on this over-the-counter (OTC) market in the United States, trading conventions developed mostly by market participants are in place. The OTC market for foreign currency trading is any currency trading done outside the confines of an exchange, such as the CME Group. You can find out what those rules are by contacting the Federal Bank of New York, which produces and regularly updates the *Guidelines for Foreign Exchange Trading Activities.* These guidelines clarify common market practices and offer "best practice recommendations." Before you become a trader, protect yourself by making sure you're working with a dealer or a broker that follows these guidelines. You can access the most current version, revised in November 2010, at `https://www.newyorkfed.org/medialibrary/microsites/fxc/files/2010/tradingguidelinesNov2010.pdf`. The New York Federal Reserve regularly issues updates to the guidelines, which you can find on its website at `https://www.newyorkfed.org/fxc/index.html`.

TIP

The OTC currency exchange market accounts for more than 90 percent of the total U.S. foreign exchange market, including spot transactions, forwards, and swaps. If you're new to Forex trading, starting out is much safer on an organized exchange, where you can trade currency futures and certain currency options. The Chicago Mercantile Exchange (CME) is one of the largest, and it offers excellent educational materials to help you get started. Find out more about the CME at `www.cmegroup.com/education`.

Organized exchanges and regulations governing them are considerably different from the OTC foreign currency market. Trading actually takes place in a centralized location rather than through a network of computers and telephones. Each of the respective exchanges regulates hours and trading practices, and their products are standardized. Organized exchanges also are equipped with central clearinghouses for payments and cash settlements.

Taking Necessary Risks in the World Money Market

Leverage, which means borrowing money to trade, is the number one risk to your portfolio when trading in Forex markets. Success on the Forex market means having to trade in large sums, because profits are made at exchange-rate differences of only fractions of a cent. Banks or brokers determine the leverage they want to offer you, but you won't find strict regulations like the ones that govern stock margin accounts.

After they're approved for trading, customers are given a set amount or allowance on which they can trade on margin. A common starting allowance for trading on margin is 5 percent (see Chapter 15 for more about margin), which means that if you put $100,000 in the bank, you're allowed to execute transactions of up to $2 million. As you gain success with more experience, that margin may be lowered to 1 percent, which means you'd be allowed to trade as much as $10 million on your $100,000 deposit.

WARNING

When trading at those high margin levels, even a minor mistake can wipe out your entire deposit.

The most conservative of banks require *full margin,* meaning you have to deposit $1 million to be able to trade $1 million. Be sure that you understand the leverage you're being offered and the loss potential you face if your trade goes sour. Just imagine starting with $100,000, which you can use to trade $2 million, and then losing half of that trading maximum with trades that have gone sour. You could end up $900,000 in the hole. Sure, lots of traders can come up with that — no problem. In reality, as long as you stick to trading, the major currencies' drastic price changes that end up in that type of loss are unlikely, but a loss of 10 to 20 percent of your holding in a matter of minutes can happen. Only trading in third-world currencies can result in losses of the million-dollar magnitude described here, and only if the country experienced a major uprising and the price of its currency dropped dramatically.

Understanding the types of risks

You also face a number of different kinds of risk, including market risk, exchange risk, interest rate risk, counterparty risk, volatility risk, liquidity risk, and country risk.

Market risk

All traders and investors face market risk. Basically, *market risk* is comprised of changes in price that adversely impact your trade or investment. Market risk, which includes overall changes in the financial markets, is in play from the moment you enter into a Forex position until the moment you exit it. The foreign exchange rate can change any time during that period, so when you're dealing in Forex, two key factors can impact the price of the currency — exchange risk and interest rate risk.

Exchange risk

Foreign exchange traders take on exchange risk (specific to the currencies in the pair chosen) the moment they buy or sell a foreign currency. Every time you take on a new foreign exchange position, regardless of whether it's through a spot, forward, future, or option transaction, you're immediately exposed to the potential that the exchange rate will move against your position, making it worth less than when you bought it. In only a matter of seconds, a profitable transaction can turn into an unprofitable one.

Interest rate risk

Foreign exchange positions can change in value not only because of the exchange rate but also because of the currency's underlying interest rate. Whenever a country's central bank (think Federal Reserve) raises or lowers the underlying interest rate for its currency, the impact on any positions you're holding in that country's currency can be a major one.

Counterparty risk

In the currency trading world, a *counterparty* is the other entity involved in a transaction — a bank or banker, a broker, or another trader. When you buy a currency option or execute a forward transaction, you risk the possibility that the counterparty to your transaction won't be able to meet his, her, or its obligations.

REMEMBER

Whenever you buy the option through an exchange, rather than directly from the counterparty, this risk isn't a factor. When that happens, you run into additional replacement costs, because you're forced to enter into another currency transaction to meet your own foreign currency needs. The key to avoiding this kind of risk is entering into contracts with known entities that have high credit ratings. Additionally, you need to investigate whether the counterparty with which you're trading has had any problems with regulators, insolvency, or questions of ethical conduct. One good place to begin your investigation is the consumer protection section of the CFTC at www.cftc.gov/ConsumerProtection/index.htm.

TIP

When evaluating a company, you first need to consider its credit risk. You can find credit rankings for many major banks at the Standard & Poor's website (www.standardandpoors.com). You can research a company's creditworthiness by investigating the requirements and standards it uses when providing credit to its customers. Companies that provide easy credit to their customers run a greater risk of not being able to meet their obligations. Conversely, companies with higher margin limits definitely are safer to do business with when you're entering into a contract.

Volatility risk

Volatility risk relates to the possibility of rapidly changing exchange rates impacting your positions in foreign currencies. As we mention earlier in the "Exploring the World of Forex" section, currency prices can change thousands of times per day. Options on currencies are valued according to volatility and underlying changes in the prices of the respective currencies. If a trader sees an increase of 100 percent in volatility, or a doubling of volatility, then the price of the option can increase 5 percent to 10 percent. If you're trading on credit, which is highly likely, your bank or broker can reevaluate the credit it's extending to you whenever it sees a dramatic increase in the volatility of your holdings.

Liquidity risk

Liquidity risk is not a major factor if you're trading in the more commonly traded currencies, but if you decide to trade in less active currencies, it can become a factor when you're unable to sell a currency you hold at the expressed time you want the sale to take place, especially when the market for that currency is not active. You can avoid liquidity risk by buying currency options or futures on an exchange.

Country risk

Country risks come in several different varieties, all of which you need to consider whenever you trade in foreign currencies. Among those aspects are

>> **Political risk:** This variety relates to the political stability of the country in whose currency you're trading. Although we haven't seen any recent seizures of commercial assets by any nations, it has happened in the past. For example, Venezuela took control of its oil industry by seizing assets of non-Venezuelan oil companies. If you trade in currencies of countries that are at risk of possible destabilization, the currency you buy can become worthless if the country changes political leaders.

>> **Regulation risk:** This variety relates to what can happen after you establish a position in a country's currency. Its government can change its regulations

and, in effect, put restraints on the ownership established by your position in the currency and by the position of your counterparty — and that can get messy.

>> **Legal risk:** This variety relates to which country has jurisdiction to rule on a contract if your counterparty happens to default. Unfavorable contract law in the host country of your counterparty can end up determining that the contract is invalid or illegal, and you can lose your position. Be sure that you understand from whom you're buying and under which country's laws any disputes will be settled. If U.S. law won't be the overriding law for the contract, be certain you understand contract law in the country of the counterparty with whom you're trading.

>> **Holiday risk:** This variety relates to the possibility that the country in whose currency you're trading has different religious, political, or governmental holidays that can shut down trading in that currency right when you need the money. Be sure you know the holiday schedules for the countries in whose currencies you trade.

Seeking risk protection

Although trading in foreign currencies often is called the modern-day Wild West, forces are in place that can help you minimize the risks — provided you take advantage of them and trade within their boundaries. The primary monitors of foreign currency trading are the world's central banks. They monitor the flow of money among countries and the balance of payments between governments and banking institutions. In the United States, the U.S. Treasury Department and the Federal Reserve monitor and regulate these types of transactions. Similar regulatory authorities exist in most major currency markets, but if you decide to do business with a nonbanking institution, you're transacting your business in unprotected waters outside the safe harbor of regulatory oversight and must do so under the often fateful guise of *caveat emptor:* Let the buyer beware.

Internationally, the Bank for International Settlements (BIS — www.bis.org/index.htm) is the leading independent agency for evaluating foreign exchange trading institutions on a global basis. BIS created risk-weighted evaluation and capital requirements for institutions that trade in foreign currencies and money-market transactions. Be certain that any institution outside the United States with which you plan to conduct trades meets BIS standards.

A number of common clearing systems assist with the transfer of foreign currencies. The two best-known ones are the Clearing House Interbank Payments System, or CHIPS, and the Society for Worldwide Interbank Financial Telecommunication, or SWIFT. Be sure you're using one of these systems when you trade because they code transactions to avoid defaults and help you identify the credit-worthiness of transactions. CHIPS is privately owned and operated by the New York Clearing House.

If you're trading in foreign currency futures, your risks are much less, because the futures industry is highly regulated. Clearinghouses for futures are efficient, and futures transactions usually are cleared hourly or in some cases even minute by minute.

Getting Ready to Trade Money

Your first step as a foreign currency trader is to develop an extensive collection of historical information not only about rate fluctuations for the currencies you plan to trade but also about interest-rate fluctuations, economic history, and political stability of the countries whose currencies you're considering. Gathering some background information about the Forex market itself doesn't hurt either. You can find more details about trading currency in *Currency Trading For Dummies*, 3rd Edition, by Kathleen Brooks and Brian Dolan (Wiley).

After collecting this information, you need to consider your own trading goals and how much you want to risk. Set your risk limits before you start so you don't get emotionally caught up in having to make these potentially disastrous trading decisions on the fly. Capital that you risk on Forex trading needs to be money that you can afford to lose without impacting your lifestyle. Do not, for any reason, use retirement savings, savings for your children's educations, or savings required to maintain your house and lifestyle.

WARNING

As is true for stock trading, when trading currencies, you need to develop a plan that determines what you trade and how much you're at risk. When your plan's in place, you need to stick to it for the entire trading day. You should not be developing the plan and executing it at the same time. Foreign currency trading requires a great deal of focus, and you can't risk breaking that focus to do additional planning in the middle of a trading day. Monitor the successes you have in meeting the goals of your plan. If you're not achieving your objectives, you may want to step back and reevaluate your plan and your decision to trade in foreign currency.

Foreign currency traders use technical analysis in a way that is similar to stock trading (see Chapters 9 and 10). Bar charts are the most common tools. The basic bar chart shows the opening, high, low, and closing prices for a given period of time.

TIP

The key difference between trading currencies and stocks is that in the foreign exchange market, a daily price chart sometimes shows the opening price in the Pacific Rim and the closing price in the United States. Because the foreign exchange market is open 24 hours a day, time periods are different for foreign currency trading than they are for stock trading. You can play with Forex charting online at `https://www.dailyfx.com/charts`.

We don't cover the basics of technical analysis for foreign currency trading here because we'd need to take up another entire book to do it right. That's exactly why John Wiley & Sons, Inc., also publishes *Technical Analysis For Dummies*, by Barbara Rockefeller. Be sure to check it out, too.

REMEMBER

Because we can't say it enough, we repeat: If you truly want to pursue this form of trading, we highly recommend that you seek additional training before you begin trading individually. You can get your feet wet by trading ETFs (exchange-traded funds) based on various foreign currencies. For more information about ETF trading, see Chapter 14.

6

The Part of Tens

IN THIS PART . . .

Read about a dozen huge trading mistakes so you don't repeat them.

Discover the ten top strategies to help you survive as a trader.

Chapter **21**

More Than Ten Huge Trading Mistakes

This chapter introduces you to ten (more, actually) huge trading mistakes that befall experienced and novice traders. We offer suggestions for helping you recognize the mistakes and for avoiding and even correcting them.

Fishing for Bottoms

Bottom fishing — trying to catch a stock as it bottoms out — is a great way to get soaked and lose a bucketful of money. In a bear market, stocks get much cheaper than most people ever expect or want. They don't stop falling until they've run out of gas.

The psychology of a bear market is perverse. As long as traders remain interested in a stock, many are the moments when it seems like the stock may recover. The thing is, stocks rarely turn on a dime and head higher. Only after the momentum crowd loses interest does the stock's downward price slide end. When value investors, who can't resist a bargain, begin nibbling, the stock begins to stabilize; however, it also may spend a very long time bouncing around in a trading range.

REMEMBER

Traders have few, if any, reasons for entering the market when a stock is trading in a range. Your best opportunity for profit occurs when the stock breaks out of its trading range. Chapter 9 shows how to identify these trading-range breakout patterns. Instead of risking your trading capital on unreliable bottoming patterns, wait until you're sure.

Timing the Top

Tops and bottoms share something in common: They rarely arrive when they're supposed to. When traders and investors are exuberant, they keep buying even after doing so no longer makes fundamental sense. That's why shorting a stock that's trending higher makes no sense, even if its price is far beyond reasonable.

You don't have to have a lengthy memory or an encyclopedic knowledge of stock market history to remember what happened to Internet stocks in the late 1990s. Those were heady days. Stocks went in only one direction — up. Some of those magically levitating companies had modest revenues, but few had earnings. Nevertheless, traders bid hundreds of dollars per share for some worthless junk. Just like the housing bubble of the early 2000s, Internet stocks were a case of mass hysteria, mob mentality, market madness, or all three.

WARNING

Call it what you will, but when a bubble is inflating, you definitely don't want to short related stocks. Sure, these stocks eventually crashed and burned, but not before depleting the trading accounts of a den full of bearish short sellers. Don't guess. Wait for reliable trading signals, like the ones discussed in Chapters 9 and 10, before entering a position.

You may be asking whether there were reliable trading signals before the Internet bubble burst. There weren't before; traders aren't fortunetellers (see Chapter 8). However, the risks at the time were well-known. And when stocks began heading lower early in 2000, you had all the information you needed to protect your profits and trading capital and begin selling short. The signals were also there in early 2008 that the market was set for another fall. Chapter 13 uses the NASDAQ bubble as an example to show how to evaluate market risk and adjust your trading strategy as the market transitions from a rising to a falling market.

Trading against the Dominant Trend

Trading against the dominant trend in the market leads to costly mistakes. Unfortunately, misidentifying the trend by focusing on the chart in front of you and forgetting to look at the next higher-level chart is an easy thing to do. You may see a promising uptrend occur with a pullback on the intraday charts. But on the daily chart, the trend you saw on the intraday chart actually turns out to be a consolidation rally during a strong downtrend. The promising pullback actually is the beginning of the next leg down on the daily chart. If you buy long in a situation like this one, hoping to capture the next leg up, your position will be swamped (and so will your trading capital) by the flood of sell orders coming from traders who recognize the implications of the stronger, longer-term trend.

TIP

Regardless of the specific indications of the chart you're looking at, always confirm your analysis by looking at charts that are one time period higher. For example, if you're studying daily charts, confirm your analysis on the weekly charts. If you're studying intraday charts, confirm your analysis on the daily charts. Always know which part of the market cycle you're in and what types of industries excel in that part of the cycle. See Chapters 10 and 13 for additional information.

WARNING

Don't try to buy long based on a brief intraday move when the dominant trend on the daily charts is down. Doing so is a great way of giving up your trading capital to someone else.

Winging It

Traders get into big trouble when they wing it. Maybe you heard the guy on business TV say the stock was hot and heading higher. Maybe you saw the news that a new product was bound to be a big hit. Although that may sound like great information, instead it's only a reason to look into the fundamental and technical conditions of a company's stock, not a reason to buy today.

Devise a strategy. We think that's such great advice, we'll say it again. *Devise a strategy.* Develop and test a trading system that matches your goals and personality (see Chapter 16). Plan your trades and execute your plan. Wait patiently for your signals to trigger your trades. Pick your entry and exit points before entering your order. Have a plan and stick to it.

Traders also get into trouble when they start second-guessing their trading plans. Sometimes, even in the middle of executing a trade, you need to make a decision but aren't sure which decision is right.

REMEMBER

When in doubt, close the position. Thinking clearly is easier when your money isn't at risk. You can always buy back the stock if further analysis confirms it's the right thing to do.

Taking Trading Personally

A losing trade is bad for your trading account, but you can't let it get to you. Sure, it makes you feel bad, but a losing trade doesn't impugn your honor or disparage your heritage. A bad trade may reduce your net worth, but it shouldn't damage your self-esteem. Entering a losing trade certainly doesn't mean that you're a nincompoop or blockhead — any more than closing a winning trade signals your brilliance and mastery of all you survey.

REMEMBER

The market isn't out to get you; it's out to get your money. Don't take trading personally. A losing trade is just another losing trade. You'll have plenty of them. Get used to it.

Falling in Love

Trading is a business. Your stocks are your inventory. Smart business owners don't fall in love with their inventory. It's there to sell, at a profit if possible, at a loss if necessary. And smart businesspeople don't fall in love with their business models. If it isn't working, they change it; otherwise, they'll be out of business before you can say "liquidation sale."

When you fall in love with your stock, you risk large losses. When you fall in love with your trading plan, you risk many more losses. It's easy to fall in love. After doing hours of research and analysis, you want to be right. You want your trades and your trading plans to generate profits, but hoping doesn't make it so.

Be smart. Don't fall in love. Your trading system doesn't have feelings, and your stock won't love you back. Be prepared to jettison positions and trading systems that don't do what they're supposed to do. See Chapter 12 for more about trading as a business and effectively managing your inventory.

Using After-Hours Market Orders

When the market opens and it's off to the races, the market order that you placed last night before going to bed is going to be swept up in a wave of frantic trading. Bad fills are sure to be the result. You're likely to pay considerably more to buy a stock that you want or to sell one for considerably less than you'd planned. You should never place a market order when entering trades after the market is closed (after hours). Instead, define how much you're willing to buy or sell a stock for by using a stop order, a limit order, or a stop-limit order. Chapter 15 discusses the mechanics of entering these types of orders.

Chasing a Runaway Trend

If you miss the breakout entry point for a stock that you want, waiting is better than entering a position as a trend accelerates. See Chapter 10 for information about identifying and trading a trend. Often, stocks will pull back and test the breakout point. Wait for that point, or wait for the stock to take a short breather after its first leg up. If you're still interested, that's a better entry point than chasing a stock as it accelerates into the trend. Like a fine wine, you sometimes need to let a stock breathe.

On the other hand, if you already have a position in a runaway stock, try planning your exit so you leave a little money on the table. Capturing every last nickel of the trend is almost impossible, anyway, so don't try. Instead, consider trimming your position as the stock reaches for the stratosphere. If you're using margin, consider taking some profit off the table and reducing your leverage a bit. We discuss this strategy further in Chapter 13, and the mechanics of using margin are covered in Chapter 15. When a runaway stock stops going up and everyone wants out at the same time, the speed at which the price falls is remarkable. Be ready to jettison stocks that rally too fast at the first sign of trouble.

Averaging Down

Averaging down is a below-average idea. You sometimes hear advisors suggesting it as a way of reducing your cost basis, but it's merely a technique to throw good money after bad. The logic of averaging down is completely contrary to the logic of trading. Traders sell losers. They don't reward them with infusions of trading capital.

However, averaging up makes some sense. Traders call it *pyramiding.* The idea is to add to your winning positions when your trading system triggers new trading signals in the direction of the trend. Pyramiding is a good way of building a large position in a strongly trending stock. Be aware of the risk, though. The larger your position, the more it hurts when the trend ends and the stock's price begins to fall. Be ready to trim your pyramid position at the first sign of trouble.

Ignoring Your Stops

Talking yourself out of honoring your stops is an easy thing to do. You'll be tempted when a trade goes against you. You'll look at your indicators and the support levels on your charts, and you'll be certain that the stock soon will stop falling. When you start thinking you want to give a position a little room to work its way out of losing territory, you're on your way toward a trading debacle. It's wishful thinking, it's hoping against hope, and it's a good way to lose a lot of money. Unless you're omniscient, close the position when the price hits your stop. Take your loss. Chapter 15 discusses stop orders and how to use them.

Diversifying Badly

Exposing all your capital in one trade is a bad idea, and so is trading hundreds of stocks simultaneously. You can find a happy medium somewhere in between.

You can monitor only so many positions and do it well. You need only so many positions to diversify your risk. And although you can have too few or too many stocks in your trading portfolio, no perfect number — one that is right for every trader — exists. That said, you nevertheless have to figure out what the right number is for you. Start with 10 or 15 positions. You may end up deciding that 8 are enough. However, unless you have an extremely large portfolio, we can't imagine why you'd need any more than 20 positions.

REMEMBER

The simple wisdom is this: Don't put all your eggs in one basket. And don't chop your eggs into little pieces and spread them across many dozens of baskets. You want to diversify — just not too much.

Enduring Large Losses

To trade is to lose. No matter how good your trading system is, no matter how experienced you are, and no matter which stocks you pick, you're going to have losing trades. Your success as a trader depends on how you handle those losing trades. If you dispose of the losers quickly, you can become a very successful trader. But if you hold on to those losing positions, you can lose so much money that it may knock you right out of the trading business.

Using margin (see Chapter 15) exacerbates the problem of losing trades. Margin is a wonderful thing because with careful application it can magnify your profits. But on the flip side, with indiscriminate use it can also magnify your losses. If you want to turn your pool of trading capital into a puddle, leverage a lot of losing trades.

WARNING

Small losses won't hurt you much, but large losses will. If you use margin and fail to cut your losses, you won't be a trader for long.

Chapter **22**

Ten Trading Survival Techniques

Trading is not a risk-free activity. Although all traders know that losses are inevitable, they want to minimize those losses and stay solvent to trade another day. In this chapter, we review ten of the top trading survival techniques that can help you enter the world of trading and enable you to continue to trade for a long time to come.

Build Your Trading Tool Chest

Before you buy that first share of stock, that first option or futures contract, or any other security, you need to have the right mix of trading software, hardware, and Internet access to be successful. You need the right tools to identify trading candidates; display and interpret charts; research trading opportunities; screen stocks for technical or fundamental constraints; and monitor and analyze your portfolio, open positions, market indexes, sectors, and trading statistics. In summary, the proper tools are critical to finding the right trades and then monitoring those positions after you've found and entered them.

Even after you've found them, if you don't have the right tools, you may not be able to enter and exit positions efficiently; control or track your orders; track your profits and losses; analyze your trading history; or monitor economic reports, earnings, and other business news.

The proper tools help you evaluate your trading system and test your trading ideas. They enable you to keep trading logs to review your trading performance. You also can use tools to stay in touch with other traders and exchange ideas that ultimately may help you improve your trading skills and discover new trading opportunities.

REMEMBER

Tools are the core of any good trader's business. Without the right ones, your chances of success drop dramatically. Don't scrimp on the tools you select for your trading activities. For more information, see Chapter 4.

Choose and Use Your Favorite Tools Wisely

As you begin sorting out your software and hardware and making contact with other traders, you'll probably find out about the hundreds of tools and charts that are out there on the market. You don't need to learn and use them all. Using too many tools can be as dangerous to your trading system and your sanity as using too few. You'll find that you get mixed signals and will probably end up in a state of analysis paralysis trying to figure out which tool is giving you the right signal.

TIP

To avoid driving yourself crazy, pick the top two or three trading tools that make sense to you and fit your trading style. Take your time getting to know how they work and how best to interpret the information they generate. Use them to build the types of charts that match your trading style and don't worry about learning all the new gadgets. If your tools are working and you're making a good profit, don't rush to add the newest tool innovation.

Keep your eyes open for new tools that can improve your trading profits, but use caution before making changes to your winning trading system. For more information, see Chapter 16.

Use Both Technical and Fundamental Analyses

You may have heard that all traders use technical analysis and think that fundamental analysis is a waste of time. Don't believe it. Although technical analysis is crucial to finding the right entry and exit points, fundamental analysis improves your ability to make the right stock choices, given market and economic conditions.

You'll find as a trader that knowing the current state of the economy and the state of the market is critical. You obviously want to buy stocks in a bull market and sell them, or short them, in a bear market, but do you know how to recognize when the market is entering a period of transition so you can make your moves when the opportunity for making profitable trades or minimizing potential losses is greatest?

Using a combination of fundamental and technical analyses, your chances of identifying bull and bear markets and finding phases of transition and consolidation improve dramatically. Your best trading opportunities are at the beginning of these phases of change, so be sure that you understand the six phases of the market and know which sectors offer you the best trading opportunities within each of those phases. For more information, see Parts 2 and 3.

Count on the Averages to Make Your Moves

You may think that using data from averages to find the right time to enter or exit a position is counterintuitive, but moving averages can be powerful trading indicators. Moving averages actually smooth out the data for you visually and help you identify any trends. Although they can't predict the future, they nevertheless help you understand the past so you can more effectively extrapolate what may happen to a stock in the future.

Traders use many different types of moving averages in hundreds of different ways. Stock closing prices are the most common data being averaged, but any value on a price chart can be smoothed for interpretation. For example, traders sometimes manipulate the moving averages by using the midpoint between the high and low prices to develop the moving average. Others look for the moving average using the open, high, or low price. It's all a matter of trading style and how the charts you're developing match your trading system.

Be sure to find out how to use moving averages and what they mean. After you understand them and what goes into them, you can manipulate moving averages to your advantage and to coincide with your trading style. Moving averages are powerful indicators, but they're not the only type of indicator you need to use in choosing your trades; use moving averages in conjunction with other indicators. For more information, see Chapter 11.

Develop and Manage Your Trading System

You need to have a road map that helps you find buy and sell signals for your trades. A trading system is such a map because it's developed using a collection of tools created from technical and fundamental analyses woven together to let you know when it's time to enter or exit positions. You can buy trading systems off the shelf, but these systems are available to thousands of others who ultimately will end up with the same buy and sell signals.

To be able to trade outside the pack, you need to develop your own trading system, using your own favorite tools. Although you can use tools provided in off-the-shelf software packages, you want to develop and adapt a trading system that fits uniquely with your personality and trading objectives.

After initially developing and testing your own trading system, your work isn't finished. You'll need to constantly monitor your system's successes and failures and look for ways to make improvements. For more information, see Chapter 16.

Know Your Costs

Trading isn't cheap. Not only do you have to worry about commissions or transaction fees, but you also must watch for any slippage in your trades. Even though you may be using stop or limit orders, you rarely end up executing trades at the exact entry or exit prices you plan. Some *slippage*, or the difference between the quoted price and the actual price for the security, is bound to occur, so be sure that you carefully monitor your commission costs, transaction fees, and slippage costs.

REMEMBER

In addition, don't forget to consider the tax man. If you're trading stocks that you hold for less than a year, any profits you make are taxed as current income instead of at lower capital-gains tax rates.

Traders must also avoid being caught by wash sale rules. Most trading losses can be used to offset trading gains and thus reduce your income tax burden, but if you sell a stock for a loss and repurchase the same stock within 30 days, you can't deduct your trading loss for that transaction. You have to wait until you sell the stock again and use any losses to reduce the cost basis of the trade, which reduces the tax owed when the position is finally closed. Full-time day traders receive special tax treatment, but you must be a bona fide day trader to qualify. For more information, see Chapters 2 and 15.

Have an Exit Strategy

Knowing when to take your profits and get out and when to accept your losses and close a position before it becomes even more damaging can be among the hardest lessons any trader must learn. All too often you're enticed by the win and want to ride it to the absolute top.

REMEMBER

Wise traders plan their exit points at the top and bottom of each position long before they ever enter that position. And more important, they stick to their plan. Getting caught up in the emotions of a winning trade is easy, but don't forget you're operating a business. Take your profits when you reach your goal and get out so you don't risk turning a winning position into a loss.

When you make a mistake, own up to it quickly, take your hit, and get out of the position. If the stock recovers, you can always reenter the position at a later time. Don't ride a stock to the bottom just to try to prove you were right. Plan your exit points before you buy and stick to them. For more information, see Chapter 12.

Watch for Signals, Don't Anticipate Them

After you make a decision to buy a stock, you may find that you're impatient to actually get into that position. You start watching the charts and waiting for the right signal to buy. Often, you'll see charts move close to your planned signal but not actually reach it.

Be patient. Wait for the signal you've designated in your plan. Don't anticipate any moves, even if the stock price is getting close to that point on your charts. You may miss the perfect entry point, but you'll be less likely to make that fatal mistake of entering a position before the signal is triggered only to see your stock reverse course and thus be forced to take a loss. For more information, see Chapters 10 and 13.

Buy on Strength, Sell on Weakness

Buy on strength and sell on weakness is a mantra you've probably heard frequently from investment and trading gurus. The reason for its popularity is a good one: It works! And it needs to become your trading way of life.

REMEMBER

When you see a stock showing strength and heading into an uptrend, it's time to buy. When you see a stock falling and showing signs of entering a weakening period, it's time to sell. If a weak stock takes a turn for the better, you can always reenter the position. For more information, see Chapter 13.

Keep a Trading Journal and Review It Often

The only way you can ever improve your trading skills is by keeping track of what works and what doesn't and trying to gauge why. After each trade, write down the details of the trade and what went right and/or wrong with that trade. You can only improve what you measure, so measure everything and put it in your trading journal.

TIP

Don't forget to review the contents of your journal every week. You may find that reviewing your successes is enjoyable but reviewing your failures is difficult. Failure, however, sometimes is the best teacher. Many people discover more from their failures than from their successes. Try figuring out why your failed trades didn't work and what you could've done to improve your results. Of course, don't ignore your successes. After all, you need to know what works and why and then try to incorporate those winning strategies more consistently into your trading system. For more information, see Chapter 16.

Index

M

About the Authors

Lita Epstein, who earned her MBA from Emory University's Goizueta Business School, enjoys helping people develop good financial, investing, and tax-planning skills. She designs and teaches online courses on topics such as accounting, reading financial reports, investing for retirement, and getting ready for tax time. She has written more than 35 books, including *Bookkeeping For Dummies* and *Reading Financial Reports For Dummies,* both published by Wiley.

Lita was the content director for a financial services website, MostChoice.com, and managed the Investing for Women website. As a congressional press secretary, Lita gained firsthand knowledge about how to work within and around the federal bureaucracy, which gives her great insight into how government programs work. In the past, Lita has been a daily newspaper reporter, magazine editor, and fundraiser for the Carter Presidential Center. For fun, Lita enjoys scuba diving and is even certified as an underwater photographer. She hikes, canoes, and enjoys surfing the web to find all its hidden treasures.

Grayson Roze has worked in the financial services industry for StockCharts.com since 2012. He now serves as a Business Manager at the company. He is the co-author of *Tensile Trading: The 10 Essential Stages of Stock Market Mastery,* published by Wiley in 2016. Grayson speaks regularly at various investment seminars, including to organizations such as the American Association of Individual Investors (AAII) and the Market Technicians Association (MTA). He holds a bachelor's degree from Swarthmore College, where he studied economics and psychology.

At a young age, Grayson began pursuing his interest in the financial markets by attending investment classes and starting to trade under the guidance of his father. At the age of 18, Grayson began investing his own account and has since become an accomplished trader in his own right. Outside of market hours, he enjoys staying fit by biking, hiking, and playing lacrosse, and he is also a passionate automotive enthusiast.

Authors' Acknowledgments

We would like to thank all the people who have been instrumental in making this new edition a reality. In particular, we'd like to thank all the wonderful *For Dummies* folks at Wiley, especially Tracy Boggier and Michelle Hacker for shepherding this project to completion and for advice and suggestions, and John Forman for keeping us accurate. Also, we want to extend a special thank you to Chip Anderson, president of StockCharts.com, for his support and encouragement throughout this process.

Publisher's Acknowledgments

Senior Acquisitions Editor: Tracy Boggier

Project Manager: Michelle Hacker

Development Editor: Georgette Beatty

Copy Editor: Todd Lothery

Technical Editor: John Forman, PhD

Production Editor: Selvakumaran Rajendiran

Cover Image: © Westend61 GmbH/ Alamy Stock Photo

Leverage the power

Dummies is the global leader in the reference category and one of the most trusted and highly regarded brands in the world. No longer just focused on books, customers now have access to the dummies content they need in the format they want. Together we'll craft a solution that engages your customers, stands out from the competition, and helps you meet your goals.

Advertising & Sponsorships

Connect with an engaged audience on a powerful multimedia site, and position your message alongside expert how-to content. Dummies.com is a one-stop shop for free, online information and know-how curated by a team of experts.

- Targeted ads
- Video
- Email Marketing
- Microsites
- Sweepstakes sponsorship

20 MILLION PAGE VIEWS EVERY SINGLE MONTH

15 MILLION UNIQUE VISITORS PER MONTH

43% OF ALL VISITORS ACCESS THE SITE VIA THEIR MOBILE DEVICES

700,000 NEWSLETTER SUBSCRIPTIONS TO THE INBOXES OF **300,000** UNIQUE INDIVIDUALS EVERY WEEK

# of dummies

Custom Publishing

Reach a global audience in any language by creating a solution that will differentiate you from competitors, amplify your message, and encourage customers to make a buying decision.

- Apps
- Books
- eBooks
- Video
- Audio
- Webinars

Brand Licensing & Content

Leverage the strength of the world's most popular reference brand to reach new audiences and channels of distribution.

For more information, visit **dummies.com/biz**

PERSONAL ENRICHMENT

Staying Sharp
9781119187790
USA $26.00
CAN $31.99
UK £19.99

Facebook
9781119179030
USA $21.99
CAN $25.99
UK £16.99

Guitar
9781119293354
USA $24.99
CAN $29.99
UK £17.99

Investing
9781119293347
USA $22.99
CAN $27.99
UK £16.99

Beekeeping
9781119310068
USA $22.99
CAN $27.99
UK £16.99

Digital Photography
9781119235606
USA $24.99
CAN $29.99
UK £17.99

Meditation
9781119251163
USA $24.99
CAN $29.99
UK £17.99

Pregnancy
9781119235491
USA $26.99
CAN $31.99
UK £19.99

Samsung Galaxy S7
9781119279952
USA $24.99
CAN $29.99
UK £17.99

iPhone
9781119283133
USA $24.99
CAN $29.99
UK £17.99

Crocheting
9781119287117
USA $24.99
CAN $29.99
UK £16.99

Nutrition
9781119130246
USA $22.99
CAN $27.99
UK £16.99

PROFESSIONAL DEVELOPMENT

Windows 10
9781119311041
USA $24.99
CAN $29.99
UK £17.99

AutoCAD
9781119255796
USA $39.99
CAN $47.99
UK £27.99

Excel 2016
9781119293439
USA $26.99
CAN $31.99
UK £19.99

QuickBooks 2017
9781119281467
USA $26.99
CAN $31.99
UK £19.99

macOS Sierra
9781119280651
USA $29.99
CAN $35.99
UK £21.99

LinkedIn
9781119251132
USA $24.99
CAN $29.99
UK £17.99

Windows 10
9781119310563
USA $34.00
CAN $41.99
UK £24.99

SharePoint 2016
9781119181705
USA $29.99
CAN $35.99
UK £21.99

Fundamental Analysis
9781119263593
USA $26.99
CAN $31.99
UK £19.99

Networking
9781119257769
USA $29.99
CAN $35.99
UK £21.99

Office 2016
9781119293477
USA $26.99
CAN $31.99
UK £19.99

Office 365
9781119265313
USA $24.99
CAN $29.99
UK £17.99

Salesforce.com
9781119239314
USA $29.99
CAN $35.99
UK £21.99

Coding
9781119293323
USA $29.99
CAN $35.99
UK £21.99

dummies.com

dummies
A Wiley Brand

Learning Made Easy

ACADEMIC

Algebra I dummies

Mary Jane Sterling

9781119293576
USA $19.99
CAN $23.99
UK £15.99

Basic Math & Pre-Algebra dummies

Mark Zegarelli

9781119293637
USA $19.99
CAN $23.99
UK £15.99

Calculus dummies

Mark Ryan

9781119293491
USA $19.99
CAN $23.99
UK £15.99

Chemistry dummies

John T. Moore, EdD

9781119293460
USA $19.99
CAN $23.99
UK £15.99

Physics I dummies

Steven Holzner, PhD

9781119293590
USA $19.99
CAN $23.99
UK £15.99

1,001 Practice Questions
SAT dummies

Ron Woldoff

9781119215844
USA $26.99
CAN $31.99
UK £19.99

Organic Chemistry I dummies

Arthur Winter

9781119293378
USA $22.99
CAN $27.99
UK £16.99

Statistics dummies

Deborah J. Rumsey, PhD

9781119293521
USA $19.99
CAN $23.99
UK £15.99

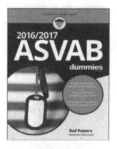

2016/2017
ASVAB dummies

Rod Powers

9781119239178
USA $18.99
CAN $22.99
UK £14.99

Includes Online Practice Tests
1,001 Practice Questions
Praxis Core dummies

Carla Kirkland
Chan Cleveland

9781119263883
USA $26.99
CAN $31.99
UK £19.99

Available Everywhere Books Are Sold

dummies.com

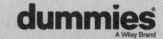
dummies®
A Wiley Brand

Small books for big imaginations

9781119177173
USA $9.99
CAN $9.99
UK £8.99

9781119177272
USA $9.99
CAN $9.99
UK £8.99

9781119177241
USA $9.99
CAN $9.99
UK £8.99

9781119177210
USA $9.99
CAN $9.99
UK £8.99

9781119262657
USA $9.99
CAN $9.99
UK £6.99

9781119291336
USA $9.99
CAN $9.99
UK £6.99

9781119233527
USA $9.99
CAN $9.99
UK £6.99

9781119291220
USA $9.99
CAN $9.99
UK £6.99

9781119177302
USA $9.99
CAN $9.99
UK £8.99

Unleash Their Creativity

dummies.com

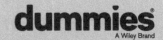